Economics as a Social Science

An Approach to Nonautistic Theory

Andrew M. Kamarck

Ann Arbor

THE UNIVERSITY OF MICHIGAN PRESS

Published in the United States of America by
The University of Michigan Press
Manufactured in the United States of America
♾ Printed on acid-free paper

2005 2004 2003 2002 4 3 2 1

A CIP catalog record for this book is available from the British Library.

Library of Congress Cataloging-in-Publication Data

Kamarck, Andrew M.
Economics as a social science : an approach to nonautistic theory / Andrew M. Kamarck.
p. cm.
Includes bibliographical references and index.
ISBN 0-472-11243-0 (cloth : alk. paper)
1. Economics—Philosophy. 2. Economic man. 3. Self-interest. 4. Social sciences. I. Title.
HB72.K354 2002
330.1—dc21 2001005531

Contents

Preface and Acknowledgments

Except when interrupted by academic appointments at UCLA and Harvard and adjunct teaching at the Johns Hopkins School of Advanced International Studies, my career as an economist was in institutions enmeshed in real world policy problems. Economics training was indispensable, but experience taught that to be useful it had to be greatly modified from conventional theory. While economics is famously, in Lionel Robbins's definition, supposed to be concerned with the relationship between given ends and scarce means, the people who are actually charged with allocating the crucial scarce investment resources in the economy find present-day theory practically useless (1981, 2, 9). Business schools that train investment managers neglect it. The investment genius of Fidelity Investments, Peter Lynch, stated flatly that his work requires a little less than fifteen minutes a year on economics (Train 1994, 22).

More kindly, Francis Bator has argued that if you take all the conventional assumptions of the pure theorist not empirically as a good description of the real world but simply as a hypothesis, the implications are interesting. The usefulness of that set of formalizations, based on this wholly and empirically unrealistic set of assumptions, enables you to identify how strong the assumptions have to be in order to make the modern version of the invisible hand theorem hold. In sum, as J. E. Stiglitz commented: "The economists of the twentieth century, by pushing the neoclassical model to its logical conclusions, and thereby illuminating the absurdities of the world which had been created, have made an invaluable contribution to the economics of the coming century" (1992, 136).

In my experience, economics can be a nonautistic discipline and really useful for understanding and coping with the real economy when it is conscious of the impossibility of grasping the world with precise accuracy; is willing to take advantage of the contribution that other disciplines can make to knowledge of the economy; and works with assumptions that are more realistic and empirically useful. Other works of mine are concerned with the first two of these conditions; this work primarily focuses on the last.

My main debt is to my colleagues over the years in the Federal Reserve, the U.S. Treasury, the Allied Control Commission in Italy, the Allied Control Council in Germany, the Senior Staff Committee of the National Advisory Council on International Monetary and Financial Problems while we were coping with the financial and monetary problems of the post–World War II period and shaping the Marshall Plan, and finally the World Bank and the financial and economic departments of governments throughout the world with which I had the opportunity to work. As readers of this work will notice, I also exploit the intuitive understanding that great authors have of the human psyche—a deeper insight into human nature than can be derived from one-dimensional economics' *déformation professionelle.*

I profited from the workshop at the Harvard Faculty Club on an earlier version of this manuscript that was organized and directed by Armand Clesse of the Luxembourg Institute for European and International Studies as part of a long-term project that investigates, using a multidisciplinary and multinational approach, the issue of the rise and decline of countries. As is evident from references throughout the book, the workshop was invaluable to me in validating and clarifying some of my thoughts, suggesting new ideas, and finally saving me from errors into which I had stumbled. For this, I am grateful to Michael Ambrosi, Professor, Department of Economics, University of Trier; Francis Bator, Professor, John F. Kennedy School of Government, Harvard University; Anne P. Carter, Professor, Brandeis University; Armand Clesse, Director, Luxembourg Institute for European and International Studies; David C. Colander, Professor, Department of Economics, Middlebury College; Peter Doeringer, Professor, Department of Economics, Boston University; Archie Epps, Dean of Students, Harvard College; Henri Étienne, Chargé de Mission, Ministère des Affaires Étrangères, Luxembourg; Mario Hirsch, Editor-in-Chief, d'Letzebuerger Land, Luxembourg; Jan S. Hogendorn, Professor, Department of Economics, Colby College; Franklyn D. Holzman, Professor, Tufts University; Charles P. Kindleberger, Professor Emeritus, MIT; Norbert von Kunitzki, President, Board of Directors, SIDMAR S.A., Gand, Belgium; David Landes, Professor, Department of Economics, Harvard University; Gustav Papanek, Professor, Boston University; John Powelson, Professor, Department of Economics, University of Colorado; Bruce Scott, Professor, Harvard Business School; Paul P. Streeten, Professor, United Nations Development Program; and Raymond Vernon, Professor, John F. Kennedy School of Government, Harvard University.

I also benefited from an additional critique that Jack Powelson, a participant in the workshop, was kind enough to undertake. The comments on my approach to the subject by Yale Professor William Parker and Boston University Professor Emeritus William M. Capron were most helpful.

Finally, I want to express my gratitude to Ellen McCarthy, the Social Science Editor of the University of Michigan Press, for her patience and for helping me keep the whole process in proper perspective. If I have gone astray in some respect, it is of course my responsibility.

CHAPTER 1

Introduction

The work of human thought should withstand the test of brutal, naked reality. If it cannot, it is worthless.

—CZESLAW MILOSZ

There is a growing perception that a new approach is needed in economics if it is to be a useful branch of learning and provide the explanatory power and guidance needed for policy. Frey and Eichenberger concluded from their survey of economics and economists that with economics' continuing emphasis on formalized, abstract, and institution-nonspecific research, its future seems rather gloomy (1993, 192).

The emphasis in contemporary economics on technical virtuosity in manipulating mathematics tends to turn students into truffle hounds—people finely trained for a single narrow function and not much good for anything else (Viner 1991, 393). In the World Bank, we found that it would usually take several years of bank experience before such economics graduates would have learned enough to be trusted to analyze real problems. For the same reason, Stephen Roche, head of the global economics group at Morgan Stanley, will not hire economics Ph.D's if they haven't had substantial experience outside of the university: "We insist on at least a three-to-four year cleansing experience to neutralize the brain-washing that takes place in these graduate programs" (Cassidy 1996, 51–52).

While economists working in the economy are coping with the rich complexities of the real world, leading theorists of the formalist economics school have limited themselves to refining mathematically the implications of a few sharply defined axioms (Solow 1997b, 43). Their subject matter consists of completely rational agents devoted to maximizing their self-interest within elegant theoretical structures that aspire to fit into a general equilibrium model.

Before World War II, mathematics in economics was usually employed as an alternative means of explanation or a means of testing the logic or rigor of an argument. It is still useful to do so. Since World War II, the temptation for economists to approach theory with the mind-set of a mathematician was strengthened by a large influx into the profession of people who had majored in mathematics or physics in college but had moved on to the greener pastures of economics in graduate school. As Gerard Debreu, who followed this career path, has recognized, when mathematics has imprinted its values on a theorist, those values "may play a decisive role. The very choice of the questions to which he tries to find answers is influenced by his mathematical background. Thus, the danger is ever present that the part of economics will become secondary, if not marginal, in that judgment" (1991, 5).

Yet, while he was warning economists of the dangers of mathematics, Debreu was also commending the axiomization of economics. But a branch of learning that consists of a structure of mathematical reasoning erected on a set of axioms is a subspecies of mathematics pure and simple. And, as the great physicist Richard Feynman observed, "mathematics is not a science." A science is concerned with reality (1995, 47). An economics that is only a branch of mathematics cannot grasp the richness of the reality of an economy constructed and run by human minds. with all of their complexity.

There is danger in drawing conclusions from logic alone that are not validated by the real world: hydrogen is highly flammable and oxygen is necessary for combustion, yet pouring H_2O on a fire extinguishes it!

To be valid, a scientific theory must meet the following tests:

- The assumptions must be isomorphic to reality.
- From these, there must be a clear chain of correct logical or logico-mathematical reasoning leading to conclusions.
- These conclusions must be testable for isomorphism to reality.
- If a single link in chain this is broken, the theory fails. (Kamarck 1983, 3–6)

Milton Friedman, of course, was right in insisting that it matters that an economic hypothesis should result in successful prediction. But this criterion does not go far enough. A scientific theory should also provide an understanding of what underlies the predicted results. Knowing, as the ancients did, that the phases of the moon predicted the tides provided only a correlation, not an adequate theory. This came only when Newton's theory of gravitation explained why and when the tides and their heights occurred.

Formalist theory is uncomfortably similar to medieval scholasticism.[1] Scholastics trusted the logical coherence of the system as a guarantee of the unrestricted relevance of their primary notions and used endless debate, unrelieved by direct observation, as their method for the furtherance of knowledge. The scholars of the Middle Ages show so much acuteness and force of mind that not a flaw in the superstructure of the theory they are rearing escapes their vigilance. Yet they are blind to the obvious unsoundness of the foundation in their data (Macaulay [1831] 1833, 211). Scholastic philosophy was dispatched to oblivion by the modern scientific approach with its emphasis upon facts, directly observed, directly employed.

Formalist theory is basically Platonic—pure, timeless, valid under all circumstances, and highly abstract. It may make some contribution by providing benchmark insights in showing the unrealistic assumptions (perfect foresight, infinite time optimization, and universal perfect competition) that are necessary and sufficient for its model to work. The theory is not an accurate representation of the complex, adaptive, learning behavior of human beings in the real economy, and its self-imposed limitations leave out important forces that affect the economy. William James called this approach "tender-minded" in contrast to the empiricist "tough-minded" emphasis on the concrete, diverse reality of the world (1907, 490–91).

Formalist theory should not be confused with the use of formal or mathematical methods of reasoning in empirical economics. Models—mathematical, verbal, or diagrams—based on empirically derived assumptions, taking account of pertinent institutions and real motivations governing economic agents, are often highly rewarding in understanding the real world (Solow 1997b). Many valuable models are based on ad hoc, essentially empirically derived assumptions. Raymond Vernon has pointed out that in the partial equilibrium oligopolistic teaching that business schools do there are all kinds of formal minimodels that are quite helpful in predicting what individual firms might do under some circumstances. They are not general equilibrium models, however, and they go astray if they are stretched too far. One drawback to model building Robert Solow describes as follows:

> [One kind of] model-builders' busywork is to refine their ideas to ask questions to which the available data cannot give the answer. . . . [P]eople are recruited . . . whose interest is more in method than in substance. As the models become more refined, the signal-to-noise ratio in the data becomes very attenuated. Since no empirical verdict is forthcoming, the student goes back to the drawing board—and refines the idea even more. (57)

Ronald Coase argues, correctly, that assumptions should be realistic, that economists can learn from observing reality, and that this is particularly necessary when we need to break our existing habits of thought (1991, 11). The ultimate justification for economics is that it may aid us in securing the relevant knowledge of the real world that can help us to understand and manage it. The right approach is to look objectively at what we need to know so as to be able to analyze more accurately.

William James emphasized testing an asserted truth against reality: to cling to facts and concreteness; grasp a generalization, and provide an example drawn from reality. But many economists are prejudiced against so-called anecdotal evidence. An awkward fact is put down by parroting "It's only anecdotal evidence". But unless theories are tested against reality what validity do they have?

Science can be defined as being either (1) an exact science such as physics, in which mathematics correctly and precisely describes and explains the reality that is its subject matter; or (2) a method of thought that obtains verifiable results by reasoning logically from observed fact. A scientist recognizes regularities and compresses their description into theories (Gell-Mann 1994, 100). Economics can never be an exact science like physics because its subject matter is not amenable to physicslike treatment (see Kamarck 1983). It can and should meet the criteria of the second definition of science.

When economics balances a whole structure of theory on a patently inaccurate, overly simplified description of human psychology, it can meet neither criteria of a science. This effort to erect a theory on an assumed narrow interpretation of the *why* of human behavior is futile and unnecessary. All we need to do is concentrate on the *what* and *how.* Physics has become the queen of sciences by explaining the what and how of gravitation and the other great laws of the universe, but it cannot explain the why—in other words, what makes it go (Feynman 1995, 107). Which is more helpful in understanding an economy, a report on the economic behavior of living human beings that tests true in experience or a theory that is internally consistent but has no basis in the real world?

An example of the latter is a theory advanced by Robert Barro (a modern economic star who was courted by both Columbia and Harvard), which suggests that government spending has no effect on the current consumption of consumers.[2] Consequently, government fiscal policy is impotent. Barro assumes that each generation is as concerned for the welfare of its descendants as for itself—the world can be taken as equivalent to being inhabited by infinitely long-lived consumers. Therefore, whenever a government increases its spending and incurs debt, taxpayers (who in essence are assumed to live forever), realizing that they will have to pay higher taxes in the future to pay off this debt, will immediately offset increased government spending by increasing their own saving by an equivalent amount.

Professor Barro apparently never asked whether he or anyone he knew had ever reacted to an increase in the government deficit in this way or whether there was any statistical basis for his thesis. His Harvard colleague, N. Gregory Mankiw, pointed out that the theorem is inconsistent with the empirical findings that consumption tracks current income and numerous households with near zero wealth could not, even if they wanted to, save more to help their descendants pay higher taxes in the future (Mankiw 2000b, 121). Paul Samuelson more devastatingly commented that "it is not without humor to hear a grown scholar allege that each new tax reduction will cause us to save more against the day when our children will be taxed to meet the entailed deficit (1989, 97). Barro's theory, imposingly entitled the Ricardian equivalence theorem, is rather an instance of what Schumpeter called Ricardian vice—jumping to policy conclusions from a highly abstract base.

Another problem, which economics can avoid by concentrating on material welfare as the classical economists did, is the logical cul-de-sac that contemporary theory has driven itself into. It adopts *intrapersonal* comparisons of utility (the psychological satisfactions derived by people from their consumption) as the basis of the theory of demand but denies *interpersonal* comparisons as a basis for welfare economics. It assumes first that people have the same psychology and then denies that they do (Blaug 1980, 89). Comparative statistics of national income and its distribution are drained of meaning, and the usefulness of economics in much policy making is largely destroyed.

Following on from this, there is a widespread view to which even some highly regarded theorists succumb to on occasion: The results of a market operating without government interference, which may lead to a Pareto-optimum (i.e., no reallocation of resources and output can make anyone better off without making at least one person worse off), is confused with an optimum optimorum (the best of the best)—a Panglossian best of all possible worlds. But this neglects the important factors of the effects of income distribution and ethical considerations.

In chapter 2, I present a quick survey of two major limitations of economics. The first flows from the inherent problems of all measurement and the particular problems that economics encounters in trying to grasp the economy, as spelled out in my *Economics and the Real World* (1983). The result is that achievable accuracy in comprehending the economy is strictly limited. The second limitation is that we can only hope to understand the economy by supplementing economics with other disciplines.[3]

Chapters 3–5 are devoted to the first two canonical assumptions of last century's economics. The canonical hypotheses are, in Robert Solow's words, "greed, rationality, and equilibrium" (Kreps 1997, 59). Greed and rationality are the components of the fundamental assumption or axiom on which neoclassical economic theory rests. My text is devoted to dissecting the fundamental axiom and supplementing its narrowness, inadequacy, and inaccuracy with more realistic assumptions. Chapter 6 discusses markets, which are more complex than the conventional theory assumes. Chapter 7 addresses change and growth. The third canonical hypothesis, "equilibrium," which is borrowed from classical mechanics, ignores real historical time and directly contradicts the most important defining characteristics of the economy: change and growth. In modern capitalist market economies, change and growth are the very essence of the system.

So far, the discussion has been concerned with the subject matter on which economics customarily focuses: exchange transactions in the market. But, although some economic theorists have tried valiantly to bring all relationships under this rubric, the world is more complex. There are two other kinds of transaction relationships, modes of relating to people, that are important. These are gift and coercion. Gift relationships characterize primitive economies, and there is a large body of writing by anthropologists on this. Gift relationships still persist to some degree in modern economies (in families, in nonprofits, and even between governments, as in the Marshall Plan and some aid to less developed countries), but these are largely peripheral to our text. The exercise of coercive power as a basis for transactions is much more important. Pursuit of personal profit is not always to the benefit of society. Economics tends to overlook the fact that often there is a choice. One may earn a living by being productive or taking advantage of the possession of coercive power and preying on or battening as a parasite on others. Chapter 8 examines this neglected aspect of economics. Chapter 9 sums up.

Modern economics is not monolithic. Empirical economists have won wide acceptance as successful policy and decision makers. Federal Reserve governors, presidents of Federal Reserve Banks, and top officials in the U.S. Treasury are routinely economists. An economist has even been governor of the Bank of England.

While economics outside of formalist theory is not as vulnerable to criticism, there are problems. In this book, I will try to show what needs to be modified or discarded in the basic theory as well as what needs to be added if economics is to become a more useful branch of learning for the twenty-first century. The general approach guiding this book responds to a concern voiced by John Hicks: "We have sought to justify our economic concepts in terms of considerations that are appropriate to the natural sciences; not observing that what economics tries to do . . . is essentially different."

CHAPTER 2

Limitations of Economics

> We must not look for the same degree of accuracy in all subjects: we must be content in each class of subjects with accuracy of such a kind as the subject matters allows, and to such an extent as is proper to the inquiry.
>
> —ARISTOTLE, *Nicomachean Ethics*

The conscious or unconscious view that many economists have of economics as a science comparable to physics tempts them to expect that it can aspire to explaining economic reality with the same precision and predictability that they believe physics has been able to achieve in explaining and predicting phenomena in the universe. This idealization of physics overlooks the fact that in modern physics Heisenberg's uncertainty principle is now accepted as describing a fundamental property of the world. We cannot measure the present state of the universe precisely. Quantum physics teaches that an electron can be a particle or a wave and an electron may suddenly appear unexpectedly. There is an absolute line beyond which it is impossible to ascertain precisely both the exact position and the momentum of a simple elementary particle. As Hawking points out, this means that we cannot have a scientific theory or model of the world that is completely deterministic (1988). Richard Feynman, one of the most brilliant physicists of our generation, commented that physics "has given up on the problem of trying to predict exactly what will happen in a definite circumstance. Yes! Physics *has* given up. *We do not know how to predict what would happen in a given circumstance,* and we believe now that it is impossible, that the only thing that can be predicted is the probability of different events" (1995, 135, italics in original).

In mathematics, Goedel proved that no axiomatic system could be complete. Economics must also realize that it too is subject to limited results. The limits to precise knowledge of an economic situation or problem are approached rapidly. The nature of an economy is such that the mesh of the net that economists can weave to catch reality is much coarser than that of the natural scientists in their realms.

It is central to the argument to make clear the distinction between the terms *accuracy* and *precision.* These are often confused in common usage, with a precise statement often being taken as evidence of its accuracy. The distinction between the two can probably best be seen in my favorite example:

> On Cape Cod, where the pace of life is relaxed, you may ask a craftsman when he can come to build a fence for you. If he answers, "sometime in the autumn," he is being accurate but not precise. If instead he promises "Eight A.M., October 2," he is being precise but not accurate. On October 2, it is highly likely that the fish will be running and he will be out in his boat or it will be a beautiful autumn day, far too nice to spoil by working.

Accuracy conveys the meaning of "correctness," of "true value." *Precision* means the "degree of sharpness" by which a thing or concept is specified, and it may or may not be accurate.

Alfred Marshall and John Maynard Keynes did not believe that it was possible to apply exact mathematical methods to economics because a pervasive part of economic life cannot be precisely measured. As Keynes stated in the footnote to his memorial for Alfred Marshall: "economic interpretation in its highest form requires an . . . amalgam of logic and intuition and the wide knowledge of facts, most of which are not precise" (1925, 25).

The virtue, and the fault, of mathematics is that the meaning of a mathematical symbol, once defined, does not change. Words, on the other hand, can flirt with meanings and coquet with relationships. Words can be deliberately ambiguous when relationships are ambiguous and it is desired to leave them so. Natural language can be more flexible in conveying meaning: it is infinitely richer in vocabulary and consequently can be more accurate, although less precise.

The first part of this chapter will present a summary analysis of why precision is unattainable in grasping the economy. Perhaps the greatest problem some economists will face in this discussion is the difficulty of shifting from the mind-set of precise numbers and well-behaved models of pure theory to the rough, inaccurate data, recalcitrant behavior, and shifting complexities of the real economy.

Although economics has prided itself on its comparability to physics, one of the basic lessons taught in physics is ignored—that it is essential to understand and express the degree of accuracy of each number used. As John von Neumann pointed out: "When a problem in pure or in applied mathematics is 'solved' by numerical computation, errors, that is, deviations of the numerical 'solution' obtained from the true, rigorous one, are unavoidable. Such a 'solution' is therefore meaningless, unless there is an estimate of the total error in the above sense" (1963).

Economists tend to overlook the need to understand how much precision is actually attainable in the accuracy of the numbers used as well as the need to express the margin of error present in an economic statistic. Sampling errors for an indifferent (i.e., not hostile) universe are estimated and stated, but the limits of accuracy in most very rough economic estimates are seldom stated and sometimes not even realized. Most of the data that economists rely on (GDP, costs, prices) are not fully reliable. Yet often economists use these numbers as though they were precisely accurate to the first or second decimal point. Norbert Wiener, the noted scientist, observed that a true science has to begin with a critical understanding of its quantifiable elements and the means adopted for measuring them (1964, 89–90).

Before looking at the errors that stem from the nature of economic data themselves, it is important to realize that there are important sources of error in all numerical computations. A mathematical formulation of reality is not reality itself. It necessarily can represent reality only with certain abstractions and simplifications. Then the model may involve parameters the values of which have to be derived directly or indirectly from observations. These parameters are affected by errors, and these errors cause errors in the result. The model usually will require transcendental operations (like differentiation or integration) and implicit definitions (such as solutions of algebraic or transcendental equations). If they are to be approached by numerical calculation, these have to be handled by elementary processes that correspond to a finite procedure that resolves itself into a linear sequence of steps. All of these steps are approximate, and so the strict mathematical statement we start with is replaced with an approximate one (von Neumann and Goldstine 1963, 482–83). Finally, a fourth source of error derives from the need to round off numbers. There has to be a maximum number of places in the numbers with which we work. These noise variables enter into the computations every time an elementary operation is performed.

Beyond these errors, which are inherent in all numerical calculations, there are special sources of error that flow from the nature of economics as a subject concerned with the economy itself. The natural sciences deal with facts that are in essence independent of human activity. Economics deals with facts that report on or are the result of human activity. This is a fundamental difference.

Several classes of errors result from this. First, economic data are gathered from people. Gathering economic statistics is a two-person game. A planet has no interest in deceiving an astronomer, but a person or economic organization may have an incentive to hold back, conceal, or distort information. Mitsubishi suppressed information on defects in its products for twenty years. For the year 2000 census, a Republican Congress forbade the Census Bureau to use the more accurate sampling procedure in counting the American population in order to hold down the number of potential Democratic seats that would result from the decennial reapportionment of the House of Representatives. When a head tax was levied in African countries during colonial times, population numbers were understated—as a government official came into a village to perform the head count, people vanished into the bush on the other side. An underground economy exists in most, if not all, countries in the world. It has become obvious that important economic statistics were distorted or completely falsified in the centrally planned countries before 1989.

There are other sources of error. Economic data are not usually secured from planned experiments but are the by-product of business or government activities. They are not usually produced by specially trained personnel and are often defined in terms of legal rather than economic categories. The data therefore tend to cover categories that are somewhat different from what an economist would like (Morgenstern 1963).

There is usually an unavoidable lag between statistics and events. Some, like stock prices, are available practically immediately, while others may take days, weeks, or months. Because of the different lags, to have key statistics in a useful time frame they have to be estimated. Then, as the data come in, there is a constant need to revise the estimates. When making policy that affects the future, as Cairncross remarked, it is necessary first to forecast the present, and in this process important mistakes can be made (Cairncross 1969).

To deal with problems in the world of reality, economics has to have a proper appreciation of what economic measurements can and cannot do. In economics, we deal with loose concepts. In handling loose concepts, the margins of precision of a statistic must widen as it slips away from describing or measuring the central area of the concept (where theoretically it can be sharp or precise) toward the gray area or penumbra in which most of the real world concepts live.

> In scientific theoretical systems like economics with a logico-mathematical framework, the basic unit is the "individual." This may be a person or a commodity like an automobile. An individual is an entity that either is indivisible into parts or loses its individuality when its parts are separated from each other. *In theory,* the individual is definite and unchangeable—sharply distinguished from its background and sharply demarcated from other individuals and in time. *In reality,* even though we may have no doubt whether a particular entity is an "individual" or not, doubt

> may enter as soon as a time or space dimension comes into play. Indefiniteness in some phase or respect of an individual is completely compatible with definiteness otherwise. . . . When does a motor car begin or cease to exist? How much exactly of its parts can we take away from a car without destroying the individual car? . . . the lack of definitiveness of the individual, either in space or in time, is important in much of economics.
>
> Second, *in theory*, classes and the concepts relating to them are exact: *A* either possesses the predicate that makes it a member of class *P* or it does not. That is, *A* must be either a member of *P* or a member of non-*P*. One cannot say A_n is a borderline case, being just barely a member of *P* and of non-*P*. This violates one of the main principles of logic—something cannot be both *P* and non-*P*. Similarly, one cannot say that A_n is just barely not a member of *P* and also just not a member of non-*P*. This violates another logical principle—a thing must be either a member of *P* or it must be non-*P*. However, once we return to reality, neutral or borderline candidates are common to most of the classes we deal with. (Kamarck 1983, 24–25)

In real life, the classes are usually inexact. Buying a house can be an investment and/or a consumption item. Purchases and mortgage costs of houses are included in the consumer price index, yet some people buy their houses partly or wholly as an investment in the hope of getting a capital gain. One man I know, who has an artist's talent and a craftsman's skill, makes his living by buying houses, improving them, and selling them at higher prices. His "profit" is partly wages and partly capital gain, and in the meantime he has been enjoying a return of implicit rent.

The indefiniteness of individuals and the inexactness of classes are both covered by Max Black's term, *loose concepts*. This describes cases in which there is no point at which a unique sharp transition can be made from a case that clearly belongs to a class and a borderline case or a case excluded from the class. In the economy, an economic empirical concept and its opposite could be regarded as lying at opposite ends of a spectrum: one can clearly distinguish between both ends, but any dividing line drawn between them as they shade toward each other can only be arbitrary. The concept and its opposite are distinct, but they are not *discretely* distinct. There is no void between them but a penumbra.

For example, "unemployment" is a loose concept. The boundaries of the concept have to be set arbitrarily when one is counting the number of persons included in the class "unemployed." An arbitrary (and not logically unique) decision has to be taken in deciding how long a person has to be without work and trying to find work to be considered unemployed. The two opposites, employed and unemployed, are clear, but there is no one point in the border area where a sharp line can be drawn between them. In many less developed countries, the unemployed are in large part people who have migrated to the city because their incomes while "unemployed" there are greater than their subsistence income in the village would have been. Similar looseness is true of other economic concepts. Central banks find it necessary to invent new measures of money supply as a growing number of different means of payment have evolved and come into use. In the last generation, these have included NOW accounts, money market fund accounts, credit cards, and so on, and today an Internet payment system is being developed.

Imprecision of concept (indefiniteness of individuals and inexactitude of classes that concepts refer to) rules in many sectors of the economy. The national accounts are a good example. Measurement of the output of primary products is close to being precisely accurate. These products tend to be generally uniform or change slowly over time and are usually sold in fairly competitive markets. Manufactures tend to be changeable in quality over time, but their markets are much less perfect. Price deflators are a problem in measuring real output over time. The difficulties are well known, and their resolution is inevitably arbitrary. In services, which now make up much more than half of total product, measurement of some is extremely difficult and unsatisfactory. General government, households, and nonprofits do not sell their output, so no proper measure of it can be constructed. In practice, output is held to be equivalent to employment costs. The figure for labor earnings is taken to measure the contribution to national income, net national product, and gross national product. In the health sector, too, because of the need to rely on the medical profession for information on the product to be purchased, third-party payments, restrictions on competition in the profession, and so on, expenditures on the sector cannot be accepted as properly measuring its output.

The balance of trade and payments accounts also have a multitude of measurement problems. Trade and exchange barriers have come down across the world, making measurement of trade more difficult; trade in services, which is hard to track, represents a growing share of total trade; and the figures on capital flows, always notoriously inaccurate, with globalization and the accompanying explosion in electronic transactions, have become even less reliable. The result is that the global balance of payments never balances (total world imports have been higher than total world exports by as much as 3 percent in recent years). Alien spaceships, rather than kidnapping terrestrials, are bringing in goods and services from outer space!

The subject matter of economics does not possess constancies and immunity to significant historical change. Not only do the structural relationships change over time, often unpredictably and irregularly, but the economy is buffeted by unpredictable, often arbitrary and irrational political and economic changes at home and abroad (e.g., consider the oil-producing countries in 1973, 1979, and 2000). The agents involved in the structural relationships often reach outside the economy and use their influence in the political sphere to get the economic parameters changed for their own benefit.

In working with loose concepts, the use of customary methods of logical reasoning forces one to make demarcations in the neutral or borderline cases that are not clear. But one must recognize that these demarcations are arbitrary or judgmental. There are no logical rules that precisely locate the borderline. As long as this is borne in mind, one can reason using loose concepts and reach useful conclusions as long as one is not deceived with illusions of precise accuracy. It is necessary to recognize that often the closest that economics can come to portraying some reality is in the form of a rough, simple model. These models need to be considered not as algorithms or effective procedures providing us with precise solutions to economic problems but as heuristics. They are plausible approaches or rules of thumb for attacking particular problems or illuminating some aspect of the structure of reality. They may give us reasonably approximate solutions. They cannot dictate or determine the precise single right decision, but they can assist us in making rational and effective decisions.

> Take the standard old-fashioned Cambridge Massachusetts Keynesian model: From the empirical evidence, its open economy variant is enormously useful for understanding the real world. It has old-fashioned micro foundations; lot of the assumptions are *ad hoc*, essentially empirical observations like the effect of changes in disposable income and changes in wealth on current consumption. (Bator 1998, 205)

> The genius of macroeconomics consists of felicitous oversimplification, which is traded off for concrete conclusions that are much harder if not impossible to obtain from less simplified models. (Baumol 2000, 11)

Paul Samuelson has written that he has learned how treacherous "economic laws" are (e.g., Colin Clark's law of a 25 percent ceiling on government expenditure and taxation) (1964, 336). However, we can ascertain particular patterns of economic behavior in quantifiable form for particular times and economies. We can ascertain tendencies and trends that provide a basis for action or prediction. Such prediction can never be as precisely accurate in its time dimensions or results as prediction in the physical sciences because a "trend" is not a law—it can change suddenly. Unlike those of physicists or astronomers, our predictions need to include the consideration of possible changes in our parameters as well as our variables. Precise data are not indispensable for the analysis of policy making. Merely knowing the probable direction of change is often important. Data do not have to be precise to make possible a prediction as to whether things will go up or down, whereas it is impossible to predict exactly how far or at what speed the change will occur. It may be vital to know whether some variable is likely to increase or decrease and whether the probable consequences are large or small, while the precise magnitude of the change is impossible to ascertain and not necessary for the decision. While it would be ideal always to be able to apply a quantitative calculus to economic analysis, when economic reality makes this impossible a qualitative calculus is often useful and may even be sufficient.

Sets of independent rough data that reinforce each other provide more assurance than a single set of precise data that are suspect. The great mathematician Karl Friedrich Gauss observed that a lack of mathematical learning is revealed by unlimited precision in computation.[1] Going beyond the possible margins of precision in an analysis involves us in the manipulation of noise and self-deception.

Limitations of Scope

The discussion so far has focused on the limitations economics has in measuring the economy. With considerable hubris, there is a trend among some economists to believe that economics is competent to analyze practically the whole of human activity, both inside and outside the economy. The claim is that "economics has been imperialistic and . . . economic imperialism has been successful" and "The most aggressive economic imperialists aim to explain all social behavior by using the tools of economics" (Lazear 2000, 103).

Gary Becker has blithely argued that economic theory explains the whole of human society, that political, legal, and social institutions can be explained as the efficient outcome of rational individuals pursuing their preferences.[2] According to Becker, "the economic approach provides a framework applicable to all human behavior—to all types of decisions and to persons from all walks of life" (1981, ix). Economics has a theoretical system capable of explaining law, crime, politics, marriage, and even parent-child and sibling relationships within a family (Stigler 1988). Poor, uncomprehending Henry James, in contrast, admonished us to "Never believe that you know the last thing about any human heart."

The "imperialistic" economics assertion that all human behavior is driven by an attempt to maximize utility in every circumstance is a good example of cultural myopia: it ignores custom, tradition, ethical restraints, and self-destructive emotional reactions and demonstrates a cramped view of human nature. Ronald Coase has a more cruel explanation: "The reason for this movement of economists into neighboring fields is certainly not that we have solved the problems of the economic system; it would perhaps be more plausible to argue that economists are looking for fields in which they can have some success (quoted in Posner 1993, 207).

Economic forces do affect human behavior in many contexts, and some economic concepts (opportunity cost, economic incentives, etc.) may help in explaining it, but there is far more to human behavior than economic theory can explain by itself (as we will explore in chapter 4). But the issue we wish to explore briefly here is the opposite of economic imperialism: the inadequacy of economic theory alone to fully comprehend and analyze the economy.

A central question that has concerned economists for centuries, certainly since Adam Smith, is what forces affect the wealth of nations. At present, a majority of the human population lives in the less developed countries, almost all in the tropics. Is this fact significant for the economic development of these countries? Economists have generally paid no attention to the effect of climate on the economy. This neglect may have been due to a reaction against Yale professor Ellsworth Huntington, who argued that human achievement was directly determined by the weather (his ideal climate bore a strong resemblance to that of New Haven). But as Charles P. Kindleberger has pointed out: "The arguments against Huntington are telling, but the fact remains that no tropical country in modern times has achieved a high state of economic development. This establishes some sort of presumptive case—for the end result, if not for the means" (1965, 78).

Kindleberger put his finger on the issue: it was right to reject Huntington's explanation but not the reality of the malevolent influence of the tropical climate. Accepting this reality as given, I took advantage of the wide-ranging knowledge and experience available to me in the World Bank to investigate why the tropical climate hampered countries in their economic development. The results were published in 1976 as a bank-sponsored book, *The Tropics and Economic Development*. Until recently, economists almost universally continued to ignore the obvious fact of the association of tropical climate and poverty. Professor Rati Ram, however, after making an empirical investigation of my "provocative" proposal that a county's geographical location in the tropics handicapped its ability to develop, concluded that: "the relationship of almost every measure of a country's well-being with its distance from the equator appears remarkably strong. In many cases, the distance variable alone can explain nearly half of the cross-country variation in income and other measures of well-being" (1997, 1443).

In the last few years, nine other economists applying sophisticated econometric tools have independently discovered that, yes, a country's location in the tropics is strongly related to its poverty. Henri Theil and Dongling Chen developed a simple latitude model to explain per capita GDPs based on purchasing power parities. They concluded: "This comparison suggests that latitude may be viewed, statistically speaking, as the principal component of the rich/poor distinction among the countries of the free world (1995, 327). Theil and several collaborators carried this study further:

> The major conclusion to be drawn . . . is that affluence tends to decline when we move towards the Equator from the temperate zones in either the Northern or the Southern Hemisphere. Needless to say, this tendency is not without exceptions nor is it constant over time. Nevertheless, its existence as a tendency in the non-Communist world in the last several decades cannot be denied. (Theil et al. 1996, 28)

Robert E. Hall studied "Levels of Economic Activity across Countries" and found that: "Distance from the equator is the single strongest predictor of long-term economic success in our specification. Being located at the equator like Zaire or Uganda is associated with a reduction in output per worker by a factor of 4.5 relative to the Scandinavian countries" (1997, 176). Xavier X. Sala-I-Martin's "I Just Ran Two Million Regressions" determined that: "Absolute Latitude (far away from the equator) is good for growth" (1997, 181). Jeffrey D. Sachs and Andrew M. Warner found that: "Countries with tropical climates and landlocked countries have lower steady-state incomes and, therefore, lower growth from any initial level of GDP per capita" (1997, 187). Finally, Paul Collier and J. W. Gunning write: "Sub-Saharan Africa is predominantly tropical. There is some evidence that this has reduced African growth" (1999, 72).

By this time, with all these authoritative studies, it should be accepted that a country's location in the tropics does contribute to its poverty. This is an important finding, but standing alone what policy recommendation does it imply? One cannot advise a government that it should move its country into a temperate zone. Only if we understand what it is about the tropical climate that creates the obstacles to development can suitable policy actions be taken. We need to know which forces at work are responsible.

The causes of this phenomenon cannot be explained by using pure economic theory. Economics by itself is helpless in coping with this highly important fact, which affects the living standards of hundreds of millions of people. It is necessary to supplement economics by drawing on other disciplines to bring out what it is about the tropics that causes the problem. Only then will it be possible to consider what can and should be done. The focus will be on Africa because that is the preeminent tropical continent in terms of area and problems.[3]

Geography and climate isolated sub-Saharan Africa from the rest of the world and Africans from one another until very recently, and they still impose high transport costs. Access is not easy. Where the desert does not come down to the sea, there is mostly swamp or lagoon. European ships visited the Nigerian coast for more than three centuries before they discovered that a major river, the Niger, emptied into the swamps and lagoons they encountered.

Of all the continents, Africa has the shortest coastline compared to area and very few natural harbors. As most rivers fall off the escarpment near the coast, it is seldom possible to penetrate the interior by sailing upriver. While the coastline of Africa was known centuries before that of North America, it was not until about a hundred years ago that the main outlines of the interior were mapped.

The tropical nature of much of the continent has also been a major obstacle. Yellow fever and malaria killed traders. Trypanosomiasis killed horses and cattle. This ruled out animal transport over most of tropical Africa. Commerce and travel had to depend on human porters, the slowest and most inefficient of all transport modes (Stanley in his search for Livingstone averaged only four miles a day). The only trade with most of tropical Africa over thousands of years was in products of great value and little bulk—gold and ivory—or slaves, a commodity that provided its own legs. The Indian Ocean slave trade lasted into the twentieth century. It still exists in the southern Sudan and Mauritania (see chapter 8). The difficulties of transport and prevalence of the slave trade account for the high degree of ethnic fragmentation that has made nation building so difficult.

The most important special characteristic of the tropics is that because of its continuous heat and the absence of frost life and reproduction go on throughout the year. The West Nile encephalitis virus threat in New York and New England in 2000 ended "with the first killing frost." In the tropics, no winter temperatures constrain continuous reproduction and growth of all kinds of life: weeds, insects, birds, parasitic fungi, spider mites, eelworms, microbes, viruses, pests, and parasites that prey on humans, their animals, and their crops.

Life across most of the tropics takes on an infinite multiplicity of forms. Fierce competition results, and only a few individuals of a species in each generation survive in any one place. The number of species in a given area is a large multiple of that found in the temperate zone (e.g., of twenty-five major insect pests that afflict maize worldwide, twenty-one are found in Africa and only five in the United States). The conditions are ideal for rapid evolutionary adaptation to exploit new opportunities. Malaria, AIDs, Ebola, and West Nile encephalitis all originated in Africa.

Insects and the parasites carried by them are poikilothermic, their speed of development varying directly with temperature. The life cycle of bacteria, protozoa, and other pathogens is also ecothermic. In temperate zones, the aquatic stage of mosquitoes takes weeks, in the tropics days; and the extrinsic incubation period of yellow fever virus, for example, varies from three weeks to a few days according to the temperature. Bacillary dysentery is spread by house flies. At 16°C, it takes forty-four days for the fly to develop from egg to adult. The timing drops to ten days at 30°C. The result is an exponential increase in the tropics compared to the temperate zone (e.g., if only ten fertile females survive in each generation, in forty-four days the resulting difference will be on the order of ten thousand to ten).

Studies in the tropics find high percentages of people harboring parasites, usually averaging around 2 infections per person. Millions of people are afflicted with hookworm (ancylostomiasis, which infects a billion people worldwide), roundworm, whipworm, tapeworm, pinworm, Guinea worm, and various varieties of filariasis (250 million people infected). About 120 million people have the grotesque elephantiasis (or lymphatic filariasis), with the number of people at risk placed at around 1 billion. Bilharzia, or schistosomiasis, affects some 200 million people; and malaria affects 500 million worldwide, with around 1 million dying annually in Africa.

Some idea of the magnitude of the African health problem is illustrated by river blindness (onchocerciasis). This disease, which affects only (!) about 20 million Africans, turns productive adults into burdens on their communities and depopulates fertile river valleys. Blood-feeding black flies inject a nematode into human beings. (A related fly afflicts northern New England and Canada, but in these regions the fly cannot carry the worm.) During a fifteen-year lifetime in her human host, the female nematode produces millions of microfilariae. Some migrate to the eyes, causing blindness. The flies reproduce near rivers, hence the name river blindness.

In 1974, I helped inspire the World Bank to begin to initiate an international program to eradicate river blindness in Africa. Success may finally be achieved by 2010. Mectizan, a livestock drug, is effective against the disease. If 95 percent of the people in an infected area take Mectizan once a year over a twelve- to fourteen-year period, the disease can be eliminated. More than 10 million people in Africa are receiving the medicine.

The total cost of eradicating this relatively minor disease has been more than $500 million so far, even though the pharmaceutical company Merck is donating the drug. Little progress has been made to date on the more important and widespread parasitic diseases; in large part because the countries are poor and it is not profitable to find and produce drugs to help treat the victims.

Most African countries are highly dependent on agriculture. Ideal conditions, under which the right amount of water is available in the right place at the right time, occur naturally only rarely in the tropics. Rainfall, which determines the seasons, is usually too much or too little. It is erratic both year to year and within each season. The billions of dollars in damage that was caused by tropical storms in North Carolina in 1999 is a graphic example of what tropical rains can do. Trypanosomiasis, which is carried by the tsetse fly, bars half of tropical Africa to cattle and horses. There is less food protein, and human muscles must do the work of the farms alone.

In the semihumid tropics, the period before the rains break is the driest, windiest, and hottest time of the year, so loss of water through evaporation and transpiration is high. This makes preparation of the dry, hard ground for planting particularly arduous. Moist soil is easier to work, and in temperate climates cold weather precipitation charges the soil with a reserve of water. In Africa, when the tropical rains do come, so do the predators and parasites, so everything has to be done at once.

Because of the multiplicity of species and the rapid evolutionary potential, there is a high probability that any new plant or animal introduced into an area by humans will attract some new pest. Without a "closed season," all sorts of pests may thrive throughout the year. Weeds, parasitic fungi, insects, spider mites, eelworms, and bacterial and viral diseases drastically reduce crop yields. Locusts may arrive in swarms up to 80 by 40 kilometers in size and devour everything where they land. Locusts are restricted to the tropics, as they can fly only when their thoracic muscle temperature is at least 25°C. After the harvest, serious losses can result from storage pests and rats.

The soil has to be protected against the sun, which burns away the organic matter, and against the direct blows of the torrential rains, which crush the structure of the soil, seal off the underlying soil from the air, and either leach out the minerals or trace elements needed for plant growth or carry them so far down that plant roots cannot reach them. Generally, soils are poor in Africa because they contain little organic material. Even in dense forests, soils are usually thin, with little fertility. The interchange between decaying and living plants is precarious, and there are very few reserves.

In much of the humid tropics, the soil is laterite, which is agriculturally poor or virtually useless. In these areas, shifting tillage cultivates fields for a few years, then allows them to revert to bush jungle to restore their fertility over periods that may last as long as twenty-five years. Alluvial and recent volcanic soils are more fertile. Forest soils that are high enough to escape the heat of lower altitudes may also be fertile and rich in humus. Tree crops, by shading the soil and protecting it from the direct impact of rain, avoid many of these problems and make permanent farms possible. Livestock is subject to most temperate zone diseases as well as tropical parasitic, nutritional toxic, and organic afflictions.

Geophysical and geochemical techniques used in mineral searches were for the most part developed for the temperate zones. Humid tropic parameters require a different structure of inference. Different instruments may be needed since extremes of heat and humidity can ruin delicate equipment.

In the humid tropics and the former humid but now arid southern edges of the Sahara, mineral formations are overburdened with soil. Rain and high temperatures have led to the formation of laterite and other soil mantles that hide the underlying rock. Dolomite, limestone, gypsum, and salts of potassium and sodium are relatively soluble and hard to locate in areas with high rainfall. Most of the minerals found are surface concentrations resulting from weathering: bauxite, some iron ores, manganese, nickel, tin, and diamond placers.

The obstacles of the tropics are not insuperable. The tropics force a rapid pace of evolution, which creates vulnerability for Africans, their crops, and their animals. But this same velocity of change could be harnessed by research. The Southeast Asian country of Malaysia, for example, basing its agriculture on tree crops and with a long-term research effort, has coped successfully with its tropical problems. Its natural rubber has been able to compete successfully with synthetic rubber. With higher rural incomes and the payoff from its oil, it has been able to move successfully into the industrial age.

Research on cures or prevention of tropical diseases, on control of natural predators, and on the other problems of tropical agriculture is clearly the answer to the question of what can be done to help tropical countries overcome the poverty stemming from their locations. It is also clear that successful results, as in the case of coping with river blindness, can only be achieved with considerable time, effort, and investment.

This discussion of the tropics illustrates that understanding an economy may require supplementing economics with other disciplines. A similar case can be made for calling on organizational theory to help us understand the corporate sector of the economy; on history and political science in the analysis of the public sector; and on other noneconomic disciplines for other aspects of an economy.[4] As David Cutler observed, "If you think only as an economist, you'll produce silly answers. And if you don't consider economics at all, you'll produce silly answers" (Powell 1998, 3).

I was surprised and pleased in the final stage of preparing this book to discover a lecture by Lionel Robbins at the London School of Economics on the same key as the theme of this chapter. He told the students that economists had it in their power to make a significant contribution to the discussion of the leading questions of the day.

> But if they are to do this, they must transcend themselves as economists. If we are to throw helpful light on the great problems of our time, still more if . . . we are from time to time to serve our term of public service, we must be prepared to go beyond our subject. . . . we must be prepared to study many other disciplines. We must study political philosophy. We must study public administration. We must study law. We must study history. . . . I would say, too, that we must also study the masterpieces of imaginative literature; . . . a man will learn more which is relevant to the study of society from the great dramatists and novelists than from a hundred textbooks on psychology—valuable as these may sometimes be. (1954, 17)

CHAPTER 3

Self-Interest

> All contradictions may be found in me. . . . I have nothing to say about myself absolutely, simply and solidly without confusion and without mixture.
>
> —MONTAIGNE

A fundamental assumption of economics is that the dominant drive in individuals is a rational striving to maximize self-interest. This behavior is in essence a constant in all human nature: it is inherited in our genes and is a characteristic of the human biogram. "It makes possible the mathematical modeling of economic problems" (Samuelson 1947, 21). Theoretical structures, rigorously worked out and using this assumption as axiomatic, fill the economic journals and innumerable texts

Self-interest is defined in the *Oxford English Dictionary* as "Regard to, or pursuit of, one's own welfare *esp.* to the exclusion of regard for others." It is equivalent to *selfishness;* which is defined as "regard for one's own interest or happiness to the disregard of the well-being of others." Bluntly, as Robert Solow puts it, this canonical hypothesis is *greed.*

As long as self-interest is not adulterated with regard for others, it is not fuzzy, blurry, or unreliable and thus can be a firm basis for mathematical modeling. Many conventional economists hold the autistic position that it is heresy to hold that the major function of economics should be to explain human economic behavior and that this behavior may not be consistent with this rational maximizing assumption (Stiglitz 1983, 999). When pressed, some economic theorists may assert that of course they know that this assumption is an unrealistic, narrow view of human nature. It is only chosen for analytical convenience. The latter statement is obviously true. But does that justify erecting a theoretical structure or model on the assumption, forgetting to mention at the end that the model cannot be taken as a realistic guide to the actual world?

In fact, self-interest is not a simple concept. Analyzed, it turns out to be a second-order desire. We have desires for various commodities—food, clothing, cars; and states of affairs—for good health, for respect. These are all primary desires. It is in our self-interest, for example, to eat when we are hungry. When you eat, you are satisfying your primary desire—to alleviate your hunger—so it is in your self-interest to satisfy a first-order desire, hunger for food. That is, self-interest is a second-order desire whose object is to satisfy a primary desire. Self-interest has as its goal the satisfaction of those first-order desires that affect us directly. And, as we shall see in the discussion, some first-order desires are for things quite distinct from oneself (Nagel 1995, 220–21)

As human beings in society and the economy, we are concerned with *what* people do and *how* they do it. It is not always necessary to know *why* people do what they do. The what and the how can be determined from observation, but the why is much more difficult or even impossible to ascertain.

William James drew a distinction between the *I* and the *Me*. The Me is the object of all of one's selfish concerns; the I is the ultimate thinker, which decides on actions. The I can make decisions directed toward benefiting the Me, or it can make decisions that will benefit others or even harm the Me. But this is counter to the economics assumption that every individual, that the I, always acts on the basis of self-interest—that it always acts to benefit the Me.

One of the great philosophical questions is whether or not human beings have free will. The economics assumption implies that humans do not. If in every circumstance the path of self-interest is always and inevitably chosen, then, you have no freedom of choice or free will. To have free will, you have to be able to choose. People are capable of forming and choosing among second-order desires. You can decide whether you want to choose the path of self-interest or some other course. Your *I* can decide what kind of person you want to be. In the words of William James, "A life is manly, stoical, moral, or philosophical, . . . in proportion as it is less swayed by paltry personal considerations and more by objective ends that call for energy, even though that energy bring personal loss and pain" (1902, 48).

Sometimes, as a last resort, the conventional assumption is defended on the basis that altruism, our choosing to help others, is in our self-interest. Thus, self-interest is stretched to contain its polar opposite, altruism. This is a classic logical fallacy, petitio principii (begging the question), that is, assuming what needs to be proved. Including opposites in one term, the concept is empty. One cannot include altruism in self-interest. In altruism, action is taken by the I and is directed not toward the Me but toward the Other.

Not all motivation is included in the span that ranges from complete self-interest through the varying mixtures of self-interest and altruism to complete altruism. There is another important dimension, selflessness. In Willa Cather's great phrase in *My Antonia,* "That is happiness; to be dissolved into something complete and great." A sure path to happiness is to lose oneself in a cause greater than oneself. One may escape from considerations of self-interest or altruism when one loses oneself in what one does—when one is completely immersed in advancing a cause, trying to master a body of knowledge, finding the answer to a formidable challenge, or creating. For many individuals, there is joy in absolute surrender to religious beliefs. In short, as John Stuart Mill wrote, "those only are happy who have their minds fixed on some object other than their own happiness." Emotion may overrun the cool calculation of self-interest. The lover may scorn prudential caution and the patriot forget his or her safety: "When the passion is extreme, suffering may actually be gloried in, provided it be for the ideal cause, death may lose its sting, the grave its victory" (James 1902, 87).

The behavior of every person is determined by the nexus of a large number of acting causes. No single cause rules the life of the individual. It is this evolving structure of multiple causal pathways that makes the complexities of the actions of a living creature so difficult to understand. People are concerned with establishing in their own minds who they are and how they wish to be seen and understood by others. An important part of personal identity is the public selfhood that is associated with the individual and has a profound influence on how he or she behaves.

> When someone is asked who, or more precisely what, he or she is, the answer is as likely to be ethnic ("a Serb"), national ("an Australian"), supernational ("an African"), linguistic ("a Francophone"), or even racial ("a white"), or tribal ("a Navajo"), and all sorts of combinations of these ("a Luo-speaking Black Kenyan") as it is religious—"a Baptist," "a Sikh," "a Lubavitcher," "a Bahai'i," "a Mormon," "a Buddhist," or "a Rastafarian." (Geertz 1998, 9)

As human beings, we spend much of our lives trying to understand ourselves and each other. To understand the behavior of someone else, we use our experience, our feelings, and our reason as our imaginative resources. Our imagination helps us to try to make sense of another person's emotions and beliefs—which we ourselves may not share—so as to try to make the other person's conduct intelligible to us. We often make mistakes in this attempt to learn what makes another person tick. We also may be mistaken in our understanding of our own actions.

As we all know, people can be unaware of their true motives. Often we do not know why we prefer one outcome to another. Research has demonstrated that a person may give a reason for an action when it was impossible that this verbalized reason was involved. The fact is that one likes to have a reason for what one does even when there is none. (Gazzaniga 1985). We have a strong inclination to justify our choices on some moral basis. In his negotiations, the great financier J. P. Morgan was guided by the conviction that there were two reasons for every action: a good one and the real one. The good reason is often the only one we acknowledge, even to ourselves. And, of course, sometimes the good reason *is* the real reason or there may be an admixture of both. Since the modern world has taken magic out of our lives, we have only science and our reason to guide us in obtaining what we want. But neither science nor reason can unquestionably tell us why we want it.

Modern formalist economic theory, however, bravely plunges forward and builds its intricate models on the assumption that it does know the motivation for human behavior. And, the why of human behavior is taken to be very simple. It is not complex, obscure, or self-contradictory, There is no ecstasy, no Dionysian music, no charismatic lightning flash of illumination. People do not alter their desires, change the motivations that drive them, or encounter a blinding light on the road to Damascus.

Most economic theorists do not even ask what self-interest is. It is part of the unconscious metaphysics that is taken for granted, and its usual interpretation is fairly narrow.

> Economics has conventionally assumed that each individual has stable and coherent preferences, and that she rationally maximizes those preferences. Given a set of options and probabilistic beliefs, a person is assumed to maximize the expected value of a utility function, $U(x)$. (Rabin 1998, 11)

Alchian and Allen state in plain words that man has an acquisitive drive or rationality that, although it may be instinctive, is a behavioral characteristic that exists whatever the economic system may be (1967, 20).

When Walras attempted to construct a theory of the economy that could mimic Newtonian physics, he confronted the problem of how there could be any regularity while the subjects, human beings, still were free to exercise autonomous choice. When humans are taken as we are, there is a richness of emotions, motives, expectations, and psychological uncertainties that affects all of us. There is a spectrum stretching from the noble to the nasty. C. S. Lewis found inside himself "a zoo of lusts, a bedlam of ambitions, a nursery of fears, a harem of fondled hatreds." Walras brushed all this aside and solved his problem by limiting human beings to a single drive, infinite selfishness. This—under the modern, more palatable guise of *rationally maximizing self-interest*—is still the fundament on which neoclassical economic theory rests.

In the United States, most young, ambitious, academic economists do not perceive knowledge of the what and the how of the economy as being important for professional success. What is felt to be important, rather, is developing the ability to apply refined mathematical techniques of analysis in solving abstract problems of economic phenomena (Frey and Eichenberger 1992; Klamer and Colander 1990, 18). Consequently, this fundamental assumption, on which all the modern complex formal theoretical structures rest, goes unexamined and unchallenged by these theorists. However, as I shall try to show in this and the following chapters, the special interpretation given by last century's economic theory to this particular assumption of constant human behavior is both wrong and damaging to the economy and society.

In our everyday life, we cannot explain every human action by applying the principle of cui bono. We know that human beings have impulses that are not completely selfish. A person (the I) can act morally when it is counter to his or her own interests (to the Me).

Human beings are not monochromatic. As Rousseau perceived, man is both bourgeois and *citoyen,* selfish and altruistic, individualistic but with the need to be a member of a community. Cicero, in his *De Legibus,* noted that "Natura propensi sumus ad diligendos homines quod fundamentum juris est" (We have a natural propensity to love our fellow men, and that is the foundation of all law). Like Walt Whitman, we don't relish undeserved compliments: "O admirers, praise not me—compliment not me—you make me wince, / I see what you do not—I know what you do not." If self-interest were dominant, we would not blush at unmerited praise.

People often fight more bitterly for what they perceive as moral or religious principle than they do for mere self-interest (Wilson 1993). Human beings are motivated by what they believe and think and not only by their self-interest. Others wonder whether life has some higher meaning (many are convinced of it), whether one lives to serve a goal beyond that of satisfying ones's personal desires.

Let me reinforce doubts about the fundamental axiom by reminding the reader that advocates of this conventional self-regarding assumption seem compelled—in order to make it acceptable to themselves and the rest of us—to argue that the pursuit of selfish self-interest is really for the greater good of all. Let me raise another doubt by asking economist-readers whether they believe that the assumption is true of the motives of economists themselves. To coin a new term, does the assumption fully explain *meta-economics*—the forces that explain the genesis of economic theories? Is the creation of economic theories driven only by the maximizing self-interest of the economist concerned? Does an economist work out a particular theory just because he or she believes, for example, that this will result in a lucrative appointment at a rich think tank, generous speaker's fees at businessmen's conferences, a well-endowed research center, or an endowed chair at a prestigious university? Surely, no one would believe that this is accurately descriptive of the full set of motivations of most members of the economic profession.

Economists who see the rest of the world as driven by self-interest indignantly repudiate such descriptions of their behavior. George Stigler, a leader of the market-idealizing Chicago school, reacted with the statement that economists

> do not relish an explanation of their own scientific behavior in ordinary economic terms. To tell an economist that he chooses that type of work and that viewpoint which will maximize his income is, he will hotly say, a studied insult. Such market oriented behavior will be characterized not with our customary phrases such as consumer sovereignty, but in terms as harsh as "intellectual prostitution." To adapt one's view to one's audience is hardly to be distinguished from the falsification of evidence and other disreputable behavior. (1982, 60)

A most remarkable aspect of the fundamental assumption is that it lacks substantiation. There is no a priori guarantee that it is true or complete. In a branch of knowledge that scorns as anecdotal evidence any reference to an individual's experience, there is no body of research that validates the basic assumption on which the whole formal conventional structure rests. It has never been established empirically that individuals always act in a rational, calculating, self-interested manner. Nor has it been established that when an individual does show calculative rationality in pursuing self-interest this behavior derives from inherent human nature rather than acculturation. (There is also no empirical basis that establishes whether behavior that does not fit this pattern is due to culture, an inherent universal human trait, personal idiosyncrasy, or personality quirk.)

An economist relying on the fundamental assumption, if he or she reflects on it at all, must believe that it accurately describes his or her motivation and accurately exemplifies the innermost essence of all human beings throughout history and in all cultures. In short, relying on the fundamental assumption is relying on the quintessential anecdotal evidence. As we shall see, there is ample justification for shying away from this particular evidence.

Historical Background

This concept of a human being as one who pursues only self-interest—narrowly defined as fully or nearly synonymous with selfishness—without regard for religious salvation is in fact an ancient one in the Western world. But the ancient concept differs from the conventional economic notion in that self-interest was perceived as malign, not beneficent. In pagan thought, present selfishness was contrasted with the myth of behavior in a lost golden age. In Christianity, reinforced by Saint Augustine's teachings on Original Sin, human beings after the Fall are seen as selfish and sinful. Jansenism in the Catholic Church and Calvinism in the Protestant censured human nature as being in extreme subjection to material and selfish ends. Secular writers, like Hobbes and Mandeville, accepted this view of human nature for their own ends (Viner 1991, 69–72).

Hobbes, in his *Leviathan,* published in 1651, used the belief as an argument for absolute government. He agreed with conventional theory in identifying self-interest as a prime motivator of man, but for him this had malevolent rather than beneficent results. With men driven by narrow considerations of self (i.e., selfishness) and distrustful of everyone else, the result is "bellum omnium contra omnes," a war of everyone against everyone else. Consequently, a strong authoritarian government with coercive power is needed—as only such a government can keep men in line and make society possible ([1651] 1914).

While the central theme of Bernard Mandeville's *The Fable of the Bees* (1714) was "Private Vices, Publick Benefits," it meant something quite different from the modern belief in the beneficent results of the pursuit of self-interest. Mandeville believed that private vices could be made to produce public benefits only through the skillful management of the clever politician.

Hobbes's conclusions were unacceptable to many. Samuel Johnson remarked that the "natural flights of the human mind are not from pleasure to pleasure, but from hope to hope." More serious refuters of Hobbes, like Cumberland, Shaftesbury, and Hutcheson, argued that man is not completely selfish; that people have nonegoistic and cooperative instincts and drives that make society and government possible without the need for an iron hand to keep them in line. Shaftesbury agreed that every creature seeks his or her private good and interest but also has a sense of public good and welfare (Viner 1991, 59).

Butler argued that man naturally tries to secure the private and public good—and that both motives are under the control of his or her conscience. He made the telling point that self-love can be served in pursuing the public good as well as the private. In addition to anticipating Adam Smith in noting that persons often serve the public good while pursuing their private ends, Butler warned—and this is directly relevant to the present discussion—against confusing possession of wealth or property with personal happiness. One can divert time or money from pursuing the accumulation of personal wealth to serving society. This may lead to greater personal happiness and is consequently in the self-interest of the individual (Myers 1983, 54–60).

It was also during this period that the modern notion began to be accepted that society is an aggregation of autonomous individuals, each of whom is endowed with rights against the claims of the group. The seventeenth- and eighteenth-century concept of natural rights and the theory of the social contract helped to liberate the individual from oppressive political systems. These ideas, by making the atomistic individual the basic unit of society, also provided a basis for liberal economics. (Pursued too far, however, the notion of the absolute priority of individual rights destroys social cohesion, civic values, and the responsibility of individuals to preserve a caring community.)

Adam Smith obviously did not agree with Hobbes that the pursuit of self-interest would necessarily have malevolent results. In *The Wealth of Nations,* he made his famous "invisible hand" remark—which is more often appealed to than understood—showing that under some circumstances self-interest has beneficial results:

> As every individual . . . endeavors as much as he can both to employ his capital in the support of domestic industry, and so to direct that industry that its produce may be of the greatest value; every individual necessarily labours to render the annual revenue of the society as great as he can. He generally, indeed, neither intends to promote the public interest, nor knows how much he is promoting it. By preferring the support of domestic to that of foreign industry, he intends only his own security; and by directing that industry in such a manner as its produce may be of the greatest value, he intends only his own gain, and he is in this, as in many other cases, led by an invisible hand to promote an end which was no part of his intention. Nor is it always the worse for the society that it was no part of it. By pursuing his own interest he frequently promotes that of the society more effectually than when he really intends to promote it. (1776, 423)

It is clear when one reads the paragraph in which the invisible hand remark is embedded that Smith was trying to show that an individual directing his or her investment to secure the greatest return results in greater national revenue as well. In anticipation of the modern calculation of gross national product (GNP), however, he was not erecting the pursuit of private gain as the only god and worship of it as the only way to secure social welfare. Note that he says that an individual pursuing his or her own interest *frequently*, i.e. not *invariably*, promotes that of society. Note also that in the last clause he recognizes that there are occasions when an individual intends to promote the interest of society rather than his or her own. In short, Smith did not subscribe to the notion that individuals always promote only their own interest and that this necessarily promotes the interests of society.

We know from Smith's empirical bent, as well as his remarks in other parts of the book, that he was also fully aware that pursuing private gain can be at the expense of public welfare. He notes: "People of the same trade seldom meet together, even for merriment and diversion, but the conversation ends in a conspiracy against the public, or in some contrivance to raise prices" (1776, 128). In another passage, he states that

> merchants and manufacturers . . . being collected into towns, and accustomed to that exclusive corporation spirit which prevails in them, naturally endeavor to obtain against all their countrymen, the same exclusive privilege which they generally possess against the inhabitants of their respective towns. They accordingly seem to have been the original inventors of those restraints upon the importation of foreign goods, which secure to them the monopoly of the home-market. (429)

Perhaps Smith's most devastating comment is his warning to regard merchants and master manufacturers with suspicion. He describes them as "an order of men, whose interest is never exactly the same with that of the public, who have generally an interest to deceive and even to oppress the public, and who accordingly have, upon many occasions, both deceived and oppressed it" (250). He scarcely misses an opportunity to condemn the "mean rapacity . . . of merchants and manufacturers, who neither are, nor ought to be the rulers of mankind" (460).

Smith is often misunderstood. Joan Robinson stated that for him it was "only necessary for each individual to act egotistically for the good of all to be attained" (1964, 53, cited in 1999, 620). Gerard Debreu in his 1983 Nobel Prize lecture commented that

> some of Walras' ideas had a long lineage that included Adam Smith's (1776) profound insight. Smith's idea that the many agents of an economy, making independent decisions do not create utter chaos but actually contribute to producing a social optimum, raises indeed a scientific question of central importance. (1984, 274–75)

For Adam Smith, it is clear that men pursuing self-interest do not uniquely and inevitably contribute to the public good. He also did not believe that man is completely dominated by self-interest; man is also controlled by conscience. The core of conscience is in our feelings for others and our reaction to their disapproval. Saint Paul's letter to the Philippians puts it succinctly: "Let each of you look not only to his own interests, but also to the interests of others." Keith Tribe summarizes Smith's concept of self-interest, as presented in his two major works, as follows:

> The Smithian conception of self-interest is not an injunction to act egoistically and without moral scruple, safe in the knowledge that by doing so the public good would somehow or other result; it is embedded within a framework of social reciprocity that allows for the formation of moral judgment. Smith . . . proposed that not only do we have a desire to be approved of, and act accordingly, we also wish to *be* what is approved of in others (1999, 621–22)

One contemporary of Adam Smith, a true believer that an individual should pursue only his selfish self-interest, is not, however, cherished as a founder of modern economics. The Marquis de Sade stated as a law of nature in his *La Philosophie dans le boudoir* that an individual's duty is only to secure his or her greatest sensation of enjoyment. Pleasure as the measure of existence should therefore be the principle on which the state and its laws should be based. This means, he argued logically, that very few acts should be considered criminal. Why should those who have nothing respect the property of those who have everything? No one can claim exclusive rights over another person, so marriage is obsolete. Adultery and incest are positively useful. In following his own teachings, this self-centered monster, the marquis, earned one death sentence, twelve years in prison, and thirteen years in a lunatic asylum.

Evolution

Many economists, with little background in the natural sciences, still believe that the conventional economic assumption is consistent with the theory of evolution. It is mostly taken for granted that evolution sanctions the common economic assumption that competition and pursuit of individual self-interest are dominant natural drives. This view dates from a century ago. Then the scientific consensus was that nature was "red in tooth and claw," that competing species battled with one another and the fittest were the aggressors who survived.

Now the consensus is different. The tiniest and most fragile of organisms dominate the life of the earth: the chloroplasts inside the cells of plants and the mitochondria inside all of the nucleated cells in humans and other animals. The chloroplasts use solar energy to produce the food and supply the oxygen on which we all depend. The chloroplasts appear to be the descendants of ancient algae that now live within the cells of higher plant forms.

The mitochondria in our cells as well as the cells of all other animals (with their own DNA separate from that of the cells in which they live) perform the vital function of turning oxygen into energy. These natural powerhouses descend from bacteria that began living within cells eons ago. Thus, evolution and cooperation go together. Cooperation among smaller units led to the emergence of more complex structures: first, cells with nuclei or mitochondria and then multicellular organisms.

This force for cooperation may even apply to more than animate life. Maja Mataric's experiments at the Brandeis University Interaction Laboratory found that when a group of ten to twenty autonomous robots are given tasks to do within a confined space they quickly learn courtesy and cooperation as social behavior (*Wired* 1995, 49).

As human beings, we consist of trillions of cooperating cells that live, do their job, and die so that we may function as conscious, thinking entities. If a pathogen infecting a human succeeds in penetrating a cell—thus protecting itself from the antibodies in the blood and lymph—the infected cell moves bits of protein from the intruder to its own surface. This draws the killer T-cells, and they kill the infected cell for the good of the whole. For artillerymen, it is reminiscent of the way a forward observer calls down salvos on his own position when the enemy is all around his foxhole. When a cell concentrates only on its own survival and reproduction, it has become a cancer, threatening the very existence of the human being. A cancer cell is a miniature neoclassical economic man.

Darwin perceived that success in survival was not solely dependent on competition. The success of many species, including human beings, is based on cooperation and altruism: "It must not be forgotten that although a high standard of morality gives but a slight or no advantage to each individual man and his children over the other men in his tribe, yet that an increase in the number of well-endowed men and an advancement of morality will certainly give an immense advantage of one tribe over another" (1952, 322).

Human beings succeeded in surviving and becoming dominant on earth through cooperation. The field studies of our relatives, the primates, conducted by post-Darwinian scholars have identified this characteristic as present in our evolutionary history (Ridley 1997). Recent research on social capital is showing that societies with high levels of trust and cooperation tend to have the most successful economies.

Cooperation is as essential for evolution as competition is in natural selection. Cooperation and competition are the twin forces that drove, and drive, evolution from the first beginnings of life on this earth. Cooperation creates more complex structures, and competition among them through natural selection determines which ones will survive (Coveney and Highfield 1995, 232).

The history of corporations in modern capitalism imitates the evolutionary chronicle of life. As Darwin perceived, socially moral behavior among people is evolutionarily advantageous. Socially moral behavior is essential if people are to live together in society. It includes justice, honesty, and nonviolence. Human beings are sociable by nature and therefore inclined to socially moral behavior, but this must be reinforced by the culture in which they live. Societies in which nobody can be trusted and nobody cooperates cannot survive.

Children die when parents ignore their needs. Yet the rewards to parenting are too uncertain to justify the sacrifices in material goods, personal efforts, and emotional commitment that most parents make. Children were cared for even in societies such as those of the San (Bushmen) of southern Africa and the Inuit (Eskimos) in which old persons were abandoned when they became a net drain on the tribe. The young are also protected and nourished in other species of mammals even though when they become adults they will compete for a limited food supply. More selfish species vanish.

What Is Self-interest?

But what exactly is "self-interest"? Adam Smith did not restrict the meaning of *self-interest* to a rational desire for command over more goods and services. As we have seen, for him self-interest included much more. Smith, moreover, did not assume that everyone understands what his or her true interests are, stating that

> though the interest of the labourer is strictly connected with that of the society, he is incapable either of comprehending that interest, or of understanding its connexion with his own. His condition . . . and his education and habits are commonly such as to render him unfit to judge even though he was fully informed. . . . Merchants and master manufacturers have a better knowledge of their own interest than the country gentleman has of his. (249–50; see also Viner 1991, 97)

Marshall, like Adam Smith, regarded economics as the study of men as they live and move and think in the ordinary business of life. He goes on to say that people in business, as elsewhere, are influenced by personal affections, their conceptions of duty, and their reverence for high ideals.

The ablest inventors and organizers of improved methods and appliances are more stimulated by emulation than love of wealth. Whatever the motive driving individuals, economics is concerned with the material rewards that people derive from their activity in business life. He comments in passing that economics cannot be compared to the exact physical sciences, for it deals with the ever-changing and subtle forces of human nature ([1920] 1952, 12).

We are born into this world with particular aptitudes and inclinations, which provide the bedrock on which our values and characters are built with the aid of our families, education, and culture. We are socialized by our parents, schools, and society to internalize the cultural and ethical standards necessary for any society to exist. Human beings can as easily be other regarding as self-regarding. W. V. Quine states that we must recognize that altruism is an existing drive and that we should nurture it in the formative years in order to fan the sparks of fellow feeling into a perceptible flame (1987, 3–5).

Altruism, in fact, is one of the innate drives in primates like the apes, the monkeys, and ourselves. One of the early classics in primate studies relates how the males of a troop of baboons that was being preyed on by a leopard organized an ambush and killed the predator, with one of the male baboons dying in the battle (Marais 1947, 33–38). In a modern set of experiments, macaques were fed if they were willing to pull a chain and electrically shock an unrelated macaque whose pain could be seen through a one-way mirror. Otherwise, they starved. After perceiving the results of pulling the chain, the macaques usually refused to pull it again. One starved for nearly two weeks rather than torture another (Sagan and Druyan 1992).

Altruism is also shown by other species. Everyone who observes birds will have seen smaller ones "mobbing," that is, harassing and attacking a larger predatory bird. They do this sometimes at considerable risk to themselves—a great horned owl may kill one of the crows that are pecking at it.

Modern psychology agrees that individuals do and should pursue self-interest. But this is only a part of individual motivation. It is also crucial to realize that self-interest is not necessarily synonymous with selfishness. Selfishness is concentration on the individual, with no regard for others. The selfish person is interested only in himself, wants everything for himself, gets pleasure from taking, not giving. A selfish individual is lacking in self-love. To make up for this deficiency, a selfish individual tries to get gratification by acquiring material possessions or power.

Self-interest is not an end but a means. The pursuit of self-interest is a means to attain the end of personal happiness. It is through self-love that happiness, self-approval, contentment, and peace with oneself are attained

(Fromm 1947, 134). A person who is absorbed in his or her own desires is often mentally ill. To become whole, such an individual has to learn to relate to others. While an individual needs self-love to be mentally healthy, psychologists emphasize that this requires more than being driven by selfishness. This is fundamental in human biology. For example, "there is one central, universal aspect of human behavior, genetically set by our very nature, biologically governed driving us along. . . . [This is] the urge to be useful. This urge drives society along, sets our behavior as individuals and in groups (Thomas 1980, 21).

Human beings learned generations ago that living in a community was necessary and desirable. This is the theme evoked in John Winthrop's famous sermon, delivered before the Puritans landed in 1630 to found the Massachusetts Bay Colony: "We must delight in each other, make each other's conditions our own, rejoice together, mourn together, labor and suffer together; always having before our eyes our commission and community in the work, our community as members of the same body."

The symbols of religion generally relate to the community of persons, not individuals. People are persons in relation to one another. The Christian church sees itself as a body, divinely called, not as a collection of individuals. The Covenant of the Israelites was between God and a people, not with individuals.

A community is indispensable, but it is also creative. A community is more than the sum of its parts. In sport, it is well known that "A team of champions will lose to a championship team." After winning the 2000 World Series, Joe Torre, manager of the New York Yankees, commented: "We might not have had the best players but we certainly had the best team." Through group interaction, one is stimulated intellectually and becomes more creative. This is why universities were created and flourish and why a place like Silicon Valley is a continuous fountain of innovation. The focus of economic theory on the individual per se overlooks this fundamental aspect of human life and the economy.

Empirical research in psychology "makes clear that preferences depart from pure self-interest in non-trivial ways. Subjects contribute to public goods more than can be explained by pure self-interest; they often share money when they could readily grab it for themselves; and they often sacrifice money to retaliate against unfair treatment" (Rabin 1998, 17).

The aim of science is truth, that is, the best approximation of the truth that one can attain and from this to secure explanatory power. The drive behind science is the great desire that drove Goethe's Faust: "Dass ich erkenne, was die Welt / Im Innersten zusammenhält."[1]

A substantial portion of research and invention is motivated by economic considerations and is subject to the economic calculus. But the research activity of academic economists illustrates that the economic motive of pecuniary gain is not necessarily the dominant or controlling motive. The desire to win prestige and respect in the profession is certainly important. Intellectual curiosity, the challenge of solving problems, the desire to make a contribution to human society, and the competitive instinct to work out an answer before anyone else are all important, nonpecuniary motives. In advancing science and technology, these motives are at work. There is pleasure, and indeed fun, in making a new machine or improving a process. It satisfies the creative instinct, perhaps as much as creating a work of art. There is pleasure in speculating about a challenging problem, coming up with a possible solution, and seeing if it will work.

When Nobel Prize winner Walter Gilbert left his Harvard laboratory to help found and run Biogen, the international biotechnology company, he explained his motives as wanting to do something socially useful, wanting to create an industrial structure, and wanting to make money. A few years later, he returned to his laboratory because he found research more fascinating than business and, as one investment analyst complained, he had run the company more as a lab than a business and apparently regarded the company's capital as one big research grant (Shapiro 1992, 218).

A survey of American college freshmen in 1992 showed that two out of three said they wanted to lead a meaningful life, which they defined as doing good in addition to doing well (Murphy 1993, 6). To devote one's life to purely selfish ends brings nothing but misery. Many maladies (cardiovascular disease, stroke), accidents, suicides, and homicides are linked to loneliness, the breakdown of human bonding, and the loss of the sense of belonging to a community. Health and wholeness require one to be connected to other people in a community (David 1993, 32). It is agony, death-provoking desperation to feel that one has been forsaken, that no one cares.

To be happy, we must live for something more than selfish ends. This is a truth discovered and repeated across the centuries by the great thinkers and philosophers. Socrates idealized the good individual in the good society, and Plato and Aristotle emphasized the importance of human interrelationships. Buddha taught that men should give up their narrow personal goals and tormenting desires and devote themselves to altruism and self-renunciation. The ideal in the teachings of Confucius was the noble man in the noble state, and he exalted behavior that ensured harmonious social relationships.

Happiness does not come from numerous possessions, an enormous income, or great success. To be happy, one must have something to do that one knows is useful to others, someone to love, and something to hope for. The work that one does must provide something more than a monetary reward—a sense of contribution, of pride in accomplishment, of joy in using one's special talents. Marshall commented that the verdict of experience is that true happiness depends on self-respect and self-respect comes only from endeavoring to live so as to promote the progress of the human race ([1920] 1952, n. 15).

William James in his *Varieties of Religious Experience* recalled that for people in all cultures religious rapture, moral enthusiasm, and cosmic emotion are all unifying states in which the sand and grit of selfhood incline to disappear. This is central in Christian theology, in which the individual is taught to submit to and find his or her center in a power or principle outside the self. Greed is strongly condemned. According to the teaching, "those who desire to be rich fall into temptation, into a snare, into many senseless and hurtful desires that plunge men into ruin and destruction. For the love of money is the root of all evils "(1 Tm. 6:10).

In Buddhist or Hindu societies, a rich man pursuing unselfish self-interest may give up all his possessions and become a beggar. The Buddhist belief teaches reincarnation, which suggests that one does not have to achieve everything in this life—there will have more lives and more chances. It is still fairly common today, even in Christian cultures, for such a person to become a monk, priest, or minister.

In modern secular countries, people who are motivated by religion or humanism often devote their lives or a portion of them to serving society rather than their own economic interests. Andrew Carnegie believed that a man who dies rich dies disgraced. He lived up to his philosophy. After selling his steel company to J. P. Morgan for around $500 million, he devoted his life to giving away his fortune, which was worth billions in today's dollars. In the few years before his death, he succeeded in giving away 90 percent of his wealth.

The warrior ethic in nonpredatory states is counter to the whole notion of selfish self-interest. Military officers are expected to place the interests of the nation and the welfare and safety of their subordinates above their own concerns. The classic military values are sacrifice, unity, self-discipline, and placing the interests of the military unit above those of the individual. To ensure that officers will live up to this ideal, military academies strive to inculcate honor and integrity—not the pursuit of selfish self-interest—into their hearts and souls. That this does result in high ethical behavior by most is indicated by the fact that the American public has consistently ranked the military at the top of American professions and institutions in terms of trust and confidence

Admiral James B. Stockdale survived eight years as prisoner of war in Vietnam. He credits the ability, shown by him and others, to resist torture without breaking to comradeship, pride, an enduring sense of self-worth, and that mixture of conscience and egoism called personal honor. A man driven only by selfishness would have succumbed to the mixture of punishments and rewards offered by his captors.

On February 21, 1916, the German army on the Western Front began the great battle of Verdun, unleashing a hurricane of high-explosive shells on the French trenches. The High Command had decided to try to win World War I by putting the entire French army through an artillery-mincing machine. General Falkenhayn chose historic Verdun, where a salient cramped the defenders but which French pride would not allow them to abandon. The plan was to erase the defenders with a hail of shells and make only limited advances while attracting French reserves into the killing field until the entire French army had been pulverized. Before the battle ended in June, more than 600,000 soldiers had died on both sides.

During the course of the four months, French divisions went into battle, suffered tremendous casualties, were taken out for rest and replenishment, and were sent back in again. Soldiers who had been wounded and healed rejoined their units in the hell. Why? Why did the millions of soldiers on both sides involved in the trench warfare for more than four years continue to fight for so long? Why did soldiers obey when ordered, as in the British attack in Flanders in October 1917, to attack over ground so swampy that many wounded drowned where they fell? The best explanation is that given in Jules Romains' *Verdun:* Jerphanion, on leave from the battlefield, explains to a friend why he will return to the slaughter.

> . . . c'est la contrainte sociale, tout simplement. La société veut, . . . que les hommes souffrent et meurent sur le front. Alors ils souffrent et ils meurent. Voilà. . . . la peur que l'homme a de la société est encore plus forte que la peur qu'il a des obus.
>
> Leur peur de la société n'est pas physique. Elle est mystique. L'homme est ainsi fait que chez lui une peur physique est presque toujours moins forte qu'une peur mystique. . . . la peur mystique de la société sait prendre des formes qui elles-mêmes ont une action immédiate. D'un côté la peur de l'obus. Mais de l'autre la peur de ce que penseront tes camarades, ton chef, ou tes hommes, si tu es chef. Il faudrait en un sens plus de courage à un homme moyen pour affronter la réputation de lâcheté que pour affronter un éclat d'obus.[2] (Romains 1938, 223–24)

More

The fundamental axiom that self-interest is the dominant human motivation usually is accompanied by the corollary that self-interest is unlimited in its demands. Alchian and Allen, for example, plainly state in their text that "We . . . assume that man is greedy—meaning solely that he wants command over more rather than less goods" (1967, 20).

Mansfield in the earliest edition of his text (1970) says that the assumption is that consumers are rational, that is, they try to maximize their utility by getting on the highest possible indifference curve. But, he says, even the Rockefellers and Mellons cannot get to their highest indifference curve since this would mean spending more money than even they have (32) In the fourth edition (1982, 49), he merely states that we assume that the consumer always prefers more of a commodity to less. This fundamental axiom depends on the inarticulate assumption that the culture within which individuals act is consistent with the desire of individuals to maximize their wealth. This unvoiced assumption is not necessarily always true.

In brief, last century's economics did not question the commercial-hedonist values of contemporary American capitalism. These are less dominant in the communitarian capitalism of Western Europe, where the earlier values of service to the state, classical humanism, and Augustine's City of God are still strong. Similar exceptions can be made for Japan and the Confucian capitalism of Singapore, Taiwan, and South Korea. And for India, R. K. Narayan drew the contrast in this way: "America's emphasis is on material aquisitions and a limitless pursuit of prosperity. . . . The quality of life in India is different. . . . From childhood an Indian is brought up on the notion that austerity and a contented life is good" (*Economist* 2001b, 88)

In material hedonism, the formula for self becomes "I am what I possess" (or, as an American bumper sticker proclaims, "I live to shop"). What I possess includes all the things that can be measured in terms of money. The overriding objective of human endeavor is to maximize material comfort and enjoyment, and there is no end or satiety to this, for humans will always have new desires for goods. This present-day social myth is so dominant that most economists—and probably most modern people—find it hard to conceive that human nature can be different. This is, in short, a demonstration of the "fallacy of false fixity," the belief that a particular social behavior is part of the nature of things and cannot be other than what it is.

Actually, the desire for material goods beyond the basic necessities of food, clothing, and shelter has to be acquired or taught. Even the demand for clothing where the climate is warm is a learned cultural custom: In Karamoja, Uganda, as late as the 1960s a man considered himself socially proper in public without a stitch of clothing but would be ashamed to appear with an uncultivated hairdo. In the northern Gold Coast (present-day Ghana), local town ordinances were needed before women would don skirts to go to town.

African tradition discouraged accumulation of all kinds. It was only after years of contact with Indian, Lebanese, and Syrian traders, who penetrated into the back country with cotton cloth, pots and pans, steel hoes, and sewing machines, that new desires were created. Only then did African farmers begin to value the opportunity to produce in order to buy directly the commodities they had learned to desire (Oliver 1991, 196–97, 242).

But this was only the first stage in creating Acquisitive Man. European employers discovered that their workers were willing to work but only in order to buy the new commodities. Employers complained about target workers, those who were interested in earning a targeted amount and once they had it stopped working. If the piece rate was raised to encourage laborers to work harder and earn more, they would work less instead. They were interested in working just enough to pay for their strictly limited requirements. The workers needed money to pay the head tax, pay school fees for their children, or purchase the few commodities.[3] This limited desire for goods was not unique to Africa; similar reactions were shown by other peoples as they came into contact with the material West.

King George III sent the first British ambassador to China with a cornucopia of British goods as gifts for the emperor in order to induce him to open China to British traders. The emperor was not swayed. It took military force in the Opium War of 1839–42 to secure a market in China for British merchants.

We now know a good deal from the direct testimony of the peasants themselves of what life was like in a small medieval community in the early years of the fourteenth century. This village, Montaillou, is near Carcassone in what is now southern France. A zealous bishop, Jacques Fornier, ran a rigorous Inquisition in his area and meticulously recorded the depositions of the people summoned. The testimony included detailed descriptions of their daily lives: what they did, conversations with others, relationships, beliefs, and so on. In this world of the 1300s, the peasants felt a deep repugnance toward "wealth." Ordinary Catholics, as well as the heretical Cathars, regarded wealth and the pleasures it bought as an inevitable source of sin:

> "Come, Master Arnaud Teisseire," said a Pamiers jailer to the doctor of Lordat, dying in his cell and refusing to confess his sinful life, "you have wallowed in such opulence! And you have lived in such splendid fashion! And you have had so many temporal pleasures! How could you be without sin?" (Le Roy Ladurie 1978, 332)

People who were relatively rich were sometimes regarded as cowards for holding on to their possessions in this world instead of seeking salvation in the next.

The people of Montaillou were not unique. Contrast the modern successive generations of Rothschild bankers with the great Augusburg bankers, the House of Fugger, of the late Middle Ages. The House of Fugger came to an early end simply because no one in a succeeding generation was interested in acquiring wealth (Mumford 1973,168). The notion that wants are unlimited is strictly a cultural stereotype.

It is, of course, an economic truism that as one acquires more of any one commodity at some point its marginal utility will decline to zero. What economic theory finds harder to cope with is the idea that one can have enough of *everything*. The consumer is usually assumed to be like the woman tourist from the Midwest who, visiting Cape Cod and seeing the vast ocean, exclaimed, "This is the first time I've ever seen enough of anything!"

Many people, even in the present-day materialistic West, do not have unlimited desires. In the successful older high-income service economies, the conventional materialistic economic motive may be weakening. When income rises rapidly enough to enable one to make all the expenditures previously beyond one's reach, often one of the luxuries granted is to give up living on a budget. An individual stops trying to live like economic man in comparing one expenditure to another. What is budgeted now is not expenditures but time. One Texas oil billionaire, who could have lived in a style that a Roman emperor would have envied, lived very modestly, dressing like a blue-collar worker and driving a beat-up pickup truck. The only luxury in which he indulged was bigamy, supporting two wives and their families.

Once their basic physiological needs are satisfied, a growing number of people turn away from consumerism and the further accumulation of goods that needlessly complicate their lives and instead turn to a less stressful lifestyle. Herbert Stein, for example, wisely advised that the way to happiness is: "Keep high aspirations, moderate expectations, and small needs."

A poll in April 1986 found that only 14 percent of the people in the United Kingdom and 15 percent in the United States had as their main goal in life to get rich. The percentage in Japan, which has only recently acquired a high standard of living, was 38 percent. Most people in the United Kingdom and the United States wished to be able "To live as I like" (60 percent in the United Kingdom, 67 percent in the United States). In Japan, this figure was 43 percent. Another goal was to "help society, gain social position" (26 percent, United Kingdom; 18 percent, United States; 19 percent, Japan).

Many people decide to give their life purpose by going into low-paid social work or the ministry. Some become members of cults that provide only the bare basics. While it may seem incomprehensible, there is satisfaction in asceticism, in denying desires. The theme that fulfillment or freedom lies in renunciation is so prevalent in religion that it must correspond to some deep, fundamental part of human nature. As early as 400 B.C.E. Antisthenes, the reputed founder of the Cynic school, was teaching that virtue, and the resulting happiness, was freedom from wants and desires.

> We have lost the power even of imagining what the ancient idealization of poverty could have meant: the liberation from material attachments, the unbribed soul, the manlier indifference, the paying our way by what we are or do and not by what we have, . . . in short, the moral fighting shape. . . . the desire to gain wealth and the fear to lose it are our chief breeders of cowardice and propagators of corruption. There are thousands of conjunctures in which a wealth-bound man must be a slave, whilst a man for whom poverty has no terrors becomes a freeman. (James 1902, 333–34)

In Asia, two of the dominant religions. Buddhism and Hinduism, teach behavior that is directly opposed to that of economic man. Hinduism idealizes asceticism and preaches self-purification through the denial of desires. The spiritual objective for a Buddhist is to learn to live with the minimum amount of material goods. The ideal is a holy, contemplative life detached from toil and worry, desire, and disturbing passions of the heart. A person is liberated from evil by means of detachment from the world. The fullness of such detachment is nirvana, a state of perfect indifference with regard to the world and its material goods and emotions. In countries with a Buddhist culture, a successful businessman does not automatically enjoy the respectability, prestige, and self-satisfaction that he would have in the United States. It is not unusual for a highly successful entrepreneur in a Buddhist country like Thailand, for example, to give it all up at the summit of his career to become a monk.

The message of Saint Francis of Assisi six centuries ago was similar. He gave up wealth and luxury for a life of poverty. A somewhat related secular theme was expressed by Emily Dickinson (Shattuck 1996):

> "Heaven" is what I cannot reach!
> The Apple on the Tree—
> Provided it do hopeless—hang—
> That—"Heaven" is—to Me!
>
> The Color, on the Cruising Cloud—
> The Interdicted Land—
> Behind the Hill—the House behind—
> There—Paradise—is Found.

Marcel Proust expressed a similar sentiment.

> Nothing is more alien to me than to seek happiness in any immediate sensation, and even less in any material realization. A sensation, however disinterested it may be, a perfume, a shaft of light, if they are physically present, are too much in my power to make me happy. (letter to Princesse Bibesco)

The modern boy who said that he preferred programs on the radio to those on TV "because the pictures are better" and the romantic movement of the nineteenth century agreed: what is imagined surpasses the real. Keats sang: "Heard melodies are sweet, but those unheard / Are sweeter."

Conventional economics never spells out the full implications of the assumption that the desires of modern man are illimitable. What kind of society does this imply? The theory depicts people as being forever unsatisfied, driven by desires that will never be fulfilled. People are supposed to seek but not find, to achieve yet always lose. Ever striving toward unattainable and unsatisfying ends, with no rational limit to his or her desires, the individual must be oppressed by anxiety, insecurity, and loss of confidence. Such individuals, isolated and disordered, in endless competition with others who are driven by the same insatiable desires, would create an anarchy and not a coherent, livable society. Nietzsche maintained that such people are "last men," animals whose horizons are limited to securing their creature comforts.

There is no doubt but that unlimited demand for goods is a dominant drive in some people. But it is wrong to assume that unlimited desire is the dominant drive in *all* people. If there is anything inherent in human nature, it is rather the tendency to be indifferent to acquiring additional goods once one's basic physiological needs are met. This is demonstrated both by the behavior of "primitive" peoples before they are subjected to modern economic conditioning and by those persons who through religion, philosophy, or reason have immunized themselves from the prevalent hedonistic influences.

Conclusion

Human beings are motivated by what they think and believe, by how they have been socialized, and not blindly, inevitably, by selfish self-interest. For Smith and the classical liberals, the idea of self-interest correctly had a crucial moral component, stemming from human nature and the needs of society. This, unfortunately, has been overlooked by modern antiliberals and market ideologues. Adam Smith was no eighteenth-century precursor of Gordon Gekko, pronouncing "Greed is good." We are social animals, and social virtues such as trustworthiness and a willingness to cooperate are essential to our well-being and a healthy economy and society. In our capitalist market economy, most of us have to make a living and hence have to pay attention to the economic motive. This is required by our economy and not necessarily by human nature. Yet the economic motive does not demand the single-minded and maximum selfish self-interest of theoretical economics. In making a living, one does not have to be greedy or insensitive to others, even though some people do go that far.

Useful and valuable results through empirical research can be secured by concentrating on the regularities of the *what* and *how* of human economic behavior. It is not necessary to assume complete selfishness to find reasonable consistency and regularity of behavior in particular situations. This requires focusing on material welfare results rather than unmeasurable psychological benefits. From these findings, as in other historical sciences, we can infer probable results solidly based on having studied the process in action. In this way, with a focus on material welfare and the real world, economics can become a true and relevant science. As usual, Marshall put the argument aptly when he noted that

> the function of the science is to collect, arrange and analyse economic facts, and to apply the knowledge, gained by observation and experience, in determining what are likely to be the immediate and ultimate effects of various groups of causes; and . . . the Laws of Economics are statements of tendencies expressed in the indicative mood, and not ethical precepts in the imperative. ([1920] 1952, v)

CHAPTER 4

Reason and Rationality

> No economist is more dangerous than the pure theorist without practical experience and instinctive understanding in the real world . . . seeking precision in a world of imprecision.
>
> —AUSTIN ROBINSON

The second element of the fundamental assumption is that every individual acts rationally in making choices to maximize his or her self-interest. This "rationality principle" (as Popper has called it) is a foundation of mainstream economics and a canonical hypothesis of economic theory (Kreps 1997, 59).[1] In Milton Friedman's words: the assumption takes "profit maximization as a central element and treats human beings as rationally directed toward the maximization of profit" (1983, 172–73).

The assertion that people always act rationally is taken by many theorists to be an axiom, that is, more than an assumption, in Aristotle's definition, "a proposition that neither can nor need be proved." Further, "Axioms . . . constitute claims about this world so widely agreed as to make further argument unnecessary (Hahn 1985, 5). This canonical hypothesis (assumption or axiom) when it is analyzed asserts that:

1. People have full knowledge of what is in their best interest
2. They should act rationally if they wish to optimize their well-being
3. They really do act rationally to optimize their well-being.

This assumption turns out to be both normative and positive: people should and do always act in their best interests. Regardless of whether it is regarded as an assumption, a self-evident proposition, or an a priori truth, as such, "rationality" is exempt from having to be tested empirically.

The conventional economic view of human nature rejects earlier classical and religious concepts. For most of Western history, the role of reason in relationship to desires was regarded as being that of the sovereign in relation to his or her subjects. Reason was relied on to control the body, to rein in or deny our appetites. Plato taught that the soul should lead the affections. Aristotle believed that the good life was one that cultivated all the human dispositions while limiting them with the Golden Mean. In the Gnostic Gospel of Philip, it was put strongly: each individual is called on to know his or her own potential for doing evil. He or she must recognize the evil within and consciously eradicate it. Thomas Aquinas instructed human beings to exercise sovereignty over desires, as morality is the master of the passions. Sufism, the mystical tradition within Islam, teaches the rejection of the ego and the self. In economic theory, things are turned upside down: desires are sovereign and reason the servant. Desires are limited not by a person's reason but only by the difficulty of securing the means to satisfy them all.

But what is acting rationally? A good working dictionary definition is that it is the most effective, most logical behavior of an agent toward attaining a desired goal or purpose.[2] Irrational behavior is that which frustrates or, in spite of the agent's belief, does not contribute to the attainment of an agent's goal or purpose. Nonrational behavior is that governed by matters of taste or value, for which no reasons are required. Note that the classification is not necessarily that which the agent would apply to his or her own behavior but that which a competent, objective observer would judge to be applicable.

In the first part of this chapter, we will undertake a quick exploration of the sweeping claim that all behavior is fully rational. Then we will focus more narrowly on economic theory.

Human Behavior

The belief that one can explain everything on the basis of a simple assumption about human behavior—which is not scientifically provable and contradicts much of what we do know and can observe about humanity—does not meet the test of reason. Certainly, human beings can and very often do act rationally. But the notion that people always demonstrate fully rational, optimizing, calculating behavior is not supported by empirical observations in any social science. Nor is it supported by psychological analysis of human behavior.

Most human beings are not atomistic individuals lacking social ties to others. Everyone has some connection to the social structures in which he or she is involved. We are not brought up in a social vacuum. Our families, our institutions, and the culture of our milieu influence the particular behavior patterns and expectations that we adopt (Bourdieu 1990). The external influences upon people exerted by institutions, history, and relationships are manifold and pervasive. Actions can be motivated by emotion, impulse, faith, or authority. The inner drives and emotions that motivate people are infinitely complex. As a result, it is highly probable that most motivations that people regard as reasonable would fail the extreme economic rationality test. Few people are as continually, calculatingly rational as Thomas Gradgrind in Dickens's *Hard Times:*

> Thomas Gradgrind, sir. A man of realities. A man of facts and calculations. A man who proceeds on the principle that two and two are four, and nothing over, and who is not to be talked into allowing for anything over. . . . With a rule and a pair of scales, and the multiplication table always in his pocket, sir, ready to weigh and measure any parcel of human nature, and tell you exactly what it comes to. It is a mere question of figures, a case of simple arithmetic. (1854, 2)

Most people are not and would not want to be a Gradgrind. And in the end even Gradgrind himself repudiated this approach to life.

Nonrational and Irrational Behavior

Since Freud, there has been general acceptance that people have unconscious thoughts, motives, fantasies, and emotions. One may have an inner self of negativity, doubt, fear, and aggression and an outer, conscious self of assumed kindness and niceness. There is often some unconscious, repressed motivation for human behavior—betrayed sometimes by Freudian slips.

Experience in early childhood frequently explains much of how a person acts in later life. Past experience and the phenomenon of transference all play a part in motivating present behavior. Carl Jung observed that the great decisions of human life are far more motivated by instincts and other mysterious unconscious factors than by "conscious will and well-meaning reasonableness." Human motivation is, in short, a highly complex and difficult subject, and psychological and psychoanalytic theories have not established a solid basis on which one can rely in trying to explain the *why* of human behavior.

People raised in a particular religion or culture tend to accept the tenets of the religion or the teachings of the culture, often without reflection or examination. One's philosophy, religious training, exposure to the raw edges of human experience, and attitudes toward life and family and the moral standards and values one acquires and seeks to observe are all likely to influence one's thinking and actions. These may act at the level of the subconscious before they are considered at the level of the conscious. A statement that is true may have little chance of being believed unless it fits within a framework of beliefs that may never have undergone rational examination.

The idea that human beings are basically rational was inherited from the Age of Reason. It took World War I to destroy this belief for many. John R. Commons, depressed by the slaughter of millions of men in the senseless conflict, put his disillusionment strongly: "Man is not a rational being as the Eighteenth Century thought: he is a being of stupidity, passion, and ignorance, as Malthus thought" (1963, 682). Keynes agreed that the a priori view that human nature is reasonable "is disastrously mistaken, overlooking the insane and irrational springs of wickedness in most men" (1949, 98–99).

Most of us would admit that we make many decisions on less than a completely rational basis. There is a Dutch saying: "If you behave normally, you are quite mad enough." Every economist who makes New Year's resolutions is confessing that the preceding year's behavior has been less than optimally rational.

Some people are slaves to a work ethic. A person, blessed or cursed by this, feels that he or she has to accomplish something in a given day—whether it is doing a piece of paid work or mowing the lawn. This is vital to one's sense of well-being—an emotional not a rational requirement.

Many of us are not rational at all for much of the time. The American government financed a three-year study (1990–92), part of the first systematic attempt to discover how many Americans had experienced a major mental disorder. The survey found that nearly half of all Americans experience a psychiatric disorder at least once in their lifetimes and that 30 percent are affected in any one year. The survey used the American Psychiatric Association's definitions of *disorder*, which includes cases of mild depression and anxiety that do not necessarily require professional care but affect function and rational thinking. Mental illness is heavily concentrated among 14 percent of the population. Eighty-nine percent of the cases of the most severe psychiatric disorders, such as schizophrenia and manic depression, are in this 14 percent group (Kessler 1994, 8).

Millions of people find solace in religious beliefs for which one would have difficulty finding any rational basis. Some cults have led to mass suicide: For example, in 1978, at Jonestown, Guyana, an American pastor led a mass suicide of 914 members of his Peoples Temple. On another occasion, 77 members of the Solar Temple died in mass murder-suicides in Switzerland, France, and Canada over the course of several years in the late 1970s. In 1997, 39 members of a computer-linked cult, Heaven's Gate, killed themselves in California in the hope of migrating to a spaceship supposed to be traveling in the wake of the Hale-Bopp comet. And in 2000 some 900 members of the Movement for the Restoration of the Ten Commandments of God died in Uganda in a mass murder-suicide.

Two great scientific revolutions drastically changed our knowledge of how human beings fit into the cosmos. The earth is not the center of the universe but only a small planet circling a small sun, one of about 100 billion stars in our galaxy in a universe of at least 50 billion galaxies. Evolution was the second great discovery. Refusal to accept these scientific facts—which are now accepted even by the Vatican—fails a test of rationality. (In October 1992, the Roman Catholic Church exonerated Galileo for having taught that the earth rotates around the sun, and in October 1996 Pope John Paul II stated that "evolution is more than an hypothesis.") Yet tens of millions of Americans believe that the universe in all its immensity and life in all its diversity was created in six days of twenty-four hours each. There are 16 million Southern Baptists, the largest American denomination favoring a literal reading of the Bible, and there are 5,000 members of the American Humanist Association, which accepts the guidance of science.

Astrology, a five-thousand-year-old Babylonian belief, still has millions of followers—many of them believers in religions whose fundamental teachings are in stark contrast to those of astrology. Newspapers carry astrology columns. Even the *Economist* has carried a full-page ad for a newsletter, *Financial Astrology,* that claims to forecast stock market indexes and major currency and commodity trends with as much as 97 percent accuracy (August 19, 1995). Astrology is pure irrationality. Edward P. Lazear claims that market tests show that "economics is the premier social science" (2000, 99). On this basis, astrology is superior to economics. Many more people consult their horoscopes regularly for advice than consult economic advisers. Boris Yeltsin of Russia had a team of Kremlin staff astrologers to guide him in making decisions (Specter 1997, 1). President Reagan was notoriously reluctant to be influenced by advice from Harvard economics professor Martin Feldstein, chairman of the Council of Economic Advisers, but the scheduling of his presidential activities was determined by an astrologer.

> The President's Chief of Staff, Donald Regan, complained: ". . . the President's schedule is the single most potent tool in the White House, because it determines what the most powerful man in the world is going to do and when he is going to do it. By humoring Mrs. Reagan we gave her this tool—or, more accurately, gave it to an unknown woman in San Francisco who believed that the zodiac controls events and human behavior and that she could read the secrets of the future in the movements of the planets." For early 1987, for example, Mrs. Reagan's

> astrologer laid down the following prohibitions for the President to follow: "Jan 16–23 very bad; Jan 20 nothing outside WH—possible attempt; Feb 20–26 be careful; March 7–14 bad period; March 10–14 no outside activity!" etc. (Regan 1988, 74, 367)

Michael Drosnin's book, *The Bible Code,* claimed that God's plan for mankind is encrypted in the first five biblical books (the Torah). When the code is cracked, accurate predictions are revealed of such events as the Kennedy assassination, Shakespeare's authorship of *Hamlet* and *Macbeth,* and other occurrences and personages of importance in modern times. All these prophecies are derived, in crossword puzzle style, by assembling letters, some upside down, some with rows between each letter, in the Hebrew text. *The Bible Code* became a best seller in 1997 in the United States, in Great Britain, and (in translation) in France, Germany, Israel, Italy, Japan, Korea, the Netherlands, Spain, and Taiwan.

Choosing the persons who will govern us is one of the most important responsibilities of voters in democracies. Certainly some people do make rational choices in the political process, carefully weighing the policies of the party and the candidate they vote for. But many, perhaps most, vote for a party and candidate because of family history, social or tribal reasons, physical attractiveness of the candidate, or a host of reasons other than the real issues involved.

In one of his experiments, B. F. Skinner fed caged pigeons small amounts of food at short regular intervals. A pigeon that had been bobbing its head when the food was first supplied began to bob its head every time food was expected. Another one, which had been turning, acted as though food and turning were related. Similar irrational practices are common among people: an executive who puts on his "lucky" tie for important occasions, for example, or a baseball player who is careful to take off and put on his cap in some special way before taking the field (Fuerbringer 1997). When I was an avid sailor, I forbade anyone on my boat to comment that a cruise was going well until we were safely made fast to a mooring.

Most people believe, wholly or partly, in some kind of irrational nonsense: the Bermuda Triangle, poltergeists, levitation, UFOs, communication with the dead, clairvoyance, mediums. Owners build hotels and office buildings that lack a thirteenth floor. Newton, Napier, and Tycho Brahe all devoted much of their time to what we regard as irrational pursuits. There is a story about the great scientist Nils Bohr that well illustrates the deep-seated influence of superstition: A visitor to Bohr's laboratory was astonished to see a horseshoe nailed over the entrance. "Surely", the visitor said to him, "you don't believe that a horseshoe brings good luck?" "Of course not!", Bohr replied. "But I have been assured that it works even if you don't believe in it!"

The success of lotteries demonstrates that large numbers of people do not rationally assess their chances of gain and loss. The probability of winning in a lottery is less than the gambler's share in the total wagered. As Adam Smith noted, people overvalue their chances of winning and undervalue their chances of loss (107–8). The same is true of other forms of gambling.

An East Coast mobster, Bugsy Siegel, built the first American gambling palace, the Flamingo, in a barren desert town, Las Vegas, Nevada, in 1946–47. Shortly thereafter, Bugsy was riddled with bullets, and his murder has never been solved. Since then, Las Vegas has become the fastest-growing city in the United States, with its million residents supported by hordes of gambling visitors.

Americans spent more than $630 billion on legal gambling in 1998, 40 percent of this at casinos that attracted more than 150 million visitors. Compare this to the $7 billion spent at the movies. In 1945, Nevada was the only state with legalized gambling. By 2000, casinos had been authorized in twenty-three states to profit from the millions of people whose strategy for their future is the pathetic hope of striking it big.

The National Gambling Impact Study Commission found in a study conducted for the U.S. Congress that as of March 1999 some 5.5 million Americans were pathological or addictive gamblers and 15 million more were at risk. It is obvious that calculative rationality is not the strong suit of millions of people.

In 1994, medical researchers at a conference at Harvard reported that there is powerful evidence that the brain and the body may alter the way they function in response to interactions with other people, to cultural symbols and imperatives, and to subjective states like belief and faith. Voodoo deaths are well documented in primitive societies: people, told that they have been condemned by magic, die even though there is no physical cause. In our culture, we use placebos.

> A patient complains to his doctor about back pain. The physician can't find anything physically wrong, so she gives the man a placebo, a sugar pill, and tells him that such "medicine" has been helpful in cases like his. A few days later he says that his pain is gone.
>
> A group of asthmatics inhale a solution that researchers warn them contains irritating and allergy-provoking substances. Half of them claim the spray makes their condition worse; 12 report full-blown asthma attacks. Researchers then give them a medication to relieve their distress, and the asthmatics report that their symptoms have disappeared.

> In both situations, they inhaled the same harmless and normally ineffective salt solution. (Cromie 1995, 3)

One review of a number of studies found that the apparent benefit of medical treatment is due to the placebo effect between 30 and 100 percent of the time (Lipman 1996)

Science has not yet produced a model of the self that can be fully relied on as a firm base for a science of any realm of human action. But cognitive science has advanced to the point where it is accepted that people possess multiple intelligences or "modules of mind." Individuals differ from one another in the relative strengths of these. These intelligences control the ways in which people perceive, retain, and use information. Each individual constructs his or her own amalgam of intelligences. Rational, logical intelligence is only one component. It is presumptuous and unjustified for economic theory to assert that calculative rational logic is the dominant factor controlling everyone's behavior.

Experiments have shown, and this is intuitively obvious to most noneconomists, that people will reject a transaction, even if it is in their self-interest, when they perceive that the transaction is not *fair* to them. Conscience is important. According to the maximizing self-interest assumption, people should cheat when they can get away with it. But most people, including good economists, do not cheat. Annual dues of the American Economic Association are self-assessed, varying with the member's income. Even though the amount paid is confidential and there is no penalty for underpaying, two-thirds to three-fourths of the members appear to respect their voluntary obligation (AEA Executive Committee 1999, 455).[3]

The amounts, totalling over $200 billion in 2000 in the United States, and scope of charitable contributions are far higher than they would be if maximizing self-interest accurately described human motivations.

Knowing what is in our best self-interest and acting accordingly does not always follow. Most of us have known people who disastrously mismanage their lives. An individual may habitually pursue self-defeating behavior. A classic example is Richard Savage, the poet and subject of a Samuel Johnson biography. Talented and charming but irresponsible, imprudent, and untrustworthy, Savage was his own worst enemy. In one instance, having been taken in off the streets by a patron and given a rich pension of £200 a year, Savage brought drinking companions into the house at all hours to pillage his patron's wine cellar and wreak general ruin. He was naturally thrown into the streets again.[4] Millions of addicts persist in self-destructive habits in spite of the cost in health, money, jobs, and family ties. They often know full well that they should quit in their own best interests but, against reason, are unable to do so.

We all are familiar with various commitment tricks that we play on ourselves to control our actions and prevent ourselves from succumbing to some temptation that we know we will not be able to resist. Ulysses and the sirens is the usual example given. People visiting a gambling casino will deliberately restrict the amount of money they take to ensure that they will not yield to temptation and risk losing more.

People arrange ways to force themselves to forego current consumption and save. Christmas savings clubs are the standard example. One young couple I knew wanted to save enough for a down payment on a house. Each year they would borrow on a personal note, put the money in a savings account and pay off the note in installments during the year. This was irrational behavior, obviously, since they had a net interest cost on the amount they saved each year. But it worked, and they finally bought their house.

Rational Behavior Is Sometimes Unreasonable and Counterproductive

The normative aspect of the fundamental assumption—that rationally pursuing self-interest always is the best policy—is also questionable. Research has found that there are a number of classes of cases in which acting as a purely rational, self-interested individual is unreasonable. That is, there are times when an individual is better off acting irrationally. One class of these cases R. H. Frank calls commitment problems. For example, a woman, the victim of a kidnapping, may promise that if she is set free the police won't be informed. If the victim is purely rational the kidnapper knows that she will go to the police, and consequently he kills her. On the other hand, if the victim feels strongly about keeping promises, even against self-interest, the kidnapper can feel safe in freeing her (Frank 1990; Schelling 1960, 43–44).

A hazard of modern life is the danger of theft away from home: the motor scooter thief in Rome or Mexico City, for example, who snatches handbags from women tourists on the streets. The thief knows that if he is caught there is little chance that he will be convicted. The tourist is not likely to return at costly expense merely to testify against him. However, if American women, for example, were well known to be so outraged at such thefts that they would pay no attention to cost in bringing the criminal to justice, this would give them a high immunity from the crime.

There are other circumstances under which the knowledge that a person has a commitment to a particular kind of irrational behavior leads to better results than a rational, maximizing, self-interest orientation. In joint endeavors such as partnerships, in which cheating is difficult to guard against, a partnership of people who have a commitment to honesty does better than one in which each partner, driven by self-interest, siphons off money into his or her own pocket. Similarly in competition or in bargaining, the individual who is known to have a commitment to self-sacrificing fair behavior will have an advantage over people who are known to be rationally maximizing their self-interest.

Economics does not have to get itself entangled in laying down obiter dicta on the complications of the why of human action. Motives, expectations, and psychological drives are difficult to quantify and hard to disentangle. When we need clues to behavior in a specific situation, we should turn to empirical surveys rather than a priori assumptions. For general guidance on human action, we can look to the psychologists, philosophers, clerics, and the great writers. Shakespeare, Tolstoy, Goethe, and Balzac have far better perceptive insights into what motivates most human beings.

Implications for Economic Man (Homo economicus)

According to neoclassical theory, people are assumed to act rationally to maximize their self-interest. They achieve this goal because in the perfect markets of perfect competition they have perfect information. They have complete knowledge and foresight of present and future prices as well as of the availability of goods and services. This assumption is obviously unrealistic. Is it not legitimate, however, to assume that when we make *economic* decisions—when we buy or sell, save or invest—that we do try to rationally maximize? Certainly, the very nature of such transactions strongly reinforces the inclination to do so.

The fundamental assumption is stated in strong terms, as a law. That is, it is a consistent causal regularity that human beings always rationally maximize their self-interest.[5] This entails the accompanying assumptions of (1) possession of perfect knowledge (i.e., that you know what will accomplish this end) and (2) that this behavior will result in optimizing equilibrium in the marketplace.

I would suggest that there are very few people, if any, whose actions and decisions are always fully determined by such rational calculation in making economic choices. There are times when there is pleasure to be derived from throwing caution to the winds and doing something foolish and irrational. When the time arrived when my wife and I no longer felt financially constrained, we derived considerable satisfaction from giving up the idea of living on a budget. That is, we gave up trying to be calculatively rational in allocating our income.

Most of us buy some commodities out of habit and some on impulse. To exploit impulse buying, supermarkets place candy, cookies, other goodies, and sensational tabloids near the check-out line. Pepsi Cola found that persuading a supermarket to display snacks next to soft drinks raised sales by 3 to 10 percent; putting the products together at the end of an aisle can provide another 3 percent boost (Byrne 2000, 178).

Taxpayers consistently make interest-free loans to the government. An overwhelming majority of Americans (nearly 70 percent) overpaid their federal income taxes by a total of $114 billion in 1998—overpaying and then receiving refunds after filing their returns with the Internal Revenue Service. This money they could have easily kept by adjusting their withholding or changing the amounts paid as estimated tax. Why didn't they? There are probably many reasons: ignorance, laziness, or as a way of securing enforced saving. Then there are the overly conscientious people who owe taxes but file early, losing the interest they could have earned by waiting until April 15 to mail their returns. Members of both categories, overpayers and early filers, are clearly not rational maximizers (Loewenstein and Thaler 1989 presents a whole litany of similar behaviors that contradict the standard economic assumption).

Another phenomenon, aptly called the "winner's curse," illustrates the often irrational basis on which buyers make their decisions. Numerous experiments have demonstrated that the winner in an auction in which the commodity's value is not accurately known more often than not finds that in winning he or she has lost, for the commodity turns out to be worth less than the highest bid. A skilled auctioneer tries to create the excitement of a competitive game. Participants can get carried away in a bidding frenzy (Lind and Plott 1991; Hansen and Lott 1991; Kagel and Levin 1991). At one art auction I attended, a woman who made the highest bid on a particular painting exclaimed rapturously to her husband, "I won! I won."

Corporations can also be swept up in competitive fervor. In fact, the concept of a winner's curse was first mentioned in studies of the outcomes resulting from competitive bidding by oil companies for oil and gas drilling rights. There are many other examples (Thaler 1988, 1992). I observed one case personally in the matter of Pan Am's 1980 success in buying National Airlines in a bidding war against Texas Air. Texas Air walked away with substantial profits on its shares in National, while Pan Am found that it had grossly overpaid. The corporate cultures clashed; National's planes were not compatible, making it impossible to centralize maintenance; and National employees' morale was low, with a psychology of bitter antagonism toward management. Pan Am never recovered from its bidding triumph. It went into Chapter 11 and then stopped flying.

Choices

Behind the belief that individuals make rational choices is the assumption that they have stable, well-defined preferences ordered on a rational scale, that these remain unchanged and unalterable during the market process, and that in this way they maximize their stable, coherent, utility function. Note that this assumption must be taken on faith—it is intrinsically unobservable.

According to the theory, people, having complete information, act in the market as if they consult their preferences on a written list, choose the commodity most preferred, pay up to the value they put on it to get it, and are willing to sell it if offered a price higher than the value they put on it. Preferences are transitive, that is, if I prefer A to B and B to C, then I also must prefer A over C. (If A, B, and C are represented by indifference curves on my preference map, they do not touch or cross. By rotating my budget line as prices change, it is possible to derive my demand curves for the commodities.)

This assumption about preference orderings is not based on any body of observable data. If not merely a convenience adopted to facilitate the mathematization of economics, it comes from idealization or caricature of an economist's personal introspection. As such, it is a weak reed on which to build a comprehensive theory.

We do not observe preference directly; we observe only the choices made for particular goods. Preferences are not observable because they are private and to a large degree unrecorded. Willingness to buy and willingness to sell may at best only be inferred from the economic agent point actions in the message space. Often we cannot even observe point messages. We may know allocations and prices but not all bids. In short, we cannot observe the behavior *functions* since we cannot observe and vary preferences (Smith 1982, 928).

> The mapping of a consumer's preferences depends on his economic experience. A consumer who has temporarily experienced a different income or a different price constellation or a different consumption pattern (say, through advertising) will have a different set of consumption preferences when these temporary influences are removed than he had

> before. The consumer cannot decide what is his most preferred combination of commodities instantaneously, only after many trials and errors. But, by then, his income, the commodities available, the structure of prices, all will have changed and the process will go on continuously. The groping manner in which a consumer decides what he prefers calls into question the basic mathematical assumption that the equations or curves representing consumer choice are analytical functions. That is, you cannot assume that because you can ascertain the relationship of quantity demanded to price for a small range of prices and quantities you can then compute the relationship over the whole range. (Kamarck 1983, 81)

Experimental tests of the theory suggest that consumers betray an inability to make coherent and consistent consumption decisions (Johnson, Kotlikoff, and Samuelson 1987). Gene Heyman, a lecturer in psychology at Harvard, states flatly: "Humans are inconsistent. Their preferences change with the setting" (Lambert 2000, 67). According to Rabin, "People misjudge the probabilistic consequences of their decisions. . . . even when they correctly perceive the *physical* consequences of their decisions, people systematically misperceive the well-being they derive from such outcomes (Rabin 1998, 33, emphasis in original)

Our choices may be unstable over time; we choose and then regret that we didn't choose differently; we make choices that are counter to our interests in the long run. This is not surprising: People in modern high-income urban societies have lost the certitudes of previous, tradition-guided communities. In observing modern society, Nietzsche noted that it is full of people who do not know who they are or what they want.

In direct contradiction to the fundamental assumption, numerous studies have reported after extensive experimentation that people often show what has come to be called preference reversal. That is, with a high probability, subjects in the experiment will choose option A over option B in a direct comparison between the two and then, when asked to price the options, place a higher value on B over A!

Tversky and Thaler illustrate this behavior with this example: offer people the choice between receiving $2,500 five years from now or $1,600 eighteen months from now. And then ask them what is the smallest immediate cash payment for which they would be willing to exchange each of the delayed payments. Experiments show that the subjects will tend to choose $1,600 in eighteen months over $2,500 in five years but then put a higher immediate cash value on the $2,500!

Consumers also demonstrate an "ownership" preference. A man pays $5 per bottle for a case of wine. Later he refuses an offer of $100 a bottle, even though he would never pay more than $35 for any wine.

Corollaries of the rational choice model are also questionable, for example, the claim that people regard wealth as fungible. That is, our decision to buy a particular commodity or service is influenced by our total wealth, not the amount in any particular account. Experiments have shown that this is not so. People seem to have a rough idea of how much they are willing to spend for different purposes. In one experiment, people were asked what they would do if they arrived at a theater and found they had lost their $10 entrance ticket. Most said they would not spend another $10 for another ticket. On the other hand, if they were going to a theater to buy a ticket but on arriving they discover they have lost a $10 bill, most said they would buy a ticket and attend. In making decisions under conditions of uncertainty, other experiments show that individuals give more weight to a prospective loss than a prospective gain. On a rational choice basis, of course, there is no difference between the two alternatives in each of these cases (Tversky and Kahneman 1981).

Other experiments confirm that many people do not ignore sunk costs in making their decisions in contrast to what the rational choice model would predict. When a person has paid a fixed amount in advance for lunch at a Harvard Club event, for example, he or she usually will eat dessert, even if it is normally skipped for diet or health reasons. The motivation is the irrational feeling, "I don't want to waste the money I've paid.

The conclusion to be drawn from the experiments and studies, which is also intuitively and commonsensically correct, is that people do not normally have a complete set of preferences for every situation. People reasonably decide their preferences when they have to, or decide to, make a choice or judgment. The context and procedures involved in making choices influence which preferences are chosen (Tversky and Thaler 1990; Smith 1994, 124).

Research in the neurosciences has found that people are cognitive misers—they tend to make choices in the easiest way available. For nonroutine and difficult consumer choices, people often make their decision rule on the spot rather than referring to a nonexistent scale of established preferences (see Hanemann 1994, 28, for references). People often use mental shortcuts that may result in irrational behavior. If you do not know enough about the quality of a commodity, you may decide that a higher price indicates higher quality.

Social Influences

The rationality optimization assumption depends on the belief that the individual's choices are his or her own; that preferences are not influenced by what others do. If people change their choices following others' actions, the demand curves dance around and become indeterminate. The pervasiveness of advertising and the large amounts of resources devoted to it give considerable weight to the belief that companies are convinced that they can influence consumers' choices. Some companies spend more on advertising their products than they do on producing them.

The existence of conspicuous consumption, advertising, packaging, and other selling techniques testifies to the fact that individual preferences are not completely internal to the individual. Amartya Sen argues that the actual behavior of human beings is affected by ethical considerations and ethics should therefore be relevant to economics (1987). This is true, but the argument can be carried further. Beliefs and emotions drive action as much as self-interest does.

Human beings live in a society. From birth, our individual personalities are affected and modified by the social practices, attitudes, and educational experiences in which we are immersed. This socialization process is internalized by us to some degree and externally expressed in more or less conforming social and economic behavior. We learn very early to tap into the collective wisdom and experience of our society—to inform us about both proper behavior and acceptable or desirable consumption and investment.

If individuals are uncertain how to behave in an unfamiliar environment, they may imitate what others do (this also helps explain why financial bubbles appear and grow in asset markets). On October 19, 1987, the U.S. Dow Jones Index fell by 23 percent, more than five hundred points. Other shares markets throughout the world fell out of bed in sympathy. There was no information that justified this behavior. In the following months, the market recovered and then went on to new heights. The behavior of the market in this episode was not unusual. In the 1920s, investors piled into auto, radio, and utility stocks, running them up beyond any long-term reasonable level; then they stampeded out in 1929. In the 1960s, the same irrational run in and out occurred with bowling and conglomerate stocks and in the 1990s with the Internet dot.com stocks. The explanation of this herdlike behavior has to be sought in the way in which people react, interact, observe others for clues as how to behave, and thus have their rational capacity affected emotionally by the behavior of others.

Tastes are often more or less socially determined and socially interdependent. Anyone who has a teenager in the household knows how effective peer pressure can be. But this is not restricted to teenagers.

A great American novelist, William Dean Howells, illustrates this point in describing one of his characters: "She was like everyone else, a congeries of contradictions and inconsistencies, but *obedient to the general expectation* of what a girl of her position must and must not be" (1890, 219, my emphasis).

Much behavior is affected by acculturation. On a trip, travelers often patronize restaurants that they know they will never visit again. Yet they leave a tip at the end of the meal as they do at restaurants where they are regular patrons. Clearly, rational self-interest would dictate that travelers should not tip the waiter, yet, because of social acculturation, most people find this impossible to do.

Market behavior is also affected by current social position and the relative position to which one aspires. Many people observe and rate or grade people by their consumptive patterns. Consumption is thus often obligatory as a way of locating oneself in society through display of the required symbols of social status. This leads to consumption driven by competition—people aspiring to higher social status purchase items that are symbolic of the people in the favored position. The latter, of course, to defend their status, move on to other items (DiMaggio 1990).

A person will tend to save less if the people with whom he or she associates have higher incomes. The rate of savings thus tends to rise as a person rises in the income distribution hierarchy in the particular social or economic terrain he or she inhabits.

A large part of our behavior is governed by social norms, by the socially conditioned reflexes we acquire in our social environment. Robert Sugden and Jon Elster have shown that it is impossible to justify the existence of such norms based on any calculative, rational, maximizing behavior. Many consumption norms seem to make everybody worse off. One example that springs to mind is the custom of men wearing neckties in the middle of a hot summer.

If you live in a small community, it may be important to behave in ways that do not lead your neighbors to believe that you think yourself more talented ("better") than they are. This discourages the gifted from using their skills. In some African villages, people who are better or more fortunate farmers are ipso facto judged to be witches.

In short, there are many influences on people's behavior. Some part of our behavior is hereditary, some is the result of deliberate intention, and some results from customs, traditions, rules, and institutions, all of which are produced by social evolution, the result of human action. The assumption that people always know and have established, stable, well-defined preferences ordered in a rational scale on which they act rationally does not stand up to examination. Consequently, one cannot argue that market results are necessarily optimal in any substantive sense.

Beliefs, Uncertainty, and Discovery

Stationary capitalism is an oxymoron. And individuals change, too. To the degree that a person is rational, he or she will learn from the decisions and experience of today to try to cope better with the different world of tomorrow. But we cannot assume that rationality results in optimization. Since the time of Frank Knight, we have known that in making decisions economic agents may be faced with "risk" and "uncertainty." Risks are represented by those events for which we believe we know the probability distribution that we may encounter. Uncertainty occurs when we do not know the likelihood that an event may take place at all, as there is no probability distribution that can be attached to the event. In making a decision when uncertainty is present, no matter how rational the process of making the decision may be, there is no way that the decision can be relied on to maximize the agent's well-being (Hutchinson 1997, 133–39). Even in dealing with risks, one cannot assume that decisions will necessarily be rational.

> It is well known from the literature on decision under risk that individual risk perceptions are often in error and tend to be systematically biased. In particular, people give too much weight to small risks, underestimate the more substantial risks, and are excessively sensitive to changes in accustomed risk levels. These biases lead to exorbitant reactions to newly discovered risks while accustomed risks are treated with comparative inattention. (Bleichrodt 2000, 127)

Contemporary economic theory has tried to get around the uncertainty problem by assuming that a person's uncertainty about the future can be represented by means of a subjective probability distribution of outcomes and that he or she can then make the decision maximizing the subjective expected utility by using that distribution. The argument is based on an analogy—the baseball fielder does not know the physics governing the trajectory of a fly ball, but he or she still understands how the ball will travel and catches it. However, the analogy is not really applicable to most decisions that people have to make about the future. A closer analogy would be if the player is blind, doesn't know what position he or she is playing, or has to make the decision about where to stand before the batter steps up to the plate. And it may turn out that the game is football, not baseball.

The future is largely uncertain; it is not reducible to a series of outcomes to which an economic agent can attach calculable probabilities on which he or she can rely. Substituting expected utility or subjective probability into a model does not eliminate the fact that real world uncertainty still remains. The outcome then is not likely to be optimal but hopefully second best (Fusfeld 1996, 310–11).

The Austrian school of economics emphasizes the importance of "discovery" in the market. There are two kinds of ignorance: ignorance when we don't have the needed knowledge but we know it is available and can be found; and "ignorance of ignorance," when we don't even know something that, when discovered, comes as a complete surprise. The discovery reveals the existence of an opportunity, a technology, something of which one was not aware that one was ignorant. It is entrepreneurial alertness that takes advantage of discovery and, in the Austrian theory, is the source of pure entrepreneurial profits (Kirzner 1997, 60–85).

On these counts alone, uncertainty and discovery, one would have to conclude that the assumption that rationality necessarily implies optimization is faulty.

Beliefs play an important part throughout the economy. They include expectations, guesses, presumptions, attitudes, hypotheses, and theories held about different aspects of the economy and the way it works. Economic decisions are affected by expectations—irrational as well as rational hopes and fears for the future. And the future is governed by incalculable uncertainty. Living beings have the ability to process information, to create, and to evolve. Acting and reacting; initiating and responding; conforming and adapting; forming and destroying coalitions; humans in an economy create ever-changing complexities. A living creature is more than the sum of its parts. An economy is far more.

Beliefs and expectations directly affect the ways in which the economy functions.

> In formal theory, an economy is usually described by endowments, preferences and technology. . . . We think it is important that something more be added: the beliefs held by the various participants in the economy. "Beliefs" include ordinary expectations and conjectures about prices, incomes, and various aggregates; we also intend the word to cover attitudes and even theories about the way the economy works. The way the economy actually does work can depend on the way agents believe the economy to work. . . . the way the economy responds to a policy move by government can depend on the interpretation that other agents place on it, and therefore on their beliefs about the way things work. An obvious example comes from central bank watching: if participants believe that every increase in the money supply will be fully translated into the price level, irrespective of any other characteristic of the situation, then they are likely to behave in ways that will make it happen. (Hahn and Solow 1997, 150)

In a modern economy, production is linked to consumption through monetary transactions in the market. By holding money or utilizing or not utilizing credit, consumers, producers, and investors have the option of deciding when to consume, produce, or invest. As a large proportion of consumption now consists of consumer durables, consumers have considerable flexibility in the timing of the expenditure of a substantial fraction of their income. Producers, too, have discretion in the size of the inventories they hold and especially in their investment decisions. In making investments in fixed capital, which may last a long time, and when the period of gestation and the time it takes to put the investment in place is also long, a considerable leap of faith is required. All of these decisions (to spend, hold money, use credit, etc.) are influenced by beliefs about the uncertainty of the future.

The Survey of Consumer Confidence is an important indicator of the state of and future developments in the American economy. The emphasis put on confidence in financial and investment decisions has been acquired through bitter experience. There were six major international financial crises in the last decade of the last century, and there has been a major effort to study their causes and determine how to prevent such crises in the future. Lawrence H. Summers, an outstanding economist and U.S. secretary of the Treasury, presented the results of one study in the 1999 Richard T. Ely lecture of the American Economic Association. It was striking how much importance he placed on the role of emotion in causing crises. He cited the influence of sentiment, bank-run psychology, international contagion, investors' irrationality, panic, herding, and reputational externalities (2000, 6).

Reasonableness

If one cannot swallow the assumption that everybody is born a self-directed rational maximizer, there are two fallback positions that defenders use for the rationality hypothesis.[6] The first is that perfect economic men influence or teach other people to follow their example. Such behavior then becomes so widespread that one can assume it applies to most people, and therefore there is little error in assuming that such behavior is universal. This might be characterized as the "adaptation" or, stretching a bit, the "Lamarckian" argument. The second, or "Darwinian," position is that calculative rationality becomes dominant through natural selection. People who are rational maximizers succeed, and those who aren't perish. This argument has been explicitly applied to analysis of firms and the behavior of investors in securities markets.

Neither of these two positions can be shown to be true. If either were true, it should prove itself in the well-organized securities markets, where the incentive is purely monetary and a large number of participants are experienced, sophisticated professionals. Alas, the informed consensus now is that the earlier efficient market theory is no longer viable in this regard: "It is extraordinarily difficult to formulate nontrivial and falsifiable implications of capital market efficiency that have not in fact been falsified" (Leroy 1989, 1614; cited in Mayer 1999, 328). In the spring of 2000, the highly skillful and outstandingly successful professional investors Warren Buffet, George Soros, and Stanley Druckenmiller all stepped out of the market because, in Druckenmiller's words, "The stockmarket is now crazy-insane, unbelievably dangerous" (*Economist* 2000a, 75). The conclusion is inescapable, for

> one would have to be extremely committed to rationality not to agree that in the area of financial economics, the heart of traditional economics, a number of important market phenomena are well explained by assuming that not all behavior is fully rational. This raises questions for other areas of economics where the preconditions for rationality are not so well established. (Russell 1997, 90)

The argument so far has been aimed at discrediting the hyper-rationality assumption that people always rationally maximize. But this is not to argue that rationality never enters into economic decisions. Of course, it may and probably usually does, to a greater or lesser extent. But one cannot assume that rationality is always unbounded, always at the extreme of the spectrum. Empirical and applied economists and even many theorists recognize that some measure of less than perfect maximizing rationality needs to be utilized in microeconomics. In short, it is "reasonable" not to try to practice unlimited rationality.

Reality appears to be consistent with cognitive science theory: The ultimate human scarce resource is mental energy (and time). It is reasonable to develop stereotypical models to call upon. When processing input from the senses, the mind tends to choose the model most readily available that seems to fit the situation. It looks for others or tries to create new ones only if the first model clearly fails. The mind employs decision heuristics and rules of thumb as another way to economize. In making decisions concerning our welfare, there is also the problem of will; people have imperfect strategies of self-managment. A person can know perfectly well what he or she should do but be unable to do it (Gazzaniga 1985; Schmid 1994; Thaler 1991).

Since Herbert Simon advanced the concept of bounded rationality, a great deal of empirical research has shown that it is very important in the real world. John Conlisk has presented a masterly exposition on this research and its implications. The following brief remarks are a partial summary of his work (Conlisk 1996).

The fundamental reasons why people limit the amount of reasoning they use when having to make a decision are:

1. They have limited analytical abilities and there is limited pertinent knowledge available.
2. They need or want to economize on the cognitive effort required.
3. They do not want to spend the time required to marshall the necessary information and come to an optimal decision.

It is often reasonable, therefore, to make decisions using decision heuristics or rules of thumb rather than working out the full logic involved. There is a tradeoff between the assurance of getting the right answer and the effort and time involved. There is a *deliberation cost* to be paid.

Similarly, whereas standard theory assumes that economic agents make an exhaustive search of all possible decisions and then optimize in picking the best, Simon observed that people do not often act that way. Instead, they adopt the reasonable course of "satisficing" by picking the first satisfactory commodity they find or making the first satisfactory decision at which they arrive. Decision makers often consciously pursue a policy of suboptimizing ("recursive programming"). That is, they make a decision, try it out, and improve it in the next round. Arrow has recently argued along the same lines that rationality should be redefined to include pursuit by individuals of gradual improvement in their decisions (1996, cited in Schwartz 1998, 172).

Thomas Russell has called attention to another type of behavior that also falls short of the full rationality assumed in economic theory. This is what he and Thaler have called "quasi rationality." Quasi rationality is the reasonable but less than fully rational behavior of individuals that conforms to regularities in decision making under uncertainty (1997, 89–90; see also DeLong et al., 1990).

The closeness of the results in an exchange transaction to perfect rational maximization, ceteris paribus, is likely to be vary directly according to:

1. The size (or importance) of the stake
2. The degree of professionalism or specialization of the agent
3. The degree of impersonal relationships among the parties
4. The pressure of competition

5. The availability of useful pertinent knowledge
6. The simplicity of the transaction

These variables are largely self-explanatory. If a large amount of money is involved in a simple transaction and the negotiators are professionals, then it is highly likely that self-interest will be rationally maximized.[7] The more of these factors are present, the more likely it is that the transaction will fit the fundamental assumption. And of course the fewer factors involved, the less likely it is that this will be true. The emphasis here is on probability, not certainty. As is evident in the financial markets where these factors are likely to be present, the results are often contrary to what should happen under rational maximization.

In our capitalist economy, most of us have to enter the marketplace if we want to make a living. This entails directing "purposeful action" toward personal objectives. But even in our market-driven economy many people succeed in enjoying lives free from the pursuit of personal gain and others join occupations such as professions in which this practice is strictly controlled. In other cultures also, which have different social contexts and historical experiences, behavior may be very different from what occurs in a modern market-driven society such as that of the United States.

It is probably accurate to observe that most people are trying to pursue personal gain in their economic lives, bearing in mind all the limitations of knowledge (including self-knowledge) and rationality and the social and ethical norms they respect. As was discussed in the preceding chapter, this does not necessarily mean being exclusively driven by selfishness or greed and disregarding the interests of others. The fact that actions may be less than fully rational does not mean that behavior is not commonsensically reasonable, that regularity may not be present, or that one cannot identify a pattern of behavior that describes what the majority of economic agents tend to do in specific situations. One could also observe that many people do reasonably well in this pursuit and many do poorly. Even though most agents in an economy are not rational maximizers as long as a substantial number are operating at the margins, while the economy could not be said to operate Pareto-optimally, it might come more or less close to it, depending on the relative weight of the different components.

In considering the "self-interest" part of the fundamental assumption, one conclusion was that as a normative prescription it should be interpreted not as selfishness but in Adam Smith's sense of including regard for others. In the "rationality" element of the fundamental assumption, one must conclude that as positive economics it falls short of precisely describing much economic behavior. The idea of *Homo economicus* inexorably maximizing his or her self-interest turns out to be just a myth; the reality is a decision maker who is guided by bounded rationality and influenced by acculturation, instincts, and emotions. The one aspect of this assumption that can be rescued is that it emphasizes the importance of end-means rationality as an approach to policy.

CHAPTER 5

Ethics and Economics

> People who have to make political or economic decisions on matters which could affect many other people's lives will, unless they have lost all sense of reason, . . . find themselves forced not only to account for their ethical motivation of conduct but also to gauge the likely consequences of their activities on the basis of their knowledge and conscience.
>
> —MAX WEBER

Even as early as Aristotle, it was axiomatic that man is a social animal. This is a universal human and historical truth. In an environment dominated by animals, which were stronger, faster, and fiercer, human beings survived and prevailed through cooperation in social groups. The Bantu-speaking peoples of Africa say, "Umuntu ngumuntu ngabantu," that is, "A human being is a human being because of other people." Even today, when a fellow human is confronted with peril, the deep instinct of human solidarity comes to the fore. At sea, a sinking boat diverts any craft close to the scene to help. In the movie, *The Russians Are Coming,* which was made at the height of the cold war, there is an instantly credible scene: an escalating American-Russian confrontation is immediately defused when a child is in danger.

The fundamental truth, and paradox, of human existence is that we can only realize our individual potential in a community. We need to live in a society—this is a fundamental inner human need. And if we are to live in a society some ethical considerations have to be embedded in our lives (Williams 1985, 13, 27, 45, 47–49, 150). There must be limits on the individual expression of human freedom and of selfishness in the interest of some ideal of justice for all within the community so that the community will continue. Behavior that increased the strength of the social group in a hostile natural environment conferred an evolutionary advantage.

Experiments have shown that people identify those individuals who cooperate and those who cheat. When people who cooperate work together, they do better than those who are guided by selfish self-interest.

John F. Welch Jr., the creative chairman of the highly successful General Electric Company, got rid of people who, even if they were highly talented, "won't block for others or play as part of a team. Their debilitating effect on the team can outweigh the benefits of their individual talent" (1994, 3).

Every society that survives has to form the character structure of its members in such a way as to make them *desire* to do what they have to do in order to fulfill their social function. In addition to the universal ethics (such as "Thou shalt not kill") that are common to all great cultures, every society has its own set of norms. These socially immanent ethics are the prohibitions and commands that are necessary to the functioning and survival of a specific society.

A society and an economy are more efficient in attaining their particular goals to the extent that the character of their members is molded to value the behavior that best suits their modes of production and life. The more effectively people are brought up to want to do what they have to do, the more successful the society and economy will be in attaining their objectives. Thus, in a hunting society courage and endurance are important virtues and in a subsistence farming community patience and cooperation are particularly prized (Fromm 1947, 199, 237–44).

There is a human inclination toward conformity; we want to fit in. We learn very early to take advantage of the accumulated experience of our society. Tapping into societal knowledge informs our social behavior and our perceptions of what is regarded as acceptable. For anyone who is not a sociopath (i.e., abnormal), social norms do affect how we behave. Thus, under some circumstances the demands of society (as of soldiers in battle) may lead us to actions that are contrary to our individual self-interest.

Selfish Behavior and the Ethical Framework

Neoclassical economics, while positing the fundamental assumption of individual selfish behavior, does not face up to the question of whether this behavior is controlled by feeling for others, that is, constrained within a framework of ethics in the society. The ethics of an individual embodied in his or her conscience—the inner voice—govern the ends an individual will try to attain and what means he or she will adopt for this purpose. For our purposes, ethics determine to what extent individuals will allow themselves to be governed by pure selfishness.

Lacking an indigenous feudal background, from the beginning the United States has emphasized the rights of individuals against their responsibilities to others. This is not as characteristic of other countries.

Most European societies as well as the Japanese have inherited some community values as well as notions of civic duty and personal codes of honor.

Great economists like Adam Smith and Alfred Marshall, who had strong ties to reality, recognized the existence and importance of ethical conduct in the economy. Marshall put the case strongly in stating that

> ethical forces are among those of which the economist has to take account. Attempts have indeed been made to construct an abstract science with regard to the actions of an "economic man", who is under no ethical influences and who pursues pecuniary gain warily and energetically, but mechanically and selfishly. But they have not been successful, nor even thoroughly carried out. For they have never really treated the economic man as perfectly selfish; no one could be relied on better to endure toil and sacrifice with the unselfish desire to make provision for his family; and his normal motives have always been tacitly assumed to include the family affections. But if they include these, why should they not include all other altruistic motives the action of which is so far uniform in any class at any time and place, that it can be reduced to general rule? ([1920] 1952, v–vi)

Marshall failed to foresee that later economists would not hesitate to construct an abstract science that regards economic man as perfectly selfish. However, he was right in concluding that such a construction would not result in a successful science.

Some pure economists, like Milton Friedman, do not recognize any limits on people acting for their selfish interests. And Gary Becker was awarded a Nobel Prize in part for assuming that economic man continues to act as such even in his family relationships. Individual selfishness preached by economics has come close to being regarded as the highest value. This was exemplified by the commencement speaker at the 1985 University of California School of Business Administration, who told the graduates, "Greed is healthy. You can be greedy and still feel good about yourself." These remarks by Ivan Boesky (made before he was fined $100 million, sentenced to prison, and barred for life from securities trading for his criminal use of insider information) were greeted with applause by the graduating class.

Boesky himself may be having second thoughts about the desirability of selfishness. While he was in prison, his wife, who held some $100 million in wealth in her name beyond the reach of the court, divorced him. On his release from jail, he had to sue her for a share. After a six-week trial, a settlement was reached, under which his former wife kept the bulk of the fortune, a huge estate in New York, and a valuable art collection. Boesky received $20 million, a house in Malibu, and alimony of $15,000 a month.

It is mainly the churches of the United States that are expected to instill respect for individual obligations to the community. Of all world's rich countries, it is in the United States that polls show the highest voluntary church membership and the highest level of religious belief. The young are taught religious values handed down from earlier epochs. The individual is taught to submit to and find his or her ends in a power or principle outside of individual. People are not isolated units, autonomous entities, but a human family, a community of persons, a body genuinely one. In Judaism also, the Covenant with God is not a contract with individuals but with a people. To live is to be united with others in a social context by bonds of family or Covenant relationships (Burghardt 1996). All the great religions teach unselfishness.

The American Roman Catholic bishops on November 12, 1996, summarized the teachings of their church in relation to the economy as follows: the economy exists for the person, not the person for the economy; a fundamental moral measure of an economy is how well the poor and vulnerable fare; all people have a duty to work, a responsibility to provide for their families' needs, and an obligation to contribute to society; and workers, owners, managers, stockholders, and consumers should act as moral agents in economic life.[1]

In neoclassical economics, there is no place for ethics. Economics teaches that one should act in one's own advantage and that by so doing one will be acting in the final analysis for the greatest advantage of all. Selfish persons interested only in themselves, who want everything for themselves, and who get pleasure from taking, not giving, are model economic men. Consistent with this, the rich are revered and heeded. That egoism is the basis of the general welfare is the principle that spokesmen for our competitive society advocate.

But at the same time we also know that this is not quite right, and we try to protect society from being destroyed by individual selfishness. In an economics concerned with the real economy, it must be recognized that the ethics prevalent in an economy affect economic behavior and must be taken into account.

The ruling ethics and the degree to which economic actors in an economy live up to them are important forces. The functioning of society and the economy is directly related to ethical behavior. How social ethical restraints are observed has a great and pervasive influence on the productivity and national welfare of an economy. Smoothly functioning markets depend on trust. If the narrow economic assumption were truly descriptive and human beings exclusively pursued their selfish interests, the community would break down. A city or a nation worth living in depends on citizens feeling a responsibility and devotion to the community and surmounting their purely selfish individualistic ends. The very existence of a society and nation is threatened when people come to believe that the institutions that are supposed to serve them are serving other ends.

As Hobbes foresaw, if individuals apply a purely selfish calculus and disregard their obligations to the wider community, the society and economy will dissolve into chaos. The bloody anarchy in Lebanon in the 1980s and the warlord-caused famine in Somalia in the 1990s exemplify this.

A classic frightening instance of this is plight of the Ik tribe of northern Uganda. The tribe's culture collapsed when it was moved from its ancient hunting grounds. The members of the tribe became atomistic individuals concerned only with individual survival. Neighbor raided neighbor, parent kept food from the child. As selfish self-interest reigned, people died (Turnbull 1972).

The breakdown of Roman law and order resulted in the Dark Ages. When community norms collapsed, people could survive only at subsistence levels.

After Sears introduced incentive pay for auto repairmen tied to the amount of charges to the customer, investigators in California, Florida, and New Jersey discovered in 1992 (and Sears acknowledged the fact) that the company's auto shops were charging customers for repairs that had not been made. This behavioral response on the part of the mechanics—unethical but correct according to the fundamental assumption—cost Sears millions of dollars in direct reparations and probably much greater sums in damage to the reputation and goodwill of the company. The firm announced in page-length advertisements that it would reinstitute the old system of fixed salaries for its auto repair staff in the attempt to win back the confidence of its customers.

The leading character in the Louis Auchincloss novel *Diary of a Yuppie* strongly believes that in the modern American economy there are no ethics to govern behavior. His law partner and his wife feel that honorable practice rules out certain behavior no matter how profitable. He maintains instead that in the moral climate in which we live today, "It's all a game, but a game with very strict rules. You have to stay meticulously within the law, the least misstep, if caught, involves an instant penalty. But there is no particular moral opprobrium in incurring a penalty, any more than there is being offside in football." Therefore, any action that serves your ends is acceptable if it is legal or if you can get away with it.

The "me-first" psychology of 1980s yuppies was merely an exaggeration of an old American traditional attitude. Benjamin Franklin's Poor Richard expressed it in his proverb "God helps those who help themselves." There is no mention of any moral obligation to help or have compassion for anyone else. But Franklin himself found it desirable (and probably essential to himself as a human being) to devote a substantial portion of his energies to service to the community. As demonstrated by Franklin, the other side of American individualism and selfishness is the intense and widespread American activity of organizing, working for, and financing volunteer associations to provide services to one or another part of the community.

Classical humanism is still an important ethic not only in recruiting college faculty—including economists—but even in influencing some corporate decisions. Donations to support community activities by some unusual corporations, like Cummins Engine or Merck ($256 million in 1999, equal to over 3 percent of pretax earnings), for example, often outweigh any possible financial benefit.

Ethics can be more powerful than the drive of selfish self-interest. The environmental movement, based on ethical considerations, has succeeded in destroying the nuclear power industry in the United States and other countries. In the past, religious values were a strong element in securing the universal education of children and in the abolition of slavery.

Under the influence of the prevailing culture, ethics and the standard of acceptable behavior may differ from country to country. The difference in behavior between Japan and other industrialized countries in this regard is striking and has economic consequences.

The day-to-day functioning of economic organizations and markets depends on the honesty, trust, and goodwill shown by people. The degree to which economic agents carry out their responsibilities without the need for external supervision and policing to keep them in line has a direct economic impact. One outstanding economic consequence of differences in moral commitment is the size and importance of the underground economy in different countries. Others are the amount of resources that has to be devoted to policing behavior (e.g., to combat shoplifting, employee theft, abuse of perks by management, or management manipulation of its power against stockholders' interests). How much has to be spent on policing to make streets safe for people is directly related to the ethical practices of the community. If the decisions of judges were to favor the side that offers the biggest bribe, reliance on contracts would suffer and much economic activity would soon come to a halt.

Research has found that the economic performance of societies is directly affected by the level of trust that people have in one another. The higher the degree of trust, the greater will be the ability of people to cooperate with one another, even if they are strangers. The higher the level of trust, the better a society and economy functions: there is less corruption, better functioning bureaucracies, better corporate performance, greater tax compliance, superior infrastructure, and lower inflation. Countries with the highest levels of trust were found to be in Scandinavia and the lowest were in Latin America (La Porta et al. 1997).

Unlike law and medicine, there is no established code of ethics included in the study of economics. In recent years, graduate business schools have found it wise to provide courses in ethics in order to get students to pay attention to underlying purposes and values. No such requirement has been made of economists, even though they exert great influence on decisions affecting social choice and human welfare.

The fundamental assumption is flawed in not recognizing that the pursuit of self-interest can have both a self-serving and an other-regarding dimension. It may include selfishness and/or altruism; regard for oneself and/or for the other, including the community. A good society and a productive economy depend on the mass of human beings behaving with a necessary minimum of virtue, accepting certain standards, and sufficiently abstaining from destructive vice. As Aristotle put it:

> As man is the best of animals when perfected, so he is the worst when separated from law and justice. For injustice is most dangerous when it is armed, and man, armed by nature with good sense and virtue, may use them for entirely opposite ends. Therefore, when he is without virtue man is the most unscrupulous and savage of the animals. (1926, 29)

Most economists would recognize that as professionals they are subject to certain binding standards of conduct that put some moneymaking activities beyond the pale.

Most people now take it for granted that public officials are an important exception to the general assumption that an individual should properly always be working for his own advantage. In industrialized countries in recent times, the assumption can be fairly made that the corruption of public officials is so rare an occurrence that economists can ignore it without any major impact on the conclusions of an analysis (but see chapter 8).[2] This was not true of these countries earlier. When Samuel Pepys was appointed to the British Admiralty in 1660, he was a poor man. He was told by his patron that it was not the salary of a place that made a man rich but the opportunity to line his pockets while he was there. Pepys took advantage of this situation and reaped a golden harvest of bribes and gratuities while supplying the Royal Navy. In the process, he built one of the most sizable fortunes of the seventeenth century (Latham 1983, 130–37).

As a public office could be a source of enrichment, it was understandable that it was often bought and sold. Even as late as the nineteenth century, when civil service reforms in Britain were being directed toward establishing a service based on merit, the duke of Wellington introduced the purchase and sale of commissions into the British Army. For him, this was a reform measure—a way of making sure that officers would be men of means and not susceptible to revolutionary temptations. Modern economists today are less courageous than the Iron Duke. Although most economists today advocate the privatization of many government-run services, no one to my knowledge has yet argued for the auctioning of government offices to the highest bidder.

Economics generally recognizes that there are certain classes of needed goods and services that will not be provided by individuals driven by personal interest and must be supplied through the public sector. These include public goods such as defense and merit goods such as public education.

Crime and Ethics

If the only motivation for individual behavior were selfish self-interest, as postulated by economics, then crime should be accepted as just another type of economic activity and no opprobrium should be borne by criminals. This is essentially the standard economic model: criminals are rational, self-interested agents whose behavior is an optimal response to the incentives set by government through its efforts in law enforcement and correction. An individual should rationally commit a crime if it presents an economic payoff. As Professor Becker explained: "The essence of the economic approach to crime is amazingly simple. It says that people decide whether to commit crime by comparing the benefits and costs of engaging in crime" (1995, quoted in Saffran 1996, 182).

Bluntly, it is simple: ethics plays no role.

> Consider an individual who would obtain a gain from committing a harmful act. If he does commit it, he will be caught with some probability and then possibly have to pay a fine or go to jail. In general, he will commit the act if and only if his expected utility from doing so, taking into account his gain and the chance of his being caught and sanctioned, exceeds his utility if he does not commit the act. (Polinsky and Shavell 2000, 47)

Accordingly, a person who commits a crime does not deserve opprobrium and, compared to an honest citizen, is perhaps merely an individual who has a higher discount rate in postponing gratifications, is less risk averse, and perhaps is capable of a better (or worse?) judgment of the personal risk of getting caught than honest citizens do. Freeman has shown that there is a relationship between crime and the collapse of the job market for unskilled labor and that a collage of evidence supports the notion that young men respond substantially to the economic returns from crime (1996).

A striking example of what purely economic selfish behavior—uninfluenced by ethical considerations—leads to is the rash of espionage cases in the United States since 1978. The director of the FBI has reported that in every case in which Americans betrayed national secrets to foreign powers "money has been the reason" (Bacon 1986). This has continued to be true for all the Americans caught spying for foreign powers in the last fifteen years.

Among the Americans who have sold their country's secrets are members or former members of the most sensitive agencies of the American government: the National Security Agency, the CIA, and the FBI. Ronald Pelton, a former employee of the top secret National Security Agency, sold some of the United States' most sensitive eavesdropping secrets to the Soviet Union for a mere $35,000 (Walcott 1987). Aldrich Ames, chief of the Soviet counterintelligence branch in the CIA, for around $2.5 million, virtually destroyed the entire American spy network in the Soviet Union.

John A. Walker Jr., an active political right winger, recruited his brother, his son, and a friend to sell U. S. Navy codes, coding machine details, and other intelligence secrets to the Soviets over a period of seventeen years. When the judge sentenced Walker in November 1986 to life imprisonment with no parole, he completely disregarded Walker's exemplary behavior as an economic man, declaring instead: "You and the others who participated in this scheme were traitors for pure cold cash. . . . I look in vain for some redeeming aspect of your character" (Hunter 1999b, 195).

In 1997, Earl Edwin Pitts, an FBI official who worked at headquarters on top secret records and personnel security, received a prison sentence of twenty-seven years for selling security information to Moscow for more than $224,000 between 1987 and 1992. In the same year, Harold J. Nicolson, a CIA official even higher in the agency hierarchy than Ames, was sentenced to twenty-three years in prison after he confessed to selling the names and positions of a large number of CIA officers to the Russians for $300,000.

Economics can explain much crime—but not all. Ethics do matter. Most people do not approach a crime opportunity in the way economic theory assumes. Most people do not refrain from crime simply because their economic analysis shows that it will not pay but because they feel that it is wrong or unethical.

One comprehensive study of criminal behavior concluded that conscience is a major force keeping people from committing crimes (Wilson and Herrnstein 1985). Conscience is related to relationships and feelings of responsibility to other people and the community. People obey the law because of their own inner voices or because they want the approval and fear the disapproval of their social groups or communities. People obey the law because they generally regard themselves as moral beings who want to do the right thing as they see it. Of the three main motives for avoiding criminal behavior (fear of being caught and punished, social pressures, and personal moral commitment), only the first fits into conventional economic theory. Like the time discount of benefits and punishments, of course, social and moral forces are matters of degree and are related to the different circumstances and cultures.

While economic theory sees crime only as rational self-interested behavior, there is no follow through. Logically, with this economic approach, crime should be one of the sectors covered in the national accounts. One could argue that "victimless" crimes should be treated differently from those that have victims (whose losses or harm would have to be regarded as an offsetting deduction).

Of course, in real life this is just another example of cognitive dissonance, of theory clashing with the recognition in practice of the importance of ethics and social factors in human behavior. Most sensible economists do not act in accordance with theory and do not really regard crime as acceptable behavior. One can be sure that Professor Becker would never dream of carefully locking all the family valuables in a safe before house guests arrive. Polinsky and Shavell, after a thoroughly masterful exposition of "The Economic Theory of Public Enforcement of Law," in a bow to reality, admit that the theory leaves out social norms (ethics and external social sanctions) "as a general alternative to law enforcement in channeling individuals' behavior" (2000, 73).

The Commons

Nearly every society in the premodern stage of development held its land in common or regarded it as a resource open to all. Whether the land was nominally regarded as the king's, as belonging to a god or gods, or as part of nature like the air or the sea, there was no private property in land. In most of today's tropical Africa, this is still true. In New England villages, the Common is the relic of these earlier times. In Switzerland, most alpine pastures are owned in common, as they have been for centuries. The Swiss grazing commons survive because the rules for determining the size of the group of legitimate users and the level of use by each are well defined and obeyed, with fines imposed for violations. Other longtime common properties continue to be viable today: Japanese forests, irrigation systems in Spain, and the Filipino Zanjera (Ostrom 1990; Stevenson 1991).

The so-called "tragedy of the commons" should rather be called the "tragedy of lost ethics" or the "tragedy of becoming economic man." This is illustrated concretely by what often happens to a pastoral society when it is affected by the modern acquisitive world. Such societies, like some of those in the Sahel south of the Sahara in Africa, appear to have worked relatively successfully for thousands of years. The people grazed their cattle or goats on common land, and generally there was grass or other vegetation enough for all. The system worked because each person felt enough social responsibility to ensure that the total number of cattle did not surpass the carrying capacity of the land. A man voluntarily restricted the number of his cattle to his fair share—what was regarded as appropriate for his position. If someone was selfish and started to become too rich, he was brought into line by various means. Some tribes had people who specialized in "smelling out witches." Obviously, anyone whose cattle herd was growing too large must be a practicing witch.

The tragedy occurs when the social constraints break down. When each person is motivated solely by selfish self-interest, each tries to put as many cattle on the commons as he can. If anyone restrains himself, it does no good because others, driven by selfishness, do not. In short order, the Commons becomes overgrazed, the vegetation cannot renew itself, the land turns into semidesert, the cattle starve, and famine ensues.

Friedrich von Hayek correctly observed that within small groups cooperation is the instinctive and dominant mode behavior. There are various ways in which groups work out the best way to use a common resource and the governance or sanctions to be applied if anyone tries to take advantage of the others. It is only as the group gets larger that altruism gets stretched too far to be a dominant motive. This is certainly true of primitive tribes, small communities, and human beings in many circumstances. It is far less true today. When numbers get large, innate altruism can no longer cope with demands and cultural reinforcement is needed.[3]

The example of the Commons has wide applicability and importance. Much of the environmental issue is a Commons-type problem. Pollution of the oceans, rivers, and lakes, depletion of the ozone layer, global warming, and the decline in ocean fisheries are all Commons problems.

The Pareto Principle, Cost-Benefit Analysis, and Values

According to the Pareto principle, a policy or action is desirable if it can make somebody better off without anybody else becoming worse off. While this appears to be an ethics-free rule, it is not. It accepts the ethical principle that *Schadenfreude,* though it may contribute to an individual's selfish enjoyment, is to be disregarded in the economic calculus and that envy should not be taken into account in arriving at the optimum (Boulding 1982, 14–15).

In real life, there are very few instances in which in a choice among alternatives one is clearly Pareto-superior, that is, when an economic change will benefit someone while leaving everyone else unaffected. In the dynamic world in which we live, each change will be better for some, worse for others. Pareto-optima consequently have little relevance in cost-benefit analysis, wherein the costs and benefits of investments or policy changes have to be assessed in arriving at a judgment or decision. Any attempt to compute the compensation necessary to ensure equality of benefits or costs founders on the inability to evaluate the justice of what is proposed without embarking on making interpersonal utility judgments. And, since according to mainstream economics it is impossible to make interpersonal utility comparisons, an economist can remain ideologically pure only by being useless. The solution, of course, is to disregard the psychological problem and apply the standard of material welfare, which is computable.

But cost-benefit analysis is a vital activity for any responsible government economist. In fact, many welfare economists and economist-practitioners have gone on to advocate the extension of cost-benefit analysis into "social C/B analysis." In social cost-benefit analysis, the project analyst assumes that the purely economic calculus of material welfare has to be supplemented with community values. These may include the desirability of reducing unemployment, giving greater weight to increasing the income of the poor, reducing regional imbalances, and so on.

Economics tries hard to be an objective, positivist science, and economists who bring any consideration of values into analysis are generally scorned. However, this does cripple economics. Paul Streeten has argued persuasively that without some value judgments national accounting becomes largely meaningless. Nuisances, or "bads," force us to expend resources and energy to remove or eliminate them. For example, dumping chemicals into the ground and polluting drinking water is a bad that may be eliminated only after a considerable expenditure. Including both the income from the polluting activity and that derived from cleaning it up in the national accounts is clearly misleading. But not all expenditures that are called forth by some one else's unasked-for activity can be classified as "antibads." An organ grinder may produce such discordant sounds that we pay him to leave us in peace. On the other hand, he may produce such lovely melodies that we reward him for the involuntary enjoyment he provided us. In short, a value judgment has to be made (Streeten 1986,140–41).

Contemporary Society

One of the results of the emergence of Europe from the Middle Ages was the sea change in perceptions of society. People began to perceive that existing law and institutions were not immutable laws of nature but human constructs, which, if unsatisfactory, could be changed. The American and French Revolutions, the new metric system, the Napoleonic Code, and Benjamin Franklin's whole career are good examples of this new view of life. Along with this came a moral change in many people. The feeling of concern that stemmed from altruistic self-interest widened beyond the family and the small community to encompass the nation. Bismarck in Germany with his invention of social insurance and Benjamin Disraeli in Britain with his concern for the working classes show that this development was even profoundly conservative. Particularly since World War II, the circle of concern felt by some has been extended to the whole of humanity. This is one of the important forces behind the growth and spread of foreign aid programs. It is also seen in the outpouring of assistance to any country that suffers a major disaster.

There is some indication that the cultivation of the altruistic motive needs to be encouraged at this stage of development in the industrialized world. Dutch prime minister Lubbers has complained that the main problem in Dutch society is the loss of a sense of the meaning of life. Members of the younger generation in particular, as a result of the country's general prosperity, are frustrated, even though they have everything material they desire. One of the appeals of the Green movement is that it gives people a goal outside of themselves. It gives people a meaning in their lives by appealing to that part of them outside of their self-interests.

Human behavior is the result not only of instinct but of culture. While altruism is as innate as selfishness in human beings, how we actually behave is strongly influenced by education in the home and school and the culture in which we live. Altruism, regard for others and the community, can be cultivated or suppressed. Families, schools, universities, and the media do much to inculcate goals and standards of success and accepted social behavior within a community. A successful society works to encourage those propensities that help and discourage those that are harmful. To the extent that economists are successful in convincing people that selfishness is an acceptable, dominant, natural motive, people will be influenced to behave accordingly and repress their innate altruism. Unfortunately, the present fundamental assumption of economic theory encourages selfishness and downplays other-regarding behavior.

As the familiar quotation from Keynes illustrates, the views of economists have far-reaching consequences for the way the world works. In his words, "the ideas of economists and political philosophers, both when they are right and when they are wrong, are more powerful than is commonly understood. Indeed, the world is ruled by little else" (1936, 383). The culture in which we live and are raised establishes for most people what is regarded as acceptable and desirable behavior. Average persons have only a limited sample of other people's experience to help them learn what they can reasonably expect of other people and what they should expect of themselves in relation to other people.

For the English classical school of economics, Viner remarked, economic man was neither ideal nor real: the classical economists did not really believe that even in the marketplace men acted only out of self-interest, nor did they believe that economic interest, the maximization of income or the minimization of unpleasant effort, was the sole form of self-interest (1991, 75).

In one of Keynes's often overlooked works, he identified "the Benthamite tradition," that is, emphasis on quantitative methods and regarding people simply as utility maximizers as the worm gnawing within modern civilization and responsible for its moral decay. He called this an economic bogus faith (1949, 96–97).

There is evidence that contemporary economists' teaching that self-interest is the dominant drive for people does have a significant effect on behavior. Economists tend to acquire what the French call a *déformation professionelle.* Several behavioral studies have shown that students of economics tend to become significantly more selfish than students in other fields. In one experiment, three sets of students were compared. The first was composed of students who took a course in microeconomics taught by an instructor specializing in industrial organization and game theory. Members of the second group took a similar course with an instructor who specialized in development in Maoist China. The third group contained students who took a course in astronomy. The experiment measured whether the students became more or less "honest" after completing their courses. The results were consistent across a range of questions: the first set of students had the largest proportion of individuals who became less honest, the second set was in the middle, and the astronomy students had the smallest proportion. The same results were found in other experiments: economics students in prisoner's dilemma games defected 60 percent of the time, while noneconomists defected 39 percent of the time. Economics professors, although generally earning higher salaries than other academics, give a smaller proportion of their incomes to charity than other faculty members do (Frank et al. 1993; see also references in Hausman and McPherson 1993, 674).

Economic forces obviously do influence the way families are formed and function. But this is not to claim that *The Communist Manifesto* was right a century and a half ago in declaring that "The bourgeoisie has torn away from the family its sentimental veil, and has reduced the family relation to a mere money relation." Nor is this correct when it is clothed in modern economic reasoning by a respectable conservative economist who was awarded a Nobel Prize for using an economic calculus in family relationships.

When the primacy of economic incentives is encouraged through such symbols as Nobel laurels, it is not surprising that some individuals do not hesitate to put satisfaction of their own desires above responsibility to children, spouses, and the community. While there are other forces involved, the legitimacy given to selfish self-interest probably has a substantial responsibility in recent years for the increase in the breakup of families, the rise in divorce rates, and the evasion of child support.

An economist, like every other human being, cannot avoid questions of personal morality. First, in our work as professionals we strive to be objective. We cannot allow any taint of self-interest to affect our findings. While a golden rain of grants and profitable lecture fees may shower upon economists who would shape their theories and arguments to serve the interests of those who will pay, anyone succumbing to this temptation is known to have violated the ethics of the profession. But economists have a deeper and more important obligation to the community—to strengthen and not undermine the public morality required of a democratic society. This society, with all its faults and shortcomings, is the best that humanity has so far developed.

The economics of a democratic society requires avoiding the Hobbesian war of all against all. The fundamental democratic principle stresses that everyone should be equally free to pursue his or her own good in his or her own way within a framework of regard for the rights of others. People have be other regarding as well as self-regarding for the society to endure successfully and remain democratic.

For the economist, this means that altruism cannot be ruled out of the fundamental assumption of the rational pursuit of self-interest. It means more. In John Rawls's theory of just institutions for a society, a basic principle is that the worst-off members of society must be protected against the worsening of their situation. This principle can almost be regarded as a classic moral principle of economics. The modern emphasis on the purely technical aspects of economic reasoning has nearly eliminated the ethical component of earlier economics. For Adam Smith, the founder of modern economics, selfishness was to be controlled by conscience, stemming from our feelings for others and our reactions to their disapproval. John Stuart Mill denied that it is normal for human beings to trample, crush, elbow, and tread on each other's heels. He felt that the best state for human nature is that in which no one is poor, no one desires to be richer, and no one fears being thrust back by others pushing themselves forward (1892, 453–54).

Marshall maintained that economic studies call for and develop that rare sympathy that enables people to put themselves in the place not only of their comrades but of other classes. He went on to say that nearly all the founders of modern economics cared for the wide diffusion of wealth among the masses. Marshall himself was in this tradition, putting the objective of making wealth "more equal in its distribution" on a par with the production of wealth itself ([1920] 1952, 38–39, 207).

The Smith-Mill-Marshall approach is not unknown even today. Jacob Viner, for example, described his idea of utopia as a society with as completely free and competitive a market as was attainable in a welfare state in which there was no mass poverty, the business cycle was under control, and opportunity was made as equal as was consistent with the survival of private property and the natural differences in capacities and motivations among human beings. Herbert Stein, chairman of the Council of Economic Advisers under presidents Nixon and Ford, repeatedly advocated that policy emphasis should be placed on positive government measures intended to reduce poverty and increase equality of opportunity.

Rawls's principle is reinforced by the analysis shared by many that the unmitigated operation of a capitalistic free market economy is unsustainable, for the resulting inequalities, insecurities, and sacrifices imposed on large numbers of people would lead to political upheaval. A nakedly capitalistic Hobbesian economy could only hope to continue with a Hobbesian absolute ruler. It is not only modern liberals who believe that naked capitalism would be intolerable; modern conservative thinkers such as George Will in the United States and David Willetts in Great Britain agree. They emphasize that a capitalist economy must have a feeling of community if it is to survive. Willetts argues that the welfare state produces the necessary sense of community to complement individualism. Without the welfare state, the insecurity intrinsic to capitalism could not be borne and would destroy the system. The modern Catholic philosopher Michael Novak also believes that capitalism cannot survive without a moral order that constrains the full working of the market system.

Conclusion

In this period in history, when the former communist countries are trying to establish market economies, economists are confronted with the pointed challenge of discovering what the prerequisites for a successful economy really are. Communist ideology called on individuals to subordinate themselves, to sacrifice themselves for the sake of the commonwealth. Conventional economics, at the opposite extreme, calls on the individual to pursue his or her own interests and disregards concern for others. Both are wrong.

In the transition from centralized planning to market economies, the former communist countries have experienced a wave of crime. The initial economy emerging in Russia has many aspects of robber capitalism. In 1995, the heads of the Proftekhbank, Tekhno-Bank, Pragma-Bank, Mosbizesbank, Kuzbassprombank, and Eurasia-Bank and the top officials of several other institutions were murdered in mafia-style attacks. Criminals own or control a large part of the banking system. The Main Economic Crime Department of the Interior Ministry estimates that 2 to 3 trillion rubles (equal to the Moscow city budget) are stolen or diverted annually from the financial system (Zhilin 1995, 9–10).

The elimination of discipline from above and from police terror exposed a Russian society and economy that lacks much of the ethical foundation needed for a market economy and democracy. Fear of the police had controlled behavior. With this gone, the new acceptable materialistic drive lacks a tempering sense of individual civic responsibility. The philosopher-president, Vaclav Havel, of the Czech Republic, has emphasized the need for the fostering of ethical values as a cure for the moral poisoning the countries now reveal as prevalent in their midst.

Pure individual selfishness leads to misery of the individual and is bad for the community. A successful society requires both the pursuit of self-regarding action and regard for the interests of others. A market economy gives such high monetary rewards to successful profit seeking that it provides a corrosive environment for social cohesion and personal responsibility. And yet a feeling of civic duty, regard for ethical values, and concern for the community are necessary for a society to be worth living in. An irreducible minimum of these virtues is even required for the economy itself to flourish. Efficient markets depend on the participants observing certain ethical norms.

For the desired open society to exist, there must be a democratic form of government that ensures orderly transfers of power, acceptance of minorities and unpopular opinion, and the rule of law. All of this is necessary in a free market economy. Unfortunately, the narrow concept of self-interest is concerned only with advancing the well-being of the individual and neglects any consideration of preservation of the whole system.

Not only is the fundamental assumption wrong as a description of and a guide to human behavior, but the anomalies in the application of the fundamental assumption in mainstream economics illustrate the need to change the theory. Modifying the assumption to take into consideration the altruistic element in self-interest will make the theory more true to reality. Accepting the fact that human actions are not exclusively driven by rational selfish motivations will make economics appear less deterministic and less susceptible to calculative rationality. This, however, will make economics more consistent with reality—a gain, not a loss. Making economics more realistic in its understanding of human motivations will improve its' predictive ability and make it a better guide to public policy.

If mainstream economists (and Marx and Engels!) were right that in our market-capitalistic society there is no nexus between man and man other than naked self-interest, then Hobbes's dilemma for society would be real: a choice between chaos and absolute rule. But following selfish self-interest is not an inevitable rule for human beings. Humans are naturally both selfish and altruistic. As Lewis Thomas notes, we are biologically a social species. We are more social, more interdependent, and more inextricably interconnected than the social insects (Thomas 1980, 20). The world is not composed of individuals standing alone but of relationships; it coheres through human connections. Our survival and success as a species depend on social cooperation. We only fall into Hobbes's dilemma through cultural choice, not by nature.

CHAPTER 6

Markets

Few people have the imagination for reality.
—GOETHE

Markets are institutions that evolved from human action in the past without initial conscious planning by anybody. As a result, there is a great deal about markets that we have tended to take for granted without being aware of what is involved. This we have learned from the attempts of the former centrally planned countries to create markets from scratch. The market is a highly useful economic instrument but idealizing it is not justified. While it is an effective instrument in helping societies generate wealth, it also favors manipulative (treating people as means) over ethical (treating people as ends) behavior. The market is not perfectly rational, its outcomes are not precisely governed by demand and supply, and, above all, it does not necessarily result in optimal outcomes or just rewards.

Modern neoclassical theory presents a model of the economy that depicts it as a series of competitive markets embracing the whole economy. Everything—commodities, services, factors of production—is included. The market for any of these is standard: the demand curve slopes downward, the supply curve slopes upward, and the point where they cross sets the market-clearing (equilibrium) price at which transactions take place. It is presumed that these markets are generally competitive.

Note that according to the rationality assumption all economic agents are successfully maximizing their self-interest in this process. Consequently, when the equilibrium price (the market-clearing price) is set by the intersection of the demand and supply curves, this is optimal for the economic agents concerned. This is a Pareto-optimum, but it is not optimum optimorum (the best of the best) since the unequal income distribution gives agents with the highest incomes more of what they desire while those with the lowest incomes may not be able to meet even their most vital needs. Francis Bator illustrates this point nicely:

> In a two-person world of Adam and Eve, depending on the initial distribution of whatever, you can have an outcome where practically everything goes to Adam and nothing goes to Eve. This is still Pareto-efficient in the sense that you cannot reconfigure any of the inputs or the outputs or the distribution in such a way as to make Eve better off without making Adam worse off. (Bator 1998, 202)

This reservation is often overlooked, however, and the results of the market are regarded as beyond criticism, a kind of utopia or even heaven on earth. As Mancur Olson observed, it is a staple assumption that the rationality of individuals makes societies achieve their productive potential; we are already therefore in the most efficient of all possible worlds (1996, 3–5). Thus, the market, in a more credulous age, could even be regarded by market-idealists as another name for God.

The major, indispensable, true contribution of the market is as a means of collecting and disseminating information among its participants. This information is provided in the form of price signals or, if prices are not allowed to fluctuate freely, by the emergence of shortages or surpluses. The market is also a coordinating mechanism. As desires, technologies, and resources change, the market provides incentives to move resources to where they are needed and divert them from uses where they are not. This view of the market as a discovery and coordinating mechanism is of course the one that Hayek stressed for years and which most economists now accept.

As we have seen in chapters 3 and 4, the assumption that people always behave as rational maximizers of their own self-interest is faulty. This substantiates Hayek's refusal to accept that the market provides a precise mathematical solution to the problem of resource allocation on the basis of exact known information or that the market necessarily leads to just outcomes.

The market economy, in truth, is a flawed, crude mechanism. Knowledge is fragmented, chaotic, and often unattainable. Participants act on the basis of their imperfect knowledge and understanding, and their influence on results is affected by their command of purchasing and market power. The future is uncertain and largely unpredictable. Learning by doing and technological innovation create profit opportunities, knowledge is limited and often ambiguous, and externalities in production and exchange are widespread.

The market, however, can be an effective tool for policy. Governments have learned that establishing a market for regulating pollution works. A maximum amount of pollution is set as a target, rights are assigned and distributed among firms, and trading is allowed in these rights.

Markets Are Social Institutions

One of the assumptions taken for granted is that the market simply exists. There is no concern for the specification of its institutional features, how it came into being, or what factors shape its development. But markets have a social and cultural history and are created or influenced in their evolution by the establishment and defense of property rights and the exercise of political power.

Most markets today are social institutions supported by a network of social practices, cultural behavior, and other institutions, including the government through regulations and laws. Living and working in a functioning market economy require public acceptance of a whole set of appropriate, conventional, and socially acceptable behaviors. The culture within which an economy is embedded has economic consequences. The market itself is both a cultural construct that influences how people behave and a system of social relations in which the participants interact.

Economic action takes place within a social context. It is usually embedded in ongoing networks of personal relationships—a regular set of relationships among individual or groups. For example, the Kamarck family has a black book listing the people we call on in times of need: the plumber, electrician, lawyer, mechanic, carpenter, and so on. We do not routinely try to find service at a lower price or even discuss price when we need help. In these ongoing relationships, each party expects and normally receives reasonable, friendly consideration from the other.

This behavior is both economic and social. It allows us to economize on the time and effort required to find the right person each time. But a social feature is present as well, for there is a perceived benefit from dealing with another human being when it is tacitly understood that neither is attempting to screw the last penny of gain out of the transaction. Similar determinants come into play between industrial firms and their suppliers and main customers. In Japanese firms, this connection is particularly intimate, but it exists elsewhere too. For example, "sticky prices" are due in part to companies not wanting to irritate their customers with frequent price changes.

Businessmen, like most people, often prefer to rely on a handshake to finalize a transaction rather than a contract that spells out the possible risks. Since it may be impossible to foresee the specific risk that needs to be guarded against, the handshake may provide more security than detailed small print. And people appreciate the fact that the other party is manifesting trust in them and showing faith that they will live up to the implicit understanding inherent in these ongoing relationships (Macaulay 1992).

People behave much the same way in consumer products markets. Most commodities are sold at prices set by their sellers. Customers have limited time in which to search for information, and once they decide to patronize a retail store they tend to continue to do so. The transaction costs for the customer of looking for a better price gives the firm some monopoly power, if only temporarily. But a sensible firm knows that to keep its customers its prices must be competitive enough to encourage new customers to sign on and to discourage its regular customers from deserting. The firm also tries to provide some incentive for loyalty by giving advance notice of sales to regular customers, facilitating purchases by them, and so on (Phelps 1981; Okun 1981).

It is obvious that for many commodities consumer demand is motivated by fashions and fads and other social considerations that override rational consideration. Even such important decisions as mergers and takeovers of corporations are subject to surges of irrational emotion. Mergers and corporate acquisitions come in waves. A favorable environment may make them more economic in some years, but this cannot be the whole explanation.

During the 1960s, the building of conglomerates was all the rage. Companies in unrelated industries were bundled into a single firm. Beatrice, a food company, acquired Avis (a car rental company), Samsonite (a luggage manufacturer), and Playtex (an underwear maker). In the 1980s, it became the fad to unbundle the conglomerates. The separate parts of most of them, including Beatrice, were sold off to improve their profitability. Both conglomerate building and unbundling were spurred by the fact that investment bankers are paid a "success fee" if the deal they are advising is concluded. If the deal fails, the fee is much less.

Limits of Markets

Observing a society and seeing only market and exchange relationships is looking with tunnel vision. In agriculture, which comes close to the classical description of a market with many buyers and many sellers, farmers in the high-income industrialized countries receive on the average 40 percent of their income from producer support above market prices or direct government subsidies.[1] Many human needs and activities are outside the market. Mediating institutions and organizations (such as churches, clubs, and associations) that are outside or beyond the market meet the needs that people have for community, the feeling of belonging, learning to live with the knowledge of mortality, and building character.

There are also moral limits—generally concurred on by all civilized peoples—to what can be traded in the market. As Arthur Okun reminded us, "Everyone but an economist knows without asking why money shouldn't buy some things." The buying and selling of human beings, the white slave trade, and assassination for hire are all outlawed. A modern taboo forbids the buying and selling of human organs. A person threatened with failure of the heart, lungs, or kidneys or threatened by blindness from a bad cornea may desperately desire the needed organ, but the supply of organs for transplants comes from voluntary donors. There is a moral revulsion against traffic in body parts. Indeed, if it were allowed criminals might murder people for their body parts, just as autos are stolen to be disassembled in "chop shops."

There is not, however, universal agreement on the inclusion or exclusion of human sperm and embryos from the market. The Canadian Royal Commission of New Reproductive Technologies recommended in November 1993 a ban on the "commercialization of baby making." The commission was critical of the United States for allowing brokers to find surrogate mothers and for allowing sperm to be sold: "It is fundamentally wrong for decisions about human reproduction to be determined by a profit motive" (Langan 1993).

The unfettered market is an inadequate instrument for coping with environmental problems, both internationally and domestically. The "wealth stock" of human-built capital (buildings, equipment, land improvements) can be measured by means of original or replacement cost, allowing for depreciation. There is no equivalent satisfactory accounting for the stock of natural resources, the quality of air and water, the absorptive and dilutive capacity of the environment, or the aesthetics of the ambiance in which we live.

There is no market in which the prices of environmental "goods" such as clean air, clean water, or beautiful beaches are quoted. Benefits and costs often run far into the future, affecting generations not yet born. Economics cannot cope with such long periods. The benefit-cost technique relies on discounting the future at an appropriate rate set by the present cost or return on capital. At a discount rate of 6 percent, a benefit of $1,000 fifty years hence is only worth $54 today (Jacobs 1991; Kamarck 1983, chap. 9; Norgaard 1992). The state can organize a market in which pollution rights are traded. While this is effective for reducing pollution, an arbitrary, nonmarket decision has to be taken on the magnitude of the problem.

There is a more fundamental problem: if monetary values are notionally assigned to environmental benefits and costs, the calculation is economically meaningless because if there were such monetary values attached in reality people would take them into account in their behavior and the results would be quite different. One ethical constraint on our decisions on the efficient allocation and use of our generation's stock of resources is that they must not irreparably harm future generations. The determination on the latter point has to be made on some other basis than straight discounting of the future back to the present.

Market Failures

The market cannot give accurate results in determining just compensation for a person's life. Financial calculations are made of expected earnings or of other economic factors, and no other satisfactory approach has been discovered. But nearly everyone will confess to a feeling of unease that nothing better has been found—and juries often repudiate the calculus and put a higher value on a human life than the amount recommended.

But the failure of the market to set a price in this instance does not rule economics out completely from being useful in this field. Decisions as to the *saving* of human lives often have to be taken on the basis of a comparison of costs and benefits of alternative possibilities. If one set of regulations, say, costs $25,000 per life saved and the alternative costs $100,000, then clearly the first alternative is preferable.

Externalities (spillover or neighborhood effects), a well-known failure of markets, are a problem because normally there are no markets in external costs or gains. An externality imposes costs on or grants benefits to third parties from an economic action in which they were not directly involved. For example, the bees belonging to a beekeeper may pollinate neighboring farms and so increase their productivity or, in the opposite case, acid rain from coal-burning power plants may destroy neighboring forests.

Externalities represent market failure since they are not included in the cost or demand schedules that determine what is produced and at what price it is sold. In an economy driven by profit, it is obviously in every firm's interest to externalize a cost whenever it can: dump waste into public water or air, get the government to build the infrastructure the firm needs, bully a city into building a stadium for a professional team, and so on. Passing labor input costs out of the firm is an omnipresent practice (note how much work a company forces you to do in paying a bill or trying to reach some entity within a firm by telephone). The market in these cases clearly does not determine what is the economically efficient amount of output at the economically efficient price. The market per se cannot cope with externalities without some special action being taken outside of the market in which they occur.

In the example of the beekeeper, if a farmer can accumulate enough land or organize a cooperative with his or her neighbors so that a hive of bees can do all its work within the boundaries of the client, a market can be created. There are migrant beekeepers in the United States who move their hives south to north during the spring and early summer under contract to fruit growers. In this case, an externality has been deliberately changed into an internality: all of the work of the bees is productive for their clients, so a price can be collected for their work.

Asymmetric capabilities or information lead to less than optimal market results. In most transactions, there is asymmetric information: between buyer and seller of most commodities and services, between a company's chief executive and its shareholders, or between employer and employee. If one party has better information, he or she can take advantage of this privileged position and strike a better bargain. Many services have unique characteristics that make it difficult or impossible for consumers to make informed decisions regarding their purchases. Health care, one of the largest economic activities in the modern world—accounting for 14 percent of GDP in the United States—appears to be one such example. Consumers are generally uninformed buyers and rely on the supplier medical profession for information on the quality and quantity of the service, there are restrictions on competition in the medical profession, payment is usually by third parties, and so on. It is not surprising that most high-income countries have a national health system.

Asymmetric information may even result in destroying a market altogether. If consumers cannot judge the quality of a commodity before they own it, sellers have an incentive to cut costs by producing an inferior product. This may result in a "race to the bottom" (with such a bad product that consumers stop buying it) or nonmarket mechanisms may have to be set up to prevent the self-destruction of the market (Akerlof 1984, 7–22).

There are similar difficulties when suppliers have imperfect or insufficient information. With imperfect information, a bank that raises its interest rates under the pressure of demand may fall victim to adverse selection, that is, it lends to high-risk customers who are willing to take on the higher rate. Insurance agencies, too, find that high premiums result in attracting customers who are most likely to file claims. In both cases, it is more sensible to keep rates below what the market would set and use administrative means to ration supply to demand (Grossman and Stiglitz 1980).

Some markets are prone to overshooting. In this case, instead of attaining and then resting at the point where demand and supply intersect, supply shoots right on past. The classic "hog cycle" is a case in point. This seems also to be true in industries that require large capital investments and a long gestation period between the investment decision and date when the first product appears. Then, when supply greatly exceeds demand, it takes a long time before excess capacity can disappear. It may take up to a decade and require an investment of hundreds of millions of dollars before a major copper mine, for example, can come on line.

The commercial real estate market in most of the industrialized world provided another instance of this in the 1980s. Following low levels of commercial construction in the late 1970s, construction of office buildings took off in the mid-1980s, stayed at a very high level, and then crashed at the beginning of the 1990s. Investors during the 1980s saw the possibility of high profits and rushed into real estate lending. Because of the long lag between the planning and the completion of a building, the supply of real estate is relatively fixed in the short run. An increase in the demand for space pushes rents above the long-term sustainable price. Since rental agreements are made for a term of several years, new tenants do not compete for the space already under lease. The new tenants are all competing for a small portion of the supply. The result is a spike in rents, which may then be regarded as representing a permanent increase. Bankers and lenders make decisions to build new capacity on the basis of the short-term spike. This euphoria about the future feeds on itself, and the result is a true bubble, with large-scale overbuilding. Sanity sets in when lenders find themselves with "see-through" skyscrapers, that is, empty of tenants, and it may take years to fill the excess space (Browne and Rosengren 1992).

Whenever information is imperfect and/or markets are incomplete, markets are inefficient. This, plus all the other circumstances that hinder the efficiency of a market, leads one to suspect that market failure is not the exception but the rule.

How Markets Work in Theory

Neoclassical economic theory assumes that buyers and sellers are price takers, with prices being set by the market. But John Hicks has called attention to a major change in markets. Markets used to be mostly flex-price markets—unorganized markets with a large number of buyers and sellers with prices directly responsive to supply and demand. There were also some organized markets formed by groups of traders to deal with one another. These also were responsive to supply and demand. Today, the dominant markets are fixed price, with prices set by producers (or some authority) and not immediately by supply and demand. Changes in costs and demand affect prices but not automatically. "Price decisions are made deliberately and are influenced by many other factors than just supply and demand" (Hicks 1977, x, xi).

When prices are set through administrative decisions, someone or some committee has to initiate action (e.g., note an unexpected piling up or depletion of inventory), consider, make a decision, and communicate it. And the decisions may be governed by some existing corporate tactical or strategic policy on how to treat a particular market or commodity and how great a change will be required before incurring the adjustment costs needed to alter a price.

In standard economics, in a market for a particular good there is a group of buyers and a group of sellers. The relationship between the quantities and prices at which purchasers are willing to buy is captured in a demand schedule. Similarly, the relationship between the quantities and prices at which suppliers are willing to sell is shown by the supply schedule. The intersection of the two curves sets the equilibrium price; the quantity demanded and the quantity supplied match at that price, and the market is cleared. And this is the largest possible quantity that can change hands at a price on which both buyers and sellers can agree.

A standard economics text, Mankiw's *Principles of Economics,* presents the accepted version of how markets work (1998, 62–85): "For every good in the economy, the price ensures that supply and demand are in balance. The equilibrium price then determines how much of the good buyers choose to purchase and how much sellers choose to produce" (85). The discussion in the text focuses on a market for ice cream cones, with the demand and supply schedules shown in table 1.

The equilibrium—market-clearing price—at which demand and supply balance at seven cones demanded and offered is two dollars. Conse-

TABLE 1. Supply and Demand for Cones in a Theoretical Ice Cream Market

	Demand			Supply		
Price	Catherine	Nicholas	Total	Ben	Jerry	Total
$0.00	12	7	19	0	0	0
0.50	10	6	16	0	0	0
1.00	8	5	13	1	0	1
1.50	6	4	10	2	2	4
2.00	4	3	7	3	4	7
2.50	2	2	4	4	6	10
3.00	0	1	1	5	8	13

quently, the theory runs, there will be a total of seven cones bought and sold at the price of two dollars each. Of course, in real life the ice cream sellers set a price and only sell at that price. But if the market *were* like this textbook example, the scenario might rather go like this:

> Catherine comes on the market and offers $1.00 for a cone and Ben sells one cone for the price. Nicholas then offers $1.00 and there is no supply, so he offers $1.50. Jerry sells him two cones, and Ben sells him one (since he already has sold one cone at $1.00 and there are only two that he was willing to sell at $1.50, one of which he was willing to sell for less). Catherine has one cone but wants more. She now has to offer $2.00, but she only wants to buy three since she already has one and she only wants four at the price of $2.00 or less. Ben sells her the only cone he has left to sell at that price. Jerry has only two left to sell. Catherine buys them.
>
> Nicholas has bought three cones at $1.50, and, while he would be willing to pay $2.00 to get three cones, he now has no reason to buy any at that price.
>
> Consequently, seven cones have been sold but only three at the market-clearing price: Catherine has bought four, one at $1.00 and three at $2.00. Nicholas has bought three at $1.50.
>
> The scenario might play out differently on different occasions. If Nicholas had made the initial purchase offering $1.50, he could have bought two cones from Ben and two from Jerry, satisfying his demand. When Catherine offers to buy, there are no cones available below $2.00 and only three at $2.00. She then has to pay $2.50 to get the fourth cone she wants. In this case, *eight* cones are sold: Nicholas has four at $1.50 and Catherine has three at $2.00 and one at $2.50.
>
> If it happens, for example, that the initial transaction begins at the high end of the price scale, Nicholas could wind up with one cone at $3.00 and two at $2.50 while Catherine might have paid $2.50 for two cones and $2.00 for another two. Seven cones will have been sold, but Ben and Jerry in this case will make out better than the "market-clearing price" would indicate.

Any of these scenarios is plausible. What is not plausible is the silent assumption in conventional theory that if Catherine buys a cone at $1.50 or Ben sells one at $3.00 they will cancel their favorable bargains in order to do business at $2.00, the notional equilibrium price.

As the Austrian school of economics points out, the conventional theory ignores the necessary process by which the theoretical equilibrium market-clearing point is supposed to be reached. Once this is taken into account, it becomes evident the equilibrium does not exist in reality.

William Squire has pointed out (personal communication, 1984) that there is a fundamental flaw in the concept of the usual demand and supply curves, that is, its disregard for time or history. For example, the amount demanded at any price is influenced by what the price was previously. If the price is rising, demand may increase to avoid a higher price tomorrow. If the price is dropping, demand may hold off in the hopes of a lower price. In other words, demand and supply are history-dependent properties.

Commodities are produced before they come to market. Producers have to hope that they can move the goods, for if they are wrong they will end up with unwanted inventories. Expectations and uncertainty are central. If the market is competitive, suppliers, driven by the profit motive, will follow the strategy of (1) constantly striving to cut the cost of their products, changing their products, or offering new products; or (2) trying to minimize uncertainty through acquiring market power by absorbing, combining, or colluding with competitors. In either case, whatever the ruling price in the market happens to be at any moment in time, the dynamic of the system operates to change it.[2] It is the exact opposite of what the concept of equilibrium signifies. In an equilibrium system, any movement away from equilibrium instantly evokes forces that restore the position.

Behavior in a market is influenced by expectations that derive from both objective and subjective factors: information and misinformation, facts and illusions, hopes and fears, optimism and pessimism, and facts and beliefs about future economic and technological trends and tendencies. The Austrian school of economics recognizes that people in the market have incomplete, and possibly wrong, knowledge and may not even be aware of what they do and do not know. Activity in the marketplace is a social learning process by means of which the participants learn and discover imperfect but useful knowledge. An important function of competition, for instance, is providing the means through which imperfectly informed firms learn about what consumers will buy. Entrepreneurs are not seeking an equilibrium position but are aggressive searchers for opportunities and weaknesses in their competitors (Horwitz 1995).

Market Power

The most efficient way to earn profits is to gain market power, ideally as close to a monopoly as possible. Neoclassical economics postulates the absence of market power (no single buyer or seller can move the price of a commodity). This is highly unrealistic for most of the economy. There is a great deal of empirical research that has found market power in the supply of many commodities (see Silvestre 1993). Competition is usually "imperfect"; market power is pervasive.[3] The long-established norm of modern market structure and behavior has been that of imperfect competition and oligopoly (Herman 1981, 1). Robert Solow agrees that generally we should assume that firms have some market power and monopolistic competition is the norm. "In any recession, it is all too obvious that most business firms would be happy to produce and sell more than they are currently able to sell at the current price. Evidently, then, price exceeds marginal cost. Why do firms not quote lower prices to increase sales?" (1998, 1). While there are many possible satisfactory answers to this question, they all involve the fact that firms must have some degree of market power (Mankiw 2000a, 427).

General Electric (GE) is the world's most successful corporation from the point of view of a shareholder, having increased its market value from $12 billion in 1981 to around $500 billion by 2000. It centers its corporate strategy on market power. It abandons any sector in which it is not now, or does not believe it can become, number 1 or number 2 in sales. This strategy is not unique to GE; it is followed or aspired to by Johnson and Johnson and many other large corporations.

Results Not Necessarily Optimal or Socially Just

For perfectly competitive markets (in those few cases in which one could argue that they exist) to be truly optimal, everyone taking part in the market should have the same perfect knowledge, the same purchasing power, and the same freedom of choice. If there is inequality in economic resources, in knowledge and skills, or even in the right skin color needed to act freely in the market, then the results of the market cannot be truly optimal. Because of imbalances in the wealth of individuals in the marketplace, the desperate need of a very poor person for a particular commodity may go unsatisfied because a wealthy person may bid more merely to satisfy a passing whim. There are large numbers of people (the disabled, the helpless, the unschooled, or other involuntary victims of society) who, through no fault of their own, do not have the money to participate on an equal footing in the market. Adam Smith perceived the inequality of power in the labor market between employer and worker even before the rise of the corporation:

> The workmen desire to get as much, the masters to give as little as possible.
>
> It is not, however, difficult to foresee which of the two parties must upon all ordinary occasions, have the advantage in the dispute, and force the other into compliance with their terms, . . . In all such disputes the masters can hold out much longer. . . . Many workmen could not subsist a week, few could subsist a month, and scarce any a year without employment. In the long run, the workman may be as necessary to his master as his master is to him, but the necessity is not so immediate. . . . Masters are always and everywhere in a sort of tacit, but constant and uniform combination not to raise the wages of labour above their actual rate. (1776, 66–67)

The market can fail or divert resources to socially undesirable ends, as in the "winner take all" or "Hollywood effect" markets.

Adam Smith noted the peculiarity of the great divergence in remuneration between the few winners and the runners-up in the profession of law (Smith 1776, 106). In today's professional sports, the few top players often receive incomes of millions of dollars a year while players rated below them sometimes have trouble eking out a living. The top rated college quarterback, on graduation, is offered a fabulous amount—millions of dollars—just to sign a contract to play. Other quarterbacks, who may be just as good but had the misfortune to play for a school with a weak offensive line, may not get any offers at all. The most popular singers are paid millions while others—nearly as good or even better but perhaps less well managed or lucky—are paid little. The same results may be observed in book publishing, investment banking, and corporate management.

In all of these cases, it is impossible to argue that the market distributes its rewards consistently with the distribution of talents. Worse, the market, because it drops huge fortunes on a fortunate few, attracts far too many others into these occupations. The sad stories of the young people who go to Hollywood hoping to become stars are commonplace. Similarly, there are thousands wasting their lives practicing basketball for every one who makes it into the professional ranks. The efficiency of the whole economy suffers from this misallocation of resources (Frank 1994).

Even if the market system did distribute its rewards according to talent, this would not make it a just system. The ability to sing like Pavarotti or Domingo or to crush opposing football linemen is largely due to inherited good fortune not earned desserts.[4] An attractive face or body or an appealing personality is rewarded in the marketplace. Handsome men and beautiful women are paid more than those who are plain (Hamermesh and Biddle 1994; Averett and Korenman 1994). Nor is it just when one's occupation suddenly becomes obsolete and income vanishes. When overseas air travel became possible, every plane had to carry a flight engineer. When jets replaced propeller planes, the remunerative flight engineering jobs vanished.

Fervent believers, however, accept that whatever a market decides is optimal. Heretics are outside the pale. Harvard economics professor Robert J. Barro, in dismissing the need for legislation to require employers to allow workers to take leave for family emergencies, stated flatly:

> Most economists (and all respectable [*sic*] economists) would agree that the amount of family leave and the trade-off between leaves and wages would be satisfactorily determined by voluntary interactions between workers and firms in our competitive labor markets. . . . there is no reason to think that the unfettered labor market generates "too little" or "too much" family leave. (1992, A13)

From 1993, when the U.S. Congress, contrary to Professor Barro's advice, passed the Family and Medical Leave Act, to 1999, around 20 million workers, both male and female, took unpaid time off for the birth of a baby or to care for a sick member of the family. Both employers and workers have been content with the law (Bernstein 1999, 42).

Professor Barro's Panglossian conclusion that the market makes optimum provision for the family concerns of workers is in stark contrast to reality. Around three-fourths of American employed mothers have children under eighteen. The first nationwide comprehensive study by researchers at Harvard's Graduate School of Education found that "The market is failing to equitably distribute affordable child care services across regions of the country, and among rich, working-class and poor communities" (*Harvard Gazette* 1993, 1, 7). In Massachusetts in March 1998, It was easier to get a child into college than into an excellent child care facility (Kornblut 1998, B8).

Inadequate child care is not a trivial matter. Poor, unstimulating environments have lasting negative effects on children's intelligence. A sick child recovers faster when cared for by a parent. A study of nine European countries from 1969 to 1994 found that "more generous leave rights reduce the death rates of infants and young children. The magnitudes of the estimated effects are substantial" (Ruhm 1998, 27). Good child care at home or at day care centers is an investment in human capital. It is absurd to argue that the market makes available just the right amount of parental leave needed by children (Sharpe 1994).

Capital Markets

Securities markets are as close as any to being perfectly competitive. Hidden in the general belief of the beneficent result of free markets is the assumption that the motives of the participants are in tune with the social purpose of the particular market. Keynes warned against the capital development of a country becoming the by-product of the activities of a casino. The proper social purpose of the financial markets is to direct new investment into the most profitable channels in terms of social yield. But this is not what occupies many of the brightest brains in Wall Street or the City of London (Keynes 1936,159). The biggest rewards—in the tens or even hundreds of millions of dollars—often go to the most successful financial manipulators.

The stock market is taken to be a prime example of an "efficient market." That is, all the pertinent information about a company (e.g., its earnings, dividends, competitive position, and future performance) is always reflected in its share price. Investors are assumed to be rational, well informed actors who absorb the available information and make objective decisions as to which shares to buy. Those investors who make decisions irrationally either learn to behave rationally or are eliminated from the market by losing all their money. The "efficient market" assumption, while comforting, unfortunately is contradicted by the real world.

The stock market is moved by emotion and fads as well as by reason. According to Warren Buffett, probably the most successful stock investor of all time, "The game is being played by the gullible, the self-hypnotized and the cynical." The very fact that his success is rare illustrates that few investors qualify as rational calculators (Lowenstein 1995a).

In Buffett's words, "market prices are frequently nonsensical." A large number of share owners have no real knowledge of the company or industry in question. Day-to-day news and rumors of ephemeral value have an excessive impact on price fluctuations while the real value of the corporation remains unchanged. If stocks were always rationally priced, stock quotations would change only when there was some reason to do so, that is, rarely. In reality, most bounce around almost constantly.

This can also be true of the whole market. On October 19, 1987, the Dow Jones Industrial Index dropped by 23 percent—almost double the drop of October 23, 1929, which heralded the Great Depression. The next day, the Dow went *up* by 5.9 percent, and the great bull market of the 1990s began. In October 1997, because of troubles in Southeast Asia, markets plummeted in Bonn, Paris, London, and New York. The Dow dropped a record 554 points (7.2 percent) on October 27 and then rebounded with a record 337 point gain the next day. Is this rational behavior?

Professional investors and speculators, with a few exceptions, are concerned with foreseeing at what level the market will value a security under the influence of mass psychology. The trick is to jump the gun and outwit the other fellow. This is, in fact, the theme of Gerald M. Loeb's enduring Wall Street classic, *The Battle for Investment Survival.*

The financial press is full of reports by "experts" pontificating on the future of the current bull or bear market. The very concept of bull and bear markets implies that the market is being affected by widespread sentiment.

There is a whole profession of well paid "technical experts" who predict what the market is going to do simply by charting what the price indices did. Their well-developed jargon includes such terms as *resistance point* (the place on the chart where the rise in the index previously stopped) and *support level* (the place where a previous decline halted). Even an investor who tries to make decisions based on fundamentals has to take into account the sentiment in the market. It may not affect which stock he or she buys or sells, but it will affect the timing of the decision: buying when a bear market has driven prices low or selling when the bull market has raised prices.

One result of all this is that assets markets are subject to "bubbles," that is, market prices that differ widely from their fundamental values for a time before suddenly bursting. The seventeenth-century Dutch tulip mania, the English South Sea bubble and the French Mississippi bubble (both of which burst in 1720), and the New York stock market crash of the late 1920s are all classic examples. Even prudent investors may participate in driving up prices while the bubble is growing. They hope to ride the market up and get out just before the bubble bursts. This is the "greater fool" theory, that is, purchasing an overvalued stock in the hope that a still greater fool will buy it at an even higher price.

It takes a lot of practice in refusing to use common sense to believe, in light of all these considerations, that the securities markets always and invariably result in optimum results or that the results are deterministic and single valued.

To perform their socially necessary role in investing their depositors' savings, banks need to be able to pick the most economically productive projects and make their decisions on purely economic grounds. Both of these criteria are not invariably met. From direct observation in a number of less developed countries, I can testify that often banks are not up to the task of making the best economic decisions. And we know from the savings and loan scandal in the United States that when government regulation was weakened, bank officials frequently took the opportunity to divert money into fraudulent investments or projects desirable only as a means of pleasing friends, relatives, or cronies.

In addition to the securities markets and banks, managers are important investors of corporate retained earnings. Their investment decisions are not necessarily optimal in terms of the whole economy.

Labor Markets

Labor is the most important market, for nearly everyone is involved. It is fairly widely—though not yet universally—accepted that conventional theory is inadequate for understanding the labor market. Conventional economics assumes that labor is a factor of production, just like capital, ignoring the fact that workers are human beings and there is therefore a social aspect to work relationships. Workers are not usually hired for a single transaction but for an extended period, establishing a relationship between employer and employee. This brings in a social dynamic often with the kind of outcomes shown in repeated games. When a worker is hired for a job, there is usually an explicit or implicit understanding of the minimum standard of performance that the worker must meet. The actual performance is affected by many factors. For example, studies have shown that the determinant of the actual performance of a worker in any group is the norm set by the group. This may be higher than the employer's minimum if the workers acquire a sense of loyalty to the company and feel that they are respected by it. A highly productive laborer may restrict his or her output out of solidarity with fellow workers. Many aspects of the employment relationship are strongly affected by social considerations (Akerlof 1984, 145–74).

The economic assumption that work is a disutility for which income and leisure are the rewards is simplistic and inadequate. Reality is much more complex. People are motivated to work by plural motives. Work per se often has intrinsic value. Many find pleasure in work. What we do is a large part of who we are. In countries with a strong work ethic, jobs provide not only income but meaning. New retirees often discover that with the loss of their work they have lost interest in life. If fired after years with a firm, the worker often feels like a piece of worn-out machinery. Unemployment increases the incidence of suicide, drunkenness, and family and personal psychological problems.

There is an underlying duality in the concept of "work" or "labor"—something we like and something we dislike. Hannah Arendt noted that every European language, ancient or modern, has two words, etymologically unrelated, for the same activity: *Work, labor; Werk, Arbeit; oeuvre, travail;* (Latin) *laborare, facere,* or *fabricare;* (Greek) *ponein, ergazesthai* (1978,

80). The first word in each pair insinuates an activity that is more pleasant, more prestigious. We speak of a work of art, a philanthropist engaged in good works, an *oeuvre littéraire,* or an *oeuvre de bienfaisance.*

Nonacquisitive drives affect effort and productivity. Recognition, pride, and satisfaction in accomplishment, freedom to make decisions, and the opportunity to make a difference or contribute something of value all matter, as do advancement within a hierarchy, pleasure in working with respected colleagues, team spirit, and a supervisor who respects the worker, listens, and cares.

There are many forces that affect wages and productivity within a modern enterprise in addition to the attempt by a rational firm to maximize profits. The history and current state of labor-management relationships within the firm have an enormous influence on the quality of labor effort, the level of work intensity, the creativity of worker suggestions, and the receptivity of management. These "social" or "sociological" factors, while they not treated in conventional theory, must be included in any analysis if we are to gain a proper understanding of the labor market and how enterprises function.

In conventional theory, all labor is equally in supply and available. The conventional assumption of "homogeneous" labor eliminates most of the important characteristics of actual labor markets. In reality, all workers are either insiders (employed workers) or outsiders (unemployed). Even without unions, employers will hesitate to replace insiders with outsiders. Not only are there costs of hiring and training but there are costs of firing (morale) and therefore productivity of the whole work force may suffer. Such action may offend notions of fairness.

In the workplace, where workers are in close personal contact, concern for fairness is an important emotional force. Workers who consider themselves unfairly treated are unlikely to want to work hard. Workers tend to feel that as long as all employees put in a "fair day's work" each should get a "fair day's pay"—in other words, equity should override sharp economic computation.

What lower paid workers consider to be fair wages in comparison with those of more highly skilled workers in the same workshop is not likely to coincide with the lower level of "market-clearing wages." The result is that if the enterprise wishes to be sure that workers do not shirk it will pay skilled workers at least as much as the market-clearing wages of the external market and will pay higher than market-clearing wages to the less skilled. In Japanese enterprises, as we know, wage compression extends throughout whole enterprises from top management down.

Market theory assumes that the unemployed are actively available outside the factory gates. But people who have been unemployed for a long period of time become demoralized, cease to look for work actively, and find ways of surviving from day to day. On the demand side, firms do not like to hire someone who has been long unemployed: skills have deteriorated and work habits become poor. The result is that the external market may have a large supply of unemployed labor with no impact on market-clearing wages (Blanchard and Summers 1988; Lindbeck and Snower 1988; Blanchard and Muet 1993). As the quotation from Adam Smith illustrates, employers usually have more power in bargaining than individual workers do. Karl Marx argued that capitalism required the existence of an army of unemployed to keep wages low. Shapiro and Stiglitz (1984) have shown that equilibrium unemployment acts as a discipline device to induce employed workers to exert more effort.

Large firms with market power and some fat in their costs set their "efficiency wages" high enough to persuade their superior workers that they are being fairly treated and to attract a queue of applicants. The result can be perfectly stable with continued existing unemployment (Blinder 1988).

Some workers get paid directly for their productive contribution: sales personnel on commission, waiters and waitresses paid through tips, the self-employed, and so on. But most workers are employees in corporations and—as Marx pointed out—are paid for their labor power not for the products of their labor. The connection between their performance and their pay is not inflexible. As the office worker, "Born Loser," in Art Sansom's comic strip explains: "There's a fine art to completing assignments at work—too late gets you fired, but too early only gets you more assignments!"

The success of an economy is related to the quantity and quality of maintaining and reproducing its labor force. Some of the costs of this are borne by individuals and families, but many are social. In addition to the provision of education through government, low-income people are often subsidized through child tax credits, child payments, earned income tax credits, and so on. The degree to which work forces are unionized affects how the social costs of labor are borne.

Most workers in the industrialized economies now work in services. When workers are producing services directly for consumers, it may be difficult to monitor productivity and quality of the service. It becomes important to motivate workers to do their best. Thus, employers may try to persuade workers that their interests and those of the firm coincide by promising lifetime tenure. There is a similar problem in firms in fields such as research and high tech, which depend on the creativity of employees.

Particularly valued employees, as in the classic case of Steinmetz at General Electric, may even be given complete freedom to choose what they do, when they work, and how much they work (Warsh 1989).

In a country's transition to industrialization, another set of forces different from today's was in play. Urban incomes and incomes in the industrialized sector are greater than incomes in the subsistence countryside. People migrate to the cities and become unemployed. These migrants, as urban unemployed, secure incomes from useful petty trade and backyard industry as well as from begging or selling unwanted services (e.g., watching your parked auto—if you refuse, your tires may be slashed). This income, plus the probability of finding regular employment, entices a continuous supply of "unemployed" to the city during the process of development. In Italy, for three or four decades after World War II the economy was growing well and putting more and more people to work but unemployment remained stubbornly constant at around two million. It was only when the Italian countryside was largely depopulated that Italian unemployment dropped (Kamarck 1965).

Markets in Land

An efficient market for land depends on the acceptance of a general belief that property rights in land stem from title rather than use. But in many parts of the world such a belief is not accepted as natural.

In Kenya, for example, the legal system, which was instituted by the British, recognizes property rights in land as passing with title, but this runs counter to traditional beliefs and practices. Farmers with holdings of less than half a hectare are the poorest but also most productive because of intensive cultivation. Efficiency would increase and poverty diminish if the small farmers could lease land from the large landlords. But these, who are mostly absentee owners, fear that leased land will be lost for good. The old tradition is still strong that farmers derive their land rights from use. The large absentee farmers could hire labor to get more intensive cultivation, but supervised, hired, multipurpose labor is not productive in Kenya for historical and cultural reasons.

Kenyan small farmers are also unable to get credit to buy land because banks worry about their ability to repossess land from a cultivator. In sum, the markets for land, capital, and labor in the rural regions of Kenya do not work according to the economic texts and rural poverty continues (Collier and Lal 1986).

The Market and the State

In neoclassical economics, the role of the state is minimal. It comes into the picture to remedy market failures that arise out of externalities but only if people cannot solve the problem of externalities privately through bargaining. The state also is there to provide or arrange for the provision of public goods—goods that are "nonrival" (one person's use does not diminish another person's) and "nonexcludable"(people cannot be prevented from using them). The transition to a market economy in the European former centrally planned countries has provided the graphic lesson that the state has a much greater role vis-à-vis the market than neoclassical economics has acknowledged. The great patron saint of the market, Adam Smith, recognized that the market needed the sovereign to maintain peace and justice, provide the physical and social infrastructure, and enforce contracts. That is, the state is essential to the market.

Competitive markets are the product of centuries of legal development of property rights, standardization of commodities and services, and evolution of nomenclature for these. Well-functioning markets need an independent legal system: a code of private property rights; bankruptcy and contract law; and a government that defines, protects, and enforces contract and property rights; a good monetary regime, developed financial markets and a good banking system; good communications; and generally observed standards and ethics. The World Bank from its experience in the European transition economies learned that the state had to establish these prerequisites for a modern market-based economy (Chhibber 1997; Gray 1997; Levy 1997; Pradhan 1997).

For markets to function well, this special set of conditions is necessary. The attempts of the former communist-ruled countries to institute a free market system have painfully demonstrated how much is demanded of government and the rest of society for such a system to function. The outcomes were remarkably different in practice. The European Bank for Reconstruction and Development found that this was primarily due to "national differences in institutional underpinnings and, in particular, to differences in legal systems and in the adherence, or lack thereof, to the rule of law" (Pistor and Sachs 1998, 2).

Property rights are not divinely established. They are set and defined by the state, established through legal action in the courts, affected by regulatory agencies, and subject to power struggles in these and other arenas. The value of a share of stock is determined not only in the marketplace but by what the management and the board of directors do in controlling the distribution of benefits from the operations of the corporation.

Investors have learned from bitter experience that government supervision is needed if a stock exchange is to prevent ramping, insider trading, and other distortions from affecting share prices. The financial crises in Asia in 1997–98 and the billions of dollars lost in the 1998 failure of the Long-Term Capital Management hedge fund led the leading American business periodical, *Business Week*, to draw this lesson:

> Expanding government oversight is critical. . . . The idea that free markets exist in a vacuum has been shattered. Without rules and regulations, they can create anarchy. Enforcing accountability and transparency is government's job. This is as true for the U.S. as for Asia. (1998a, 162)

The history of each country makes each business environment unique to that country. When the European Community embarked on its policy of creating a single internal market among its twelve members, it had to be laboriously constructed. Nearly three hundred specific subjects had to be harmonized by changing the existing laws, rules, and procedures. Product health and safety standards (what constitutes a sausage, how beer is brewed, and so on) and rules for the treatment of intellectual property and the service sector all had to be negotiated.

In addition to creating and monitoring the legal and social structures essential to the market, the state is needed to create the physical infrastructure for a successful market economy. Adam Smith recognized that the state had to create those infrastructures the productivity of which cannot be properly recognized during the too short horizon of private entrepreneurs. The canal and railroad building that was financed or subsidized by the government in the nineteenth century created the American national market. Publicly financed research in agriculture has been a large contributor to the enormous increase in productivity on farms. Public investment in feeder roads and irrigation has yielded high returns in many cases, and investment in health research has stimulated the biotechnology industry.

In modern times, in addition to the need to rely on the government to see to the provision of certain types of physical infrastructure, government investment in human beings has also been necessary. Educated, healthy workers and consumers underpin the market. There is no way that the pure market system could have eradicated the scourge of smallpox.

When a competitive market does exist, external authority (the state, strong custom, etc.) may be needed to keep it so. Profits can be won through superior efficiency or market power. Market power can be exerted on suppliers or buyers. The Standard Oil Trust not only secured lower rates than its competitors on the railways, but it forced the railways to give it a kickback on all the payments made by its competitors. Microsoft forced computer manufacturers to pay it a fee even on computers they produced that did not use MS-DOS, Microsoft's operating system at the time.

In a modern democratic society, it is necessary to guard against a highly skewed distribution of income. There is nothing preventing the market system from creating such an undesirable distribution. Great disparities in income and wealth may threaten the successful functioning of a democracy. A democratic government appears to be a necessary condition for the long-term survival of a market economy. It is quite possible, of course, for governments to change the distribution of wealth without interfering with the effectiveness of markets. A progressive income or expenditure tax at the top and a negative income tax at the bottom, generous provision of financing for students in higher education, technical training, and so on are all ways of offsetting wide disparities in income.

With the increasing complexity of modern life and higher population densities, government regulation of the social conduct of firms has become pervasive. This includes regulation of the health and safety of work places and products, the accuracy of the information that firms disseminate about their products, and the noise and other pollution that the firm produces. The economic conduct of firms—pricing, methods of distribution of products, control of entry and exit, and so on—is also commonly regulated.

Finally, a modern market economy needs wise economic management to mitigate economic cycles and maximize economic growth potentials.[5] A poorly managed public sector or ill-advised government intervention can cause substantial damage to the market economy.

The market and academia

Adam Smith said that in universities where the teacher receives a salary and is prohibited from receiving any fee from his pupils his interest is set as directly in opposition to his duty as it is possible to set it: the teacher will either neglect his job altogether or perform it in as careless and slovenly manner as he can get away with. In the university of Oxford, the greater part of the public professors have, for these many years, given up altogether even the pretense of teaching (716–18).[6]

Many present-day economics professors are avid advocates of market forces to be used to decide issues from agriculture to government policies but refrain from advocating the creation of an academic market for themselves—abolishing tenure and fixed salaries and compensating professors out of the fees paid by the students they attract.[7] In such a case, there would be no need to concoct an imaginary market to illustrate the way demand

and supply work, since fees would vary according to them. If a fee-based system were regarded as too much of a good thing, there are other market conditions that could be allowed: when job benefit of tenure is granted, in such a market an offsetting cut in salary might be appropriate.[8] Younger economists could be allowed to bid for positions—allowing the senior members, of course, to defend their jobs if necessary by offering to take salary cuts.

Free market ideology does have its limits, however, and this is one. Tenure protects freedom of inquiry. Abuses can be avoided through the nonmarket ethos of professionalism. As professionals, economists in academia expend their energy in pursuits that fall outside the impersonal market: acting as gatekeepers to professional acceptance; judging, mentoring, and recommending students; refereeing manuscripts and reviewing books; and conferring, voting, and politicking over the choice of new members in their departments and the awarding of tenure.

Concluding Remarks

The market is an important, vital institution in our enterprise system. It is better than any other instrument human beings have been able to devise to mobilize the scattered partial bits of information possessed by buyers and sellers to set prices, organize the exchange of goods, and indicate where resources should be utilized. But the market is not a god to whom unquestioning obeisance is due. It was made to serve us, not vice-versa.

The market has severe limitations. It works, but it works imperfectly. It is not a precise, deterministic instrument. Market outcomes, particularly in the most important market, the one for labor, are affected and sometimes even determined by nonmarket factors. The defects, shortcomings, and failures of the market are sufficiently great and widespread that one cannot legitimately claim that the results of the market lead to just social rewards. Actual rewards to participants in the market depend on an unforeseeable combination of ability, effort, chance, market power, and just plain luck.

The market is a social construct, a product of social evolution. To work well, it requires state management and a suitable framework of laws, rules, habits, and informal accepted norms. As Ronald Coase famously remarked, "Without appropriate institutions no market economy of any significance is possible."

The intervention of the state or other public authorities in the market, or in creating or structuring it, cannot be counted on to always act wisely to make the market work more ideally. Yet nonintervention is also a policy, and it is certain to have imperfect results. In developing countries and restructuring economies such as those of the former communist nations, if the government sits back and waits for market institutions to evolve from the bottom up it may take generations, just as it did in Western Europe. And in the meantime, as in Russia, the initial results can be crime, corruption, chaos, and a mortality crisis resulting in huge losses of men and women at their most active and productive period of life.[9] Guided by good economic analysis, public intervention can set up the institutions, provide the necessary laws, and codify the informal rules that can result in improved markets and market results. The contrast between those capital markets (the heart of market capitalism) that are well regulated and those that are badly regulated or not regulated at all is a graphic proof of this claim.[10]

CHAPTER 7

Change and Growth

When you are criticizing the philosophy of an epoch, do not chiefly direct your attention to those intellectual positions which its exponents feel it necessary explicitly to defend. There will be some fundamental assumptions which adherents of all the variant systems within the epoch unconsciously presuppose. Such assumptions appear so obvious that people do not know what they are assuming because no other way of putting things has ever occurred to them.

—ALFRED NORTH WHITEHEAD

. . . economics adheres strictly to the importance of equilibrium as part of any theory . . . equilibrium is a central concept in economics. Virtually all economic theories have as primary desiderata that the behavior described must be consistent with some notion of equilibrium. . . . it is the interest in equilibrium itself that distinguishes economics from other social sciences. To be sure other social sciences discuss spillover and feedback effects but among social scientists, only economists insist on a physical-sciences-style equilibrium as part of the analysis.

—EDWARD LAZEAR

Equilibrium is a concept of statics (a branch of Newtonian mechanics), which is concerned with bodies at rest or moving at a constant velocity. It is a condition in which all acting influences cancel each other out, resulting in a stable, balanced, or unchanging system. *Equilibrium* is a polar word—there is more than a whiff of something desirable about it.

Adam Smith, writing during the first stages of a historic transformation, was highly aware of the existence of change in the economy in real time. A century later, the historian Henry Adams observed that the central fact of the modern world was the acceleration of change. A perceptive observer, one who is not blinkered by outmoded theory, is instinctively aware that the most important characteristic of our capitalistic market economy is change, which powers growth. Change is the very essence of the system: "The essential point to grasp is that in dealing with capitalism we are dealing with an evolutionary process. It may seem strange that anyone can fail to see so obvious a fact which moreover was long ago emphasized by Karl Marx" (Schumpeter 1942, 82).

In this chapter, we will examine the canonical paradigm of equilibrium in economic theory; general equilibrium theory, which is the overarching theoretical concept of neoclassical economics; and the ways in which these relate to growth. The thrust of the argument is that the assumption that the economy is a stable system, that there are forces that move the system toward equilibrium values after any disturbance, frustrates the ability of theory to arrive at a correct understanding of the dynamic real economy. The argument will probably be difficult to accept since it runs so directly counter to the mind-set that has been embedded in economics for well over a century.[1]

Today's Worldview

The genesis of the concept of equilibrium and its dominance in economic theory are perhaps understandable in light of the cultural and intellectual environment of the nineteenth century. But with the progress of science in the last century—correcting our concept of reality—Schumpeter's insight is irresistible.

It is only very recently in historical time that human beings have become aware that we live in history—that there is a past that differs from the present and we proceed into an unknown future. Earlier most people tended to regard the passage of time as a recurrence of familiar moments. The cycle of seasons and the phases of the moon and the sun were all representative of the cycle of time. The repetition of the familiar provided the framework for human experience (Boorstin 1979, 229–34).

Most people now accept the idea of history and realize that day-by-day we move on into the novel, the untrod new world of the future. We are not, as the concept of equilibrium implies, at or continually returning to a destination. We are on a journey into the unknown. Today's intellectual environment is more in harmony with Schumpeter's insight than it was in 1912 when his message was largely ignored. It should be difficult now for a modern mind to deny his thesis that changes "are theoretically and practically, economically and culturally, much more important than the economic stability upon which analytical attention has been concentrated for so long" (1912, 255).

Physics itself is now a historical science. With Hubble's discovery in 1929 that the universe is expanding, the universe could no longer be considered a system in equilibrium. It has a beginning and changes over time.

Our own sun will eventually swell into the solar system and put an end to all its planets. Before then, an asteroid randomly smashing into our earth may kill us off, just as 65 million years ago the dinosaurs were eliminated. During its limited life span, our solar system is not immutable: the spin axes and orbits of planets change, comets come zooming in and out, and asteroids and fragments of comets smash into planets. Our whole solar system is moving at 40,000 miles per hour in the direction of the star Vega. And our galaxy, the Milky Way, is traveling in the direction of the constellation Hydra at a speed of 1.4 million miles an hour.

Our very earth, we now know, is no longer firm or reliable (a lesson easily learned by anyone who lives on the West Coast of the United States or in Japan). We cannot understand our planet if we refuse to recognize that the continents are moving, carried by sliding plates that collide or ride up over one another. Here new land is forming; there the ground is disappearing into the fiery bowels of the globe.

In biology, as in economics, the lure of the Newtonian equilibrium metaphor initially overrode reality. As late as the 1970s, ecological textbooks still taught that highly diverse systems were stable. When disruptions occurred, built-in forces would bring the system back to the normal equilibrium. It is only very recently that this approach has been superseded and it has been realized that "the over-all system, instead of being in equilibrium, may be in a state of more or less continuous upset—reeling from one disturbance to another, and never reaching a well-ordered normal state" (Ford 1988, 54).

Darwin's theory is now supreme. Present life forms can only be understood in terms of their past. New species develop, and others disappear. The environment, with which individuals and species must cope, is itself evolving due to the struggles of all species to survive. The process is open-ended and stochastic. In reproduction, DNA is copied, but never perfectly, and mutation is constantly taking place. Change is inevitable. As Darwin commented,

> natural selection is daily and hourly scrutinizing, throughout the world, the slightest variations; rejecting those that are bad, preserving and adding up all that are good; silently and insensibly working, *whenever and wherever opportunity offers,* at the improvement of each organic being in relation to its organic and inorganic conditions of life. (Darwin 1952, 42; italics in original)

The relationship between the sexes is fundamental in human society, yet even gender roles are in flux. For most of human existence, the difference in reproductive responsibility resulted in a difference in the social and economic roles the two sexes performed. In today's technologically advanced economies, with extremely low birth rates, the connection between the reproductive and gender division of labor has been broken. In most high-income countries, the proportion of men at work has fallen: young men stay in school longer and older men retire sooner. In the United States, the proportion is dropping toward 50 percent. The number of women taking paying jobs has been constantly rising. Whereas a hundred years ago less than a fifth of American women had such jobs, now the proportion is beginning to approach 50 percent. Within a few years, there is likely to be very little or no difference in labor participation rates between men and women. So, again, there is nothing permanent.

Social changes and demographic trends affect the economy. In the high-income countries, retirement has become a normal expectation, the nonworking elderly currently relying on nonearned incomes represent a large proportion of the population, and whole areas of the country are peopled by older, nonworking individuals.

For most of human history, population numbers grew very slowly. From 8000 B.C. to around 1750 A.D., it took between one and three millenniums for the world's population to double. Then the rate began accelerating, doubling first in a century and then in around thirty-five years after World War II. Now, while population numbers in some countries are still rising, the rate of growth is slowing and in some countries the numbers are starting to drop.

History, geology, astronomy, biology, and physics now accept the concept of process as central to understanding. Ceaseless change, the day-by-day move into the novel, and the untrodden world of the future also characterize the modern economy.

Change and the Economy

Before modern times, economic change, if it occurred at all, was very slow and was often even repressed by despotic governments. The situation is very different now. Marx and Engels's summary description of the first phase of the capitalist market economy in the *Communist Manifesto* is classic. The bourgeoisie

> has been the first to show what man's activity can bring about. It has accomplished wonders far surpassing Egyptian pyramids, Roman aqueducts, and Gothic cathedrals. . . . The bourgeoisie cannot exist without constantly revolutionizing the instruments of production. . . . Constant revolutionizing of production, uninterrupted disturbance of all social conditions, everlasting uncertainty and agitation distinguish the bour-

geois epoch from all earlier ones. In place of the old wants, satisfied by the productions of the country, we find new wants, requiring for their satisfaction the products of distant lands and climes. In place of the old local and national seclusion and self-sufficiency, we have intercourse in every direction, universal interdependence of nations. The bourgeoisie, by the rapid improvement of all instruments of production, by the immensely facilitated means of communication, draws all,even the most barbarian, nations into civilization.

The bourgeoisie, during its rule of scarce one hundred years, has created more massive and more colossal productive forces than have all preceding generations together. Subjection of Nature's forces to man, machinery, application of chemistry to industry and agriculture, steam navigation, railways, electric telegraphs, clearing of whole continents for cultivation, canalization of rivers, whole populations conjured out of the ground—what earlier century had even a presentiment that such productive forces slumbered in the lap of social labor? (1848, 5–6)

The sweep of the economic change since the *Communist Manifesto* was published in 1848 has been even more astounding. Beginning in England and Scotland in the eighteenth century, the Industrial Revolution spread to the United States, Western Europe, Japan, and Eastern Europe, and since World War II it has affected most of the rest of the world.

During most of the period since the beginning of the Industrial Revolution, the number of weekly, annual, and lifetime work hours has decreased. Modern workers scarcely realize how short their workweek is compared to that of workers during the initial stages of industrialization. In the 1820s, mill girls in Lowell, Massachusetts, were awakened at 4:30 for a fourteen-hour day, six days a week, with short breaks for meals. They were on their feet all day tending the deafening spindles and looms. When the native-born Americans called for a ten-hour day in the 1840s, they were replaced with successive installments of immigrants: Irish, French Canadians, and Southern and Eastern Europeans. It was only on the eve of World War II that British workers were granted a week's paid annual leave through an act of Parliament. Now workers in the high-income countries work less than half as many hours a week as a century ago and have several weeks of annual vacation to boot.

Veblen and Myrdal, who like Schumpeter were outside of the accepted economics canon, noted that economic processes have positive feedback, with small effects reinforcing each other. This results in a cumulative impact on an economy, driving it farther and farther away from any initial assumed equilibrium.

It is well known to development economists that if a region can in some way "get the jump" on other regions in its economic development, it is likely to attract additional capital, entrepreneurs, and better qualified labor and thus increase the initial disequilibria among other regions (Myrdal 1968). While in some cases the clustering of an activity in some defined place is clearly logical; in many instances it is purely a matter of chance that an initial entrepreneur happened to pick a particular town. The town may have been the entrepreneur's birthplace, there may have been a strong university department nearby, or a key person may have simply liked the climate or the proximity of beaches or ski resorts. Eastern Uttar Pradesh became (and still is) India's carpet belt when the Moghul emperor Akbar imported carpet weavers from Persia in the sixteenth century.

Microsoft, the dominant company in the computer industry, is located in Seattle simply because founder Bill Gates likes it there. There may have been innumerable locations that would have been just as good. Whatever the cause, once growth begins in a specific place, the forces drawing people and enterprises there become cumulative. Each arrival attracts others until some kind of saturation point is reached.

In the economy, just as Darwin observed in nature, speed in making changes is essential to survival. Sony's Beta video cassette recorder may have been technically superior to the dominant VHS model, but VHS won a slight market advantage by coming first to the market. This became cumulative as customers, fearing to wind up with an "orphan" instrument, chose the market leader. Quite soon, VHS became the standard. As most motion pictures were soon available only on VHS, the beta VCRs became unsalable.

A similar network dynamic rules in many products for which the learning curve is important. The high-technology sector, by its nature, is able to exploit increasing returns. It may cost immense sums in research to produce a new product in the drug, computer, or airplane industries. Boeing's new 777 aircraft, for example, took eight years to research and design and it cost $8 billion to produce a prototype. After a product is developed, the cost of an additional unit is relatively cheap and the average cost falls rapidly as more are produced (Arthur 1993). The producer that aggressively exploits its increasing returns can gain a great advantage over its competitors and later entrants. Compaq, a producer of computers, having gained market share through advertising, began in 1992 to cut its prices by around 30 percent a year. Its increasing volume made possible improvements in design and manufacturing costs. By 1994, it had cut its combined labor and overhead costs by 75 percent over the two-year period. Labor costs were reduced to an absurd 2 percent of total cost for some of its products (*Economist* 1994c, 59).

As a country becomes industrialized, massive structural shifts take place. In 1776, probably 90 percent of the American labor force was engaged in agriculture. Today that figure is less than 2 percent. After the mechanical cotton picker was introduced in the 1940s in the cotton-growing Mississippi Delta, the number of farms fell from 105,000 in 1940 to 6,000 by 1990 and the number of sharecroppers working on the farms fell by 98 percent, sending millions of blacks north. The number of persons resident on farms, 40 percent of the total American population in 1900, had dropped so far by 2000 that the government no longer bothered to count them annually. Now American tourists visit farms (organized for the purpose) to marvel at what agriculture is like.

Sweeping changes characterize all countries in the course of industrialization. In the European Union by 2000, less than 5 percent of the population remained in agriculture, contributing less than 2 percent of GDP. Economic forces push surplus labor out of agriculture. Sometimes, new jobs are created in the process of industrialization rapidly enough to absorb the people squeezed out of agriculture. At other times, countries experience large-scale unemployment or underemployment for decades. However the transition occurs, it proceeds with enormous dislocation and secondary economic and social impacts.

Great Britain's industrialization was built on coal, iron and steel, and textiles. In 1920, there were 1,250,000 miners of coal; at the end of World War II, there were 700,000 and by 2000 coal mining in Britain was no longer a significant economic occupation. In France in 1948, there were almost 200,000 coal miners. By 2000, there were only 6000, and the industry is expected to be discontinued by 2005. In the British steel industry, 80 percent of the workers lost their jobs from 1974 to 2000 and thirty-three out of the thirty-seven steel facilities of British Steel PLC were closed permanently. By 2000, pop music was contributing more to British export earnings than the steel industry and Indian-style restaurants employed more people. In textiles, the 1930s were one long agony as spindles and looms were scrapped and Great Britain switched from being a net exporter to an importer of textiles.

In another great structural change, the share of manufacturing output as a percentage of GDP in industrial countries has declined and is now under a fifth of the total. Everywhere in the high-income countries, the fraction of the labor force in manufacturing is decreasing. Workers have been moving out of factories into services. The share of manufacturing in the American nonagricultural labor force fell from 34 percent in 1950 to 14 percent in 2000. By 2000, there were around 2 million more workers employed in government than in manufacturing. Early in the twentieth-first century, it is safe to predict, manufacturing employment in the United

States will have dropped to under 10 percent of the labor force. In Great Britain, the proportion of jobs in manufacturing dropped from 37 percent in 1970 to under 18 percent in 2000; there are now some 3 million fewer jobs in manufacturing. In the same period, the labor force in manufacturing dropped by 17 percentage points in Germany and Italy. Similar drops have taken place in Australia, Austria, Canada, France, and Japan. WalMart, a discount retailer, has been the greatest creator of American jobs in recent years: in 2000 it employed 1.1 million workers—600,000 more than DaimlerChrysler, the largest industrial employer.

The net changes taking place among sectors conceal even greater changes occurring within each industry. A pervasive finding of recent research using longitudinal establishment level data is that:

> Seemingly similar plants within the same industry . . . behave quite differently in terms of real activity at cyclical and longer-run frequencies. Even in the fastest-growing industries, a significant fraction of establishments decline substantially; similarly, a large fraction of establishments in the slowest-growing industries grow dramatically. During severe recessions virtually all industries decline, but within each industry a substantial fraction of establishments grow. Likewise, during robust recoveries, a substantial fraction of establishments contract. Simply put, the underlying gross microeconomic changes in activity dwarf the net changes that we observe in published aggregates. (Haltiwanger 1999, 4)

Creative destruction, Schumpeter's term, remains characteristic of successful capitalism: corporations that do not keep up with change die. From the beginning of the rubber tire industry in the United States, Akron, Ohio, was at its center. Akron firms dominated the world tire industry during most of the twentieth century. But in 1982 the last tire was made there. By 2000, of the three largest firms in the American industry one was Japanese (Bridgestone-Firestone) and another French (Michelin). The third, Goodyear, was still American but closely allied to Sumitomo, a Japanese firm. As in Darwin's observation, the corporation that is most responsive to change is the one that survives.

The world, in which human beings live, is not Platonic but Heraclitean. As Heraclitus perceived, "nothing endures but change." Everywhere the essence of vitality is change and conflict.

A friend once told me that when she was a young mother with a family of small children she had continually longed for a normal day. That is, a day when no child had an earache or was late, no one had lost his mittens or forgotten her homework, the car's gas tank wasn't on empty, the children liked their lunches, all the bills were paid on time. She finally realized that her days *were* normal days—chaos and unpredictability were simply the routine of life. After she grasped this, that the real world was not Platonic, she was able to see the world as it is and enjoy her family life.

There is no utopia of order, stability, and harmony but a world of flux, constant change, and disorder. The Papal Curia eventually accepted that Galileo was right, and his remark applies to the economy, too: "Eppure si muove."

General Equilibrium Theory

Well into the twentieth century it was taken for granted that the universe was in an unchanging state of equilibrium that was either created at some point in the past or had existed forever. It is understandable that the ideal of eighteenth-century rationalists was to discover the laws governing society. Just as Newton had worked out the laws governing physical nature, they felt it should be possible to explain the behavior of human beings using similar methods. Once everything was measurable, it would be possible to secure the answer to any problem, "Calculemus," as Condorcet said (Berlin 1969, 57).

In the last quarter of the nineteenth century, while the economy of Western Europe was transforming itself in the second Industrial Revolution, Léon Walras concentrated on producing a theory of general equilibrium for the economy. Walras was the first economist to succeed in erecting a theoretical system inspired by this approach. His effort was motivated by Newton's achievement in celestial mechanics.[2] As Walras stated in the letter in which he applied for the chair at Lausanne, he was devoted to constructing "the science of economic forces, analogous to the science of astronomical forces" (Jaffé 1965,1:210). From the time when Walras was nineteen years old and read Louis Poinsot's *Elements de statique,* he was determined to construct economic theory as a physico-mathematical science on the same model, and with the same formal properties, that characterized classical mechanics and astronomy (Ingrao and Israel 1990, 88–89, 379, nn. 4–5). In his words: "One evening I opened Poinsot's Statique, and this theory of equilibrium through the composition and decomposition of forces and couples appeared so clear and logical that I read the first half in one breath; the next day, I finished off the second half" (Jaffé 1965, 3:148). Walras saw an analogy between the functioning of a system of interdependent markets and the equilibrium of the system of celestial bodies in classical mechanics. Therefore, he thought he could build a theory assuming that maximizing by consumers and producers under certain conditions would result in a general equilibrium of the economy where amounts produced and demanded in every commodity and factor market would be equalized. Modern economic theorists have followed Walras's model, though in recent years there has been less acknowledgment of inspiration from Newtonian mechanics.

The general equilibrium model of Walras, modified and improved by Cassel, Zeuthen, Neisser, von Stackelberg, Schlesinger, Wald, Hahn, Arrow, and Debreu, dominates modern economic theory, resisting the influence of the latest developments in modern science. Economic theory still mimics the seventeenth-century Newtonian mechanistic cosmos, with economic theorists intellectual slaves to long defunct and superseded natural scientists.

The major essentials of the general equilibrium theory are that a general equilibrium exists, that it is unique, and that it is stable. Perfect competition is assumed to prevail in all markets; economic agents are assumed to have unlimited, perfect knowledge and foresight and to be limitlessly greedy. Economic agents

> are assumed to maximize their benefits relative to costs. Starting from a given set of assets, each agent trades and exchanges until an optimum position is reached. Trading will cease when all agents have reached their individual optima because no agent will have any incentive to change position, and the system as a whole will have reached an equilibrium. This is the essence of the complex body of mathematical general equilibrium theory that dominates today's economics. (Fusfeld 1996, 307)

An equilibrium system is one in which each acting influence is offset by another, resulting in a stable, balanced, or unchanging system. Continuous growth within this framework can only be as a steady state, where everything grows in exact proportions. In equilibrium theory, there is a unique point toward which the forces of the system move, and this point can be calculated from the data, the set of axioms, variables, and parameters that belong to the system. The system operates in logical not historical time. In Newtonian mechanics, equilibrium was built to be a working description of the actual universe; in economics, general equilibrium is rather a Platonic ideal that the economy might achieve if messy uncontrollable real world forces and misguided human beings did not intervene.

The paradigm of general competitive equilibrium remains central in modern economics theory. Worse, it has become dogma. Contributions to macroeconomics that are guilty of a concern with real life have been criticized as ad hoc because they are not derived from the general equilibrium model (Hausman and McPherson 1993, 683). With no basis for the theory in reality, belief in it is akin to a religion.

The general equilibrium model has been worked on without any investigation at any stage, whether its basic axioms correspond to reality and whether the propositions derived from them by deduction can be verified (Kaldor 1985, 11–12). Weintraub goes further and says that the theory "is one in which empirical work, . . . facts and falsification, played no role at all" (1983, 37). Blaug agrees that it has no empirical content and the theory "would seem to lack any bridge by which to cross over from the world of theory to the world of facts" (1980,191). That is, the general equilibrium theory, a mathematical structure erected on a small number of basic axioms, is mathematics rather than a science whose truth is tested against the world of reality.

Note how desperately John Hicks was forced to stretch to try to salvage something from the theory once realism entered in the form of the recognition of imperfect competition. In his words,

> it has to be recognized that a general abandonment of the assumption of perfect competition . . . must have very destructive consequences for economic theory. . . . It is, I believe, only possible to save anything from this wreck—and it must be remembered that the threatened wreckage is that of the greater part of general equilibrium theory—if we can assume that the markets confronting most of the firms with which we shall be dealing do not differ very greatly from perfectly competitive markets. If we can suppose that the percentages by which prices exceed marginal costs are neither very large nor very variable, and if we can suppose (what is largely a consequence of the first assumption) that *marginal* costs do generally increase with output at the point of equilibrium (diminishing marginal costs being rare), then the laws of an economic system working under perfect competition will not be appreciably varied in a system which contains widespread elements of monopoly. At least, this get-away seems well worth trying (Hicks 1946, 84, 85; see also Wiles 1983, 72)

The theory assumes that if all individuals make the right decisions equilibrium and optimum conditions will be established. This supposes that there exists some independently given and determinate set of right decisions. Such a set does not exist. What happens depends on what individuals do now. What individuals do now depends on what has happened in the past, how they understand the present, and how they forecast the future. When prices are determined by price expectations—and these may induce changes in wage and supplier costs, which in turn justify the price expectations—the optimum is obscured by ignorance of the future. And, moreover, it is indeterminate (Balogh 1973, 83).

In defense of general equilibrium theory, however, it might be argued that it is not meant to be a help to comprehension and explanation of the economy. The theory is meant to be a demonstration that a free market economy leads to the highest level of consumer satisfaction (consistent with the given distribution of wealth). There is no doubt that a market-guided economy has many advantages, but this does not guarantee that it is a utopia. Free markets can do much in providing optimum or superior solutions to many economic problems, but they are not a unique philosopher's stone that can cure all economic ills.

General equilibrium theory is not necessary to convince economists and laymen that competition and free markets are effective economic methods to secure a better use of resources. Experience, economic history, and awareness of the results of economic policy demonstrate this. A general equilibrium model for a capitalist economy is misleading, pointless, and irrelevant since it leaves out the very essence of the market economy, relentless, never-ending change.

Lest the reader be led to believe that no virtue can be found in the general equilibrium model, I should acknowledge that it has made one contribution to economics. Because of their exposure to the model, economists learn that changes in one part of the economy are likely to have repercussions in other parts (Solow 1997a, 108). When an economist is confronted with a real problem, the model reminds him or her to look beyond the margins of, say, the industry with which he or she is concerned. But general equilibrium reasoning is likely, then, to lead the economist astray since the tendency is to believe that the industry should be moving toward a tidy equilibrium. In the real world, there is not likely to be a tidy equilibrium: technology is changing, competitors are reacting, new products in another industry are making a product redundant, and so on. In fact, if an economist's training includes economic history and a good exposure to empirical economics, he or she will have an even better idea of the repercussions and influences likely to result from any particular change and how much more comprehensive the model needs to be than what flows out of the general equilibrium mind-set. It should not require a theory of an imaginary economy to convince economists that in the real economy there is interdependence among its parts.

General equilibrium theory fits well with central planning, in fact better than with a capitalist market economy. By suppressing or ignoring individual variation, planners can command and maintain the attainment of their planned equilibrium. A general equilibrium model can be constructed for a centrally planned socialist market economy with a set of assumptions no more heroic than those for a capitalist market economy. One simply has to assume that workers, managers, and consumers will fully accept the decisions of the planning board as being the best for them and the economy. As in orthodox general equilibrium theory, *n* equations with *n* unknowns can be solved to determine the prices that will simultaneously clear all markets. Actually, one does not even have to assume that the central planning board has perfect knowledge of the demand and supply curves. Just as in a market economy, the agency can adjust prices by raising the prices of goods that are in excess demand and lowering the prices of goods for which demand is too low. As Oscar Lange argued, such a socialist economy would be better than capitalism because the state can distribute income more equitably, it can handle the problem of externalities better, and it can avoid monopolies.

In other words, if a successful general equilibrium model with realistic assumptions for a capitalist market economy could be built that would demonstrate that unrestricted competition necessarily leads to the highest possible level of consumer satisfaction under these conditions, this would not be enough. One must also prove that a similar model constructed for a centrally planned economy with parallel assumptions would not produce more consumer satisfaction.

The effort that highly intelligent economists have devoted to trying to construct general equilibrium models resembles the quest for the Holy Grail by the knights of the Round Table. In 1983, Professor Debreu was awarded the Nobel Prize for his general equilibrium model. The advanced version of the theory for which he won the prize turns out, as with all previous general equilibrium theories, to be of no help in understanding economic reality. His model assumes that there is no government, there is no money; and investors can perfectly protect themselves against uncertainty. There is perfect competition, consumers and producers have perfect knowledge of all prices and markets for contingent goods, consumers are never satiated (they always want more), there is perfect certainty about the future, and everyone obeys the rules of the game.

The theory and model as it exists today is truly a magnificent intellectual achievement. Future scholars are also likely to regard it as one of the inexplicable human obsessions of the past, ranking perhaps with the search for the fountain of youth but less productive of useful by-products than the thousand years' vain attempt to find the magic philosopher's stone

One has to admire the persistence and even perhaps the near genius manifested in the ingenuity of the model makers as they have worked for generations in an attempt to perfect the theory. But one also has to mourn the waste and futility manifested in such a quest. The century-long journey down a blind alley diverted some of the most brilliant economic brains from work on diagnosing and correcting the real problems of the world and enticed them into the bogs of purely abstract and nonempirical economic reasoning (Blaug 1980,192; 2001, 160). Imagine what could have been accomplished if these economists had been inspired instead to work on the problems of the actual evolving economy.

Equilibrium

Whereas classical economists were concerned with the economics of a stationary state toward which the economy was believed to be evolving, modern economists use as their central concept the economics of an economy in equilibrium. This ignores the fact that the real economy is always in motion. It not only fails to arrive at equilibrium, but any notion of what equilibrium could be at a given moment is irrelevant to the changes driving the economy. Understanding the major force that drives change in market economies is fundamental. In stagnant, unchanging economies like those of ancient Egypt and classical China as well as in command economies the concept of equilibrium may be useful. This catches the immobility of such economies over time, since any movement away from equilibrium is self-correcting or results in action that brings the economy back into equilibrium.

One of the central consequences of an equilibrium model is stability. Any disturbances that move an economy or an industry away from equilibrium must have negative feedback or are overmatched by other equilibrating forces or causes that will restore the equilibrium. With negative feedback, small effects die away (as in diminishing returns and falling marginal utility), so equilibrium reestablishes itself. In reality, change usually drives the economy farther away. This is most clearly manifested in industries with increasing returns. Here it is obvious that the movement is away from notional equilibrium. Equilibrium does not recognize the economic consequences of growing knowledge and increasing returns. These are related to one another since a very large part of the increase in knowledge comes from learning by doing or is inspired by the need to overcome problems that arise in the course of production.

Keynes noted that it was Hume who began the economist's practice of stressing the importance of the equilibrium position rather than the ever-shifting transition to it. However, Hume believed that it is in this transition that we actually live (1936, 343 n. 3). But Keynes did not fully grasp the fact that we do not live in a transition to an equilibrium position. The basic characteristic of a market economy is evolutionary change. That is, the economy is not in transition to a fixed, definitive equilibrium position any more than biological evolution is in transition toward some ideal creature. Evolution and change in the economy are processes driven from behind rather than pulled ever closer to a fixed goal. At any moment in time, one may be able to say, all things being equal and with no unforeseen changes, that such and such will be the outcome. What is misleading is calling this projected outcome equilibrium. This implies that if the outcome does come about the forces involved will maintain it or, if it moves away, there are forces to restore it. The implication, also, is that attaining equilibrium is desirable.

In the premodern religious era, Christians and Moslems believed that this life was a time of trials and tribulation in preparation for the next world, where existence would be eternally happy and heavenly perfect. In a more secular age, Leibnitz and Voltaire's Dr. Pangloss preached that this is the best of all possible worlds. The same idea of perfection as a goal was accepted by many believers in the theory of evolution. It was felt that evolution governs a path that leads ever upward and survivors must be the fittest in some transcendental sense. In economics, the same unconscious state of mind leads market idealists to believe that the economy is already in the optimum state (equilibrium), is groping for such a state, or would achieve equilibrium if it were not for wicked or ignorant human interference.

Unfortunately, neither in evolution, as Darwin observed, nor in the economy is it true that the optimum will result. It is perfectly possible that some species, the fittest by all measures, may have been destroyed simply because they happened to be in the wrong place at the wrong time. Those now occupying the niche of the extinct species may simply have been more lucky at the decisive time. If it is true that the dinosaurs became extinct as the result of a massive meteor smashing into the earth, this simply means that dinosaurs were less fit than the small ratlike mammals to survive an event that occurred once in sixty-five million years. Had the meteor missed the earth, dinosaur scholars might now be worrying about preserving primates as a species, with the most sensitive dinosaurs arguing that simply because one cannot find any use for them, does not mean that primates should be eliminated.

In the world of human institutions and relationships, if one must have a natural science metaphor it should come from biology or meteorology rather than seventeenth-century physics. And, of course, Marshall did use the biological metaphor in thinking about economics. In the course of his life, he became increasingly convinced that biology was more closely related to economics than Newtonian mechanics was. He observed that human societies, like biological nature, are constantly evolving. Since neither the precise direction nor the speed of a change can be precisely predicted, the "laws" of economics are no more than statements of trends or tendencies (See Kamarck 1983, 21–22; and Kaldor 1985, 58).

In a biological metaphor, the central fact is change, and clearly this is the dominant fact in an economy as in all human events. An enterprise in every aspect of its operations has to consider the changes that are happening within it and the economic environment in which it operates. In a competitive environment, the objective is the constant search for more sales, lower costs, improvements in products, or more saleable products; it is not trying to achieve a stable equilibrium.

The tropical rain forest provides a helpful metaphor. As was described in chapter 2, in the forest life and reproduction go on throughout the year among weeds, insects, birds, parasitic fungi, spider mites, eelworms, microbes, viruses, and other pests and parasites. Life takes on an infinite multiplicity of forms, with fierce competition for survival and only relatively few individuals in every generation surviving in any one place. There is rapid evolutionary change in the face of new opportunities (Kamarck 1976, 17).

The biological metaphor, while it is better than that of Newtonian mechanics, is not perfect for the economy. It fails in that the agents in the economy are conscious players on their own account, not merely entities acted upon by the environment. As every economist worth his or her salt knows, the economy is a complex, constantly changing, *adaptive* system in which each agent—individual, firm, industry, or nation—is constantly acting and reacting to what the other agents are doing. The key to understanding is to grasp that the whole process is one of constant change. As an opportunity is grasped and exploited by one agent, this may open up opportunities for others as competitors, partners, parasites, or predators. In the final analysis, the equilibrium optic obscures the real economy.

Just as physics has reconciled itself to the fact that one cannot have a scientific theory or model of the world that is completely deterministic, it is equally true that we cannot have a scientific model of the economy that is completely deterministic.

An equilibrium is a position of rest or the final coherent state of balance. But the economy is never static, and both it and the society in which it exists are constantly moving. At most, equilibrium is only a mathematical concept lacking existence or experience in the economy. In the real world, time is a continuing, irreversible process. Time's arrow points in only one direction. Everything changes over time. Commodities in the market "commonly go through a cycle of initiation, exponential growth, slowdown and decline" (Vernon 1971, 70). Even the most apparently stable institutions are at best merely in a temporary stasis among dynamic forces. The structures or institutions within which a market exists are also in flux. An economy is not a rationally organized, objective system but a dynamic process that is continually in motion and constantly changing, with millions of participants acting on knowledge, most of which is on its way to becoming out of date.

Amartya Sen has pointed out that equilibrium reasoning is logically deficient: (1) equilibrium may not exist; (2) if it does exist, it may not be unique; (3) if it exists and is unique, it may not be stable; and (4) if it exists and is unique and stable, it may be inefficient in the sense of not achieving Pareto-optimality. Finally, the fact that competition exists does not imply the existence, uniqueness, stability, or efficiency of a general equilibrium (1991, 70, quoted in Streeten 1997, 50).

The Austrian school of economics correctly believes that, in terms of the equilibrium concept, all prices are disequilibrium prices and no equilibrium position can be achieved. The market works to discover information, make adjustments, and shift resources to cope with changing conditions. As there is no omniscient auctioneer who controls the market and establishes the point of equilibrium, transactions must take place at nonequilibrium prices (Kirzner 1997; Rosen 1997). The market process results in outcomes, not in equilibria.

In recent years, formal theoretical work has been conducted that does not fit into the accepted canon, for example, the work at the Santa Fe Institute on complexity, nonlinear dynamics, evolutionary game theory, and inductive rationality. Almost all of the models developed deal with multiple equilibria, which creates the problem of how equilibrium selection will be decided (through institutions or public policy).[3] However, in this pioneering work, instead of reporting that the models result in multiple outcomes (avoiding the implication that these are desirable or likely to persist) for which some criteria for choice will have to be developed, the equilibrium mind-set still dominates.

The very idea of equilibrium is a notion that has no place for the influence of real time. The exogenous variables and the formal equations that determine the nature of the equilibrium are independent of time and history (Kaldor 1985, 62).[4] "Sicut erat in principio, et nunc, et semper, et in saecula saeculorum. Amen."[5]

> the model into which time as a logical variable has been incorporated is formed in such a way that the mathematical structure is unaffected by the passing of real time. The forms of differential equations that structure the system are themselves time invariant. The dynamic model that might be expected to have some explanatory relationship to the real world is therefore able to be started and restarted at any of differently assumed time dates and the nature of its behavior inspected. It is in this sense that logical time is capable of movement both backward and forward. For the dynamic scheme can be restarted and the relations

> between the implications of time-invariant equations of motion can be inspected at any point of its logical time or its logical phases of development. (Vickers 1995, 5–6)

In focusing on the concept of equilibrium, real historical time is neglected. This deemphasizes the uncertainty and ignorance of the future that real life entails. In the economy, decisions take place in real time. Agents take decisions based on their unique knowledge and experience. This is dated knowledge, based on what is known of the past and perceived of the present. As for the future, an experienced and knowledgeable agent can make some guesses with varying degrees of confidence about particular aspects of the situation. While risks can be assigned probability distributions based on experience, there is always the element of uncertainty, which is not only unknown but unknowable. Theory usually tries to finesse this fact by assuming perfect knowledge or assuming that the future economic data could be interpreted as random variables that could be described by objective or subjective probability distributions. The idea that genuine uncertainty could be transmuted to probabilistically reducible risk is untenable. It assumes knowledge when essentially there is ignorance.

Growth

A realistic understanding of economic growth is hampered by the mechanics equilibrium optic. It's as though geographers insisted on working with the concept of a flat rather than global earth. It's not surprising that economic theory has had problems in accounting for growth. A solar system or galaxy evolves but does not learn. An economy is a complex, adaptive system evolving from learning or adapting to experience. Applying the physical equilibrium model to the economy is consequently a categorical mistake. Nearly everywhere one looks one can perceive the economy mutating, transforming, and changing.

Economics cannot neglect history. The present is influenced by the past. There have been divergent roads, and the present path was not inevitable. There were many possible worlds, and to understand the one we have we need to know how it evolved.

Adam Smith observed that growth of the market led to specialization and this in turn led to increases in productivity. With lower costs, markets could be further extended, and more specialization became possible. With the specialization, the division of complex tasks into simpler ones led to the development of machinery, further cost reductions, and more growth in the size of the market. In this process, specialized firms become possible and come into existence. With the growth of specialized labor and specialized firms and the stimulus that comes from the exchange of knowledge and experience, there arises a concentration of activities in a particular locality and even a particular country. This is the phenomenon illustrated by Silicon Valley today.

When in the eighteenth century in Great Britain production moved from the putting-out system to the factory, change accelerated. The mill owner was a production man, alert to the possibilities of changing techniques and the reorganization of work so as to cut costs or speed up output. The inducement to change inherent in the new technology—its calculus of efficiency, its systematizing of empirical research, and its growing ties to the discoveries of science—was greatly strengthened (Landes 1970, 122).

The evolution of economic growth theory has proceeded roughly as follows. In the early standard model, it was simply an increase in the aggregate quantities of labor, capital, and the use of land, which resulted in increased total output (recognizing, however, the existence of diminishing returns to inputs). This model was improved by recognizing that there was more to the story: there was growth in productivity (beyond that from specialization), the result of growth in capital per worker and spillover from exogenous innovation in the rest of the economy. In recent years, theorists have brought the innovation process into the model, making it endogenous, by assuming productivity growth from investment in human capital and research and development (Taylor 2000, 90–91). All this helps to explain growth, but it leaves out that which drives the process in competitive free market economies.

The advantage of a capitalist competitive market system is that in its essence it is driven to change, while a central planning system, like a secure monopoly, tends to become static. Capitalism is, as Schumpeter observed, "by nature a form or method of economic change and not only never is but never can be stationary" (1942, 42). It is this characteristic of capitalism that the Soviet and Eastern European socialist countries lacked, and it was one of the principal causes of their lag behind in spite of the tremendous sacrifices they imposed on their peoples.

Adam Smith's contribution, in what was almost an offhand comment that has largely been overlooked, showed that he perceived that competition is the deus ex machina of growth in a competitive market economy:

> The increase of demand, . . . though in the beginning it may sometimes raise the price of goods, never fails to lower it in the long run. It encourages production, and thereby increases the competition of the producers,

> who, in order to undersell one another, have recourse to new divisions of labour and new improvements of art, which might never otherwise have been thought of. (1776, 706)

Schumpeter, in a more sophisticated analysis, essentially came to the same conclusion: the force that powers the system's incessant transformation in a competitive market is the fact that profits derive only from change. In competitive equilibrium, price must equal costs to the entrepreneur. He or she makes a profit only through competitive change: finding a new way to cut costs, producing a different product, finding a new market not yet exploited by competitors, and so on. Profits drive change—and growth through change is the essence of the system (1912, 128–56).

Schumpeter believed that his emphasis on the innovating entrepreneur might make his theory obsolete in a world in which production was dominated by large corporate organizations (Stolper 1942, 69). However, he built better than he feared. In the modern corporate economy in the industries that are subject to competition, intensive effort is devoted to organizing and engineering change. Tens of thousands work in the research laboratories of corporations, the government, and the universities, all of them focused on generating change.

The most successful corporations, such as Dupont, 3M, Hewlett-Packard, and GE, are those that are most devoted to innovation and change. IBM noted that in 1997 more than half of its revenue came from products that had been on the market for less than twelve months. Johnson and Johnson describes its top priority this way: "Continuous, non-stop, endless, relentless innovation" (Larsen 2000, 3).

In my own experience, I have seen the dramatic results that occur in economies when competition and economic incentives are introduced. The growth explosion in Spain in the 1960s that followed the freeing of the Spanish economy from fascist-mercantilistic restrictions is a graphic example. The outburst of innovation that followed the breakup of the Bell system monopoly in the United States is another.

To better understand the economy, we have to include Smith's and Schumpeter's insights in the conventional analysis. Baumol has it right:

> Because the analysis is macroeconomic, it cannot easily take account of the market forces and fierce competition among firms for priority in new products and processes. Yet these, arguably, are among the key determinants of the magnitude of the resources the economy devotes to innovation and are at the heart of the explanation of the historically unmatched production and growth performance of free-enterprise economies. (2000, 13)

CHAPTER 8

Predators and Parasites

> Deception and detecting deception both gave evolutionary advantage to greater brain size.
>
> —THE MACHIAVELLI HYPOTHESIS

> Man, biologically considered, is the most formidable of all beasts of prey, and, indeed, the only one that preys systematically on his own species.
>
> —WILLIAM JAMES

Goods and services may be bought in the market as exchange transactions or may be secured by the exercise of coercive power through predation and parasitism (P&P). P&P are transactions in the economy that are as driven by self-interest, as conventional theory assumes, but are dominated by power relationships. It is difficult or impossible to argue that in pursuing self-interest in such cases the predator or parasite, as if "led by an invisible hand," serves the general interest. Economic self-interest exercised through power can at times result, as is illustrated most poignantly in the discussion below on slavery, in immoral and humanly destructive outcomes or in other instances in economic regression or stagnation.

Predation and parasitism receive little notice in mainstream economic theory, but unless they do our understanding of the economy is deficient. They are interwoven with all life, and economic life is no exception. They have been important in all economies, including those of today. To understand how economies work, it is essential to include P&P in economic analysis. At present, national accounts statistics make no distinction between income earned through the provision of productive services and gains and income earned through predation or parasitism. Only the former add to the national welfare. A country blissfully free from most predatory activities may be better off than one that has a higher per capita income but suffers from widespread predation.

Predation and parasitism are inherent in nature. Human beings, at the top of the food chain, are the most successful of all predators; even vegetarians exist by devouring vegetable life. Both parasites and predators live off others without making useful contributions to society. Predation is abrupt or intermittent, it implies actual or potential violence, and usually the prey dies. A parasite, on the other hand, not only lives off its host but has an interest in its survival. Parasites are often permanently attached to their hosts. Parasitism is common throughout nature.

Human beings are hosts to a range of fauna and flora. We are colonized by some 100 trillion bacteria, some of which have symbiotic relationships with us, and a host of viruses and mites. The AIDS disease has revealed how intense this colonization is. The weakened systems in AIDS patients not only allows the common tuberculosis and bacterial pneumonias to flourish but also the rare fungi, yeasts, viruses, and hostile bacteria that are usually tightly controlled by our immune systems. In poor tropical countries, human beings are regularly hosts to numerous parasites: lice, fleas, roundworms, tapeworms, whipworms, hookworms, schistosomes, nematodes, flukes, and a wide range of protozoans, bacteria, and fungi.

Parasitism may even have been responsible for the evolutionary invention of sex. While dandelions and 360 species of bdelloid rotifers (multicelled freshwater invertebrates) propagate successfully without DNA exchange (i.e., without sex), most life appears to find sexual reproduction necessary. While biologists have no firm, established theory to explain why this is so, the Red Queen hypothesis has considerable evidence in its favor. Just as the Red Queen in *Through the Looking Glass* has to run to stay in place, DNA is changed each generation through sexual reproduction to foil pathogens that attempt to prey on the species. The remixing of the parents' genes in the offspring increases the rate of genetic variation and so changes the genetic set of immunological locks of the cell, blocking the previous method of entry a bacterium or virus may have used to penetrate the cells of a parent.

If this hypothesis is true, then in order to minimize the danger of parasitism nature has imposed a large, continuing, and immeasurable cost on most species, for sex is a costly means of reproduction. The sexual process is shot through with inefficiency. Being forced to take time and energy from seeking food and evading predators to search for a partner is a great waste of time and energy. Some species, like the bees and ants, have to produce, feed, and dispose of a vast number of idle males—drones—only a few of whom serve any useful purpose and that for a brief moment. In other species, including some males of the human species, the male fertilizes the egg but makes no further useful contribution, abandoning the care and upbringing of the young to the female. Then there are all the costs of making oneself attractive to prospective sexual partners, either through dress and ornament, as humans do, or through physical change such as the stags who have to grow massive antlers to dispose of rivals or the peacocks with the great feather displays that make them vulnerable to predators. Finally, the act of sexual intercourse facilitates the spread of many pathogens and parasites.

P&P in Economics

Most of modern neoclassical economics ignores the influence of power and tends to silently assume that economic reward is usually related to the productive contribution that an individual makes. Theory does recognize, however, that power can be used in a few special instances to secure unjustified economic rewards. It recognizes the existence of monopoly and oligopoly and circumstances under which an individual or firm may succeed in using power to raise prices above those that would rule in a freely competitive market. But economic theorists usually prefer to operate on the assumption of perfectly competitive markets. In the real world, where perfectly competitive markets are rare, companies with a dominant position in a market have opportunities to increase their profits through predation.

Economic theory recognizes the existence of predatory pricing; that is, the uneconomically low prices a large or wealthy company might charge to drive a smaller or more poorly financed competitor out of business. Usually this has been downplayed, however, on the reasoning that the low prices benefit consumers, that the predatory price fixer is not likely to succeed in maintaining the market power advantage it won as soon as it tries to profit by raising prices, and that consumers won't accept a lower priced or free product if this exposes them to the danger that in the long run their range of choice will be narrowed. In fact, the experience of several industries argues otherwise.

In the high-tech sector, once a company succeeds in dominating a market its product tends to become the dominant standard and consumers incur extra costs if they switch to a rival. Further, in industries with increasing returns due to technology or learning curves, the additional volume that predators acquire puts them on a lower section of the cost curve and helps to insulate them from potential entrants. Again, in products for which brands are important, a new entrant has higher costs to create brand loyalty than an established firm has in maintaining its position. In the American airline industry, whenever a small start-up airline tries to compete with a major airline it is usually driven into bankruptcy by the major lines, which drastically cuts fares on the small line's routes. In both this and the high-tech case, the aggressive behavior discourages other entrepreneurs from daring to challenge the predator in its other markets as well. Finally, the idea that consumers today will pass up a cheaper or free product (like Microsoft's browser, which was initially given away in its attempt to dominate this market) because of long-term fears of the consequences of a predator's success is naive. The economist's notion that "contestability" mitigates oligopoly may thus be diametrically wrong (*contestability,* in brief, is defined as the idea that potential competition is as effective as actual competition in influencing a company's market behavior).

Conventional economics also recognizes that in periods of violent or runaway inflation, economic motives do not work normally. In such periods, nearly everyone has to divert time and energy away from trying to earn income through producing goods or services to coping with inflation by extraordinary measures. Inflation distorts normal economic calculations, and to survive people have to adjust. Individuals and corporations find that they may be rewarded more from juggling finances and profiting at the expense of someone else than from producing goods and services or worrying about how to improve their productive efficiency. It may pay to take on as much debt as possible so as to expropriate less nimble creditors. Managers of corporations often find that speculating on rises in inventory values is more rewarding than trying to produce goods efficiently.

Economics generally ignores the existence of human predators or parasites. It could be argued that they are properly outside the realm of economics, which should be only concerned with the productive activities of human beings rather than the whole spectrum of ways in which humans make a living. When this narrow focus is adopted, the impact of predators on the economy is overlooked. For most of human history, leaving P&P out of the economy is like presenting *Hamlet* and omitting the king.

Aristotle, the first economist, accurately observed that in making a living some men are producers and some are predators. Of the latter, some hunt wild birds and beasts, some fish, and some prey on other men (1926, 39). Aristotle regarded predation as a far more honorable occupation than commerce. Wealth was an essential need of the state, and it should properly be won by means of piracy, brigandage, and waging war to round up slaves. The state should depend on slave workers (Viner 1991, 40).

There has been recognition of predatory activity by other economists. As mentioned in chapter 3, Adam Smith, in his remarks about the benefits to society of the "invisible hand," left open the possibility that at times society may suffer from an individual's pursuit of his or her own interest. He also argued that when there are accumulations of valuable property in a society and "the affluence of the few supposes the indigence of the many," then the poor, "driven by want and prompted by envy," are tempted to invade the property of the rich (1776, 670).

Alfred Marshall noted (in his preface to the eighth edition of *Principles of Economics*) that he was omitting any discussion of times "when trusts are striving for the mastery of a large market; when communities of interest are being made and unmade; and, above all, when the policy of any particular establishment is likely to be governed, not with a single eye to its own business success, but in subordination to some large stock exchange maneuver, or some campaign for the control of markets" ([1920] 1952, xii). Schumpeter, too, was highly aware of predatory activity and as a result was pessimistic about the survival of capitalism because "the beneficial competition of the classic type seems likely to be replaced by 'predatory' or 'cutthroat' competition or simply by struggles for control in the financial sphere. These things are so many sources of social waste" (1942, 80).

Keynes, with his deep experience in finance, sounded a warning against one special type of predatory behavior: financial manipulation. He cautioned against productive enterprise in an economy becoming "a bubble on the whirlpool of speculation" (1936, 159). And, like Aristotle, Pareto understood the fundamental fact of economic life: men use their energies in two different ways, either producing economic goods or trying to appropriate the goods produced by others ([1927] 1971, 341).

In recent years, it has become respectable for economists to recognize one category of economic parasitism, rent-seeking behavior.[1] There is now a large volume of research in the "public choice" literature on this subject. Since "economic rent" is any payment made to a factor above the amount necessary to keep that factor in its present employment, individuals who secure income higher than the necessary payment are receiving rent. Thus, *rent seeking* is usually defined as use of the power of the state to transfer wealth by means of taxes or regulation from one group to another or to some individual when there is no social end involved. It does not include action by the state to secure a more equitable distribution of income but rather those actions for which the purpose is personal and purely mercenary and the individuals benefiting are the ones manipulating the state.

The fact that some individuals acquire wealth in this way rather than by a productive contribution is not the worst aspect of this kind of parasitism; the primary harm stems from the fact that when resources are diverted to this activity the gain to those who are profiting is less than the loss to other people or the whole economy. There are no hard data to indicate how prevalent and important rent seeking is in the high-income economies, although some estimates have been made of the cost of government restrictions in countries like Turkey and India. There are many indications that lead one to believe that this kind of behavior can be richly rewarded and accounts for some significant fraction of the acquisition of wealth in today's world.

While most of the focus on rent seeking has been on government activities, the private sector is not immune. A most glaring instance is the remuneration of corporate chief executive officers (CEOs). One study found that the remuneration of CEOs in firms in which there was no large shareholder present on the board of directors appeared to be characteristic of skimming, that is, of CEOs controlling the remuneration process and paying themselves as much as they can (Bertrand and Mullainathan 2000, 203–8). Such CEOs are receiving payments above the amounts that would keep them in their present employment. Baumol and Blinder, in fact, used the salary of Lee Iacocca, then chairman of the board of Chrysler Corporation, to illustrate the concept of economic rent (1988, 783). An indication that this is fairly widespread comes from the great chasm between CEO pay in the United States and that of workers on the factory floor. American CEOs in the Standard & Poor's five hundred leading companies in 2000 took 475 times more pay than manufacturing workers did. In European countries, bosses take only 10 to 24 times the pay of their workers. The discrepancy between American and German CEO incomes was highlighted in the Daimler Benz merger with Chrysler in spring 1998. Although Daimler was taking control of Chrysler; Chrysler's CEO's pay in 1997 was seven times that of Daimler's (Ryback 1998, 86).

A somewhat wider category of predation and parasitism is covered by the term *directly unproductive profit seeking* (DUP). This includes rent-seeking behavior and all other ways of seeking a profit that do not contribute to production. While DUP describes activities in the private as well the public sectors, most of the interest in it has also been to demonstrate the evil consequences of government action.

During the Middle Ages, "robber knights" made a living by controlling access to a pass in the mountains or a ford or bridge over a river and levying a charge on everyone who wished to use it. Rent seeking focuses on the benefits derived by people who have passed the gate (and who may have been largely responsible for the gate having been erected) and can then exploit the reduced competition from people kept outside. But there is another important predatory gain involved: the profits from what I call gatekeeping.

Gatekeeping focuses on the "toll" extorted by the gatekeepers for allowing or influencing access. A large portion of modern corruption falls into this category. For example, in 1989 and 1992 the financial adviser of the

Massachusetts Water Resources Authority fed crucial internal information to Merrill Lynch, making it possible for that firm to secure the top position in the agency's securities underwriting team. Merrill Lynch was thus able to earn millions of dollars in fees and commissions. In return, it steered bond business, preferably outside of New England, to the adviser, who at the time was head of the Boston office of Lazard Frères (Kurkjian 1993, 1, 44).

When Communist China introduced economic reforms allowing private investment, party members went into business to make money. The easiest way to make money for a high-placed party member or a member of his family was to become a gatekeeper, that is, a trafficker in influence. With the Communist Party above the law, there is no guarantee of equitable justice or security of property rights except through the influence of an important party member. With this system, widespread corruption was inevitable.

Not all gatekeeping tolls are illegal. In Boston, near where I live, newspapers have documented instances in which lawyers have become millionaires several times over in a few years simply by using their political influence to secure for developers from public offices lucrative zoning exceptions, building code variations, and so on. This is one of the profitable ways in which the "courthouse gangs" in many rural counties throughout the southern United States used to finance themselves.

Exploiting the control of access is not a practice restricted to the public sector, although it is best known there. As the public sector is normally judged by higher ethical standards, the private sector escapes the same degree of scrutiny.

When a corporation is interested in acquiring another, a key player is the CEO of the target company. If a generous enough personal settlement is arranged for the CEO, he or she may be induced to promote the deal rather than evaluating it on its merits. In 1997, Drew Lewis, the CEO of Union Pacific, agreed to a merger with the Southern Pacific Rail Corporation and received a $4 million bonus and a five-year, $3.75 million consulting contract. The merger turned out to be an economic disaster for the southwestern United States. The merged company could not cope with the traffic; snarled rail transport cost businesses and regional economies billions in unnecessary costs.

In 1999, when BankBoston was taken over by Fleet Bank in a $16 billion deal, the agreement promised Charles K. Gifford, BankBoston's CEO, a package that included stock and stock options totaling an estimated $26 million; a three-year contract guaranteeing him the same income as the CEO of Fleet Bank (which in 1998 amounted to more than $4 million a year); a severance payment worth up to $15 million if he was forced out of the new bank; and a pension on his retirement of $1.25 million a year for life, with his wife getting $937,500 a year for life if she survived him. The new company also expected to dismiss five thousand employees of the combined work force (Browning 1999, C1, 10).

Even the business press has questioned the justification for the "eye-popping" packages arranged for some CEOs when their companies are taken over. When ITT was taken over by Starwood Lodging, ITT's CEO received $20 million in cash and stock and an option grant of 162,500 shares of Starwood. The company also agreed to pay the "gross-up" taxes due on his cash severance payments. When MCI was taken over by WorldCom, Bert Roberts, the chairman of MCI, remained chairman but was paid a "retention bonus" of $10.5 million. These are just two of a large number of similar cases (Reingold and Wolverton 1998, 33).

The Columbia/HCA Healthcare Corporation became the world's largest health care company in 1997 through growth and an aggressive policy of buying other providers. In its successful battle to gain control of a cancer care center in El Paso, Texas, the company secretly paid a key player, one Dr. Abboud, $152,000 for "outstanding expenses" that he had not incurred and $120,000 for used medical equipment without any appraisal of its true value. In February 1997, a federal jury found that the money was part of an unlawful conspiracy and awarded a business partner in the center $6.5 million in damages (Eichenwald 1997, 25, 27). In another case, until forced to desist by an antitrust suit in 1994, Microsoft Corporation forced computer manufacturers that used its MS-DOS operating system to pay it "royalties" on computers they shipped that used other operating systems.

The modern global economy is so complex that it is difficult for investors to secure and master enough information to make optimum decisions. In addition to the long-standing role of banks in meeting this need, there are now "financial advisers" who specialize in providing counsel to investors. While an attempt is being made to "professionalize" this occupation, many such advisers profit from commissions paid by the companies to which they steer their unwary clients. In the financial press, one finds advertisements such as the following (the company's name has been changed):

> **Introducers Wanted by Credit Paris de Berlin (CPB)**
> The Credit Paris de Berlin is a Luxembourg open-ended fund which offers investors three specialist sub funds in a range of currency denominations. Following recent strong performance, CPB now seek to appoint additional high quality introducers to complete their global net-

> work. The fund offers an extremely attractive commission structure and intermediaries with the ability to make a substantial placement are invited to contact.

Occasional instances of gatekeeping tolls in other industries surface from time to time. In the investigation of the Atlanta, Georgia, branch of the Banca Nazionale del Lavoro, which was active in financing Iraq before the Gulf War, the manager admitted that he had received a $300,000 loan from a Turkish trading company and never repaid it. The company also paid $100,000 to his father for unrelated services (Fialka 1993, B12).

Buyers for large retailers and other large corporations control the spending of millions of dollars. Securing an order is important and sometimes vital to a supplier or manufacturer's agent. It is not rare for a buyer to use his or her influence to secure commissions, kickbacks, or bribes from the avid sellers. Some set up front companies through which transactions are channeled to conceal their interests.

J. G. Locklear, a buyer for the J. C. Penney Co., when caught, confessed, "I became captive to greed." He supplemented his salary of $56,000 a year with $1 million in bribes and kickbacks from vendors and sales representatives in the course of four years. It is unusual for a retail buyer who is caught in this sort of practice to be prosecuted. Usually, the retailer, concerned with its image, obtains some restitution from the buyer and sweeps the matter under the rug. In Locklear's case, he was sentenced to eighteen months in prison and fined $50,000 (Gerlin 1995, B6A).

Scandals in the late 1970s revealed that some of the most respected American corporations regularly paid influential people (gatekeepers) in other countries (in business and government) to use their influence to steer orders to the bribing corporation. The American government passed legislation forbidding American companies from paying such bribes. Other governments were slow to take similar action. France and Germany were opposed to banning bribery because of fear that this might hurt their companies' sales abroad. Germany, Canada, and a number of other countries even allowed companies to take tax deductions for foreign bribes as a cost of doing business. A French court went even further, extending this tolerance to bribing the French government itself. On February 6, 1997, the French Cour de Cassation reversed a lower court that had convicted a corporate executive for bribing a relative of the minister of trade. The court held that the executive was not guilty of misusing corporate money since the bribe of 760,000 francs resulted in a reduction of 10 million in taxes on the company (*Economist* 1997b).

In December 1996, the United Nations adopted a declaration condemning the practice of bribery. On February 15, 1999, an international convention agreed on by all the twenty-nine members of the Organization for Economic Cooperation and Development (OECD) and five other nations went into force, criminalizing bribes paid by their companies to public officials and officers of parastatal corporations in foreign countries and ending the tax deductibility of bribes. The OECD nations also agreed to work for an international treaty against such bribery. Some progress has therefore been achieved toward cutting back on this kind of predation. Note, however, that the corruption of private citizens and companies was deliberately excluded from this agreement.

Gatekeepers, that is, persons who influence decisions on allocating resources that are not theirs, are pervasive in large-scale bureaucratic organizations, both private and public. And wherever there are gatekeepers there is parasitism or the potential for it. Bathed in an environment in which moneymaking is revered and central to the operations of the economic system, it takes a gatekeeper with strong moral character to overlook temptation.

Although rent seeking and gate tolls are important instances of the exploitation of power, there are numerous other kinds behavior that profit from coercion. Many of these have been and still are important in modern economies.

Slavery, Piracy, and Crime

Slave owning is a classic form of the exercise of coercive power. It has existed in virtually every known historical society, and it still exists today. Slaves have been one of the most important commodities in international commerce for thousands of years. In the ancient world, slavery was of course practically synonymous with the labor market.

A largely unfamiliar slave trade that went on for several centuries was the export of captives from the Slavic lands of the Commonwealth of Poland and Lithuania, the Ukraine, and Russia and from the Caucasus to the Ottoman Empire. Capturing people for export was a principal occupation of the Tartars of the Crimea during the sixteenth and seventeenth centuries. The route trodden by the slaves to the coast through the Ukraine became known as the Trail of Tears. Until the fall of Constantinople in 1453, Venetian and Genoese merchants purchased slaves from countries bordering the Black Sea. These slaves were sold throughout the Mediterranean. Male Circassian slaves transported to Egypt were recruited into the Mameluke (slave) forces that ruled Egypt for two and a half centuries until

1811. The trade in Slavs was sufficiently widespread for many centuries to cause the Latin word *sclavus,* for "Slav," to transmute into the modern *slave.*

Trading slaves developed naturally as one of the few commodities available for export from Africa. From the beginning of dynastic Egypt right down to modern times, slaves, gold, and ivory were principal exports of sub-Saharan Africa. After the rise and spread of Islam across North Africa, the demand for slaves increased and the normal supply was augmented through slave hunts. By the late ninth century, slave merchants from as far away as South Asia were established in the Fezzan (southern Libya), dealing with suppliers from across the Sahara. Islam provided the slave hunts with the ideology of *jihad,* which justified aggression against black animist believers. At times, the slave hunts (*razzias*) resembled large-scale military operations, lasting two or three months at a time.

The explorer Heinrich Barth reported on one *razzia* that he accompanied in 1851 in the western African middle belt (between the desert and the forests). After two months, the expedition returned to its base with between three and ten thousand captives. These were mostly children under the age of eight and women. Nearly all the men were killed as soon as they were captured (Oliver 1991, 118).

From eastern Africa, Arab slavers exported their captives by sea directly to Arabia. Dr. Livingstone, an involuntary spectator, described one eastern African slave hunting *razzia* in 1871 on the upper Congo River: The Arabs' Swahili gunmen fired without warning on the people in a market, killing and drowning hundreds. They burned some seventeen villages, rounded up the survivors that were marketable, fitted them into slave-sticks and marched them to the Indian Ocean coast. (Livingstone 1871, 86–88).

The export of slaves to Asia lasted in all about twelve centuries. A substantial commerce in slaves continued across the Sahara and the Indian Ocean until the end of the nineteenth century. The trade in slaves and ivory was the basis of the coastal Swahili and Arab economy of Zanzibar. Large-scale trade in slaves across the Indian Ocean was only ended by the European occupation of the Sudan and East Africa.

The Atlantic slave trade from West Africa started when the Portuguese began to import slaves into Western Europe around 1442 and the Spanish brought slaves to the New World after 1517. The large-scale Atlantic trade run by American, British, and other European merchants into North America, the Caribbean, and South America continued for three centuries. The British abolished its slave trade in 1807. At that time, the Royal Navy, and later the French Navy, began to enforce a ban on the slave trade. It was not until after the American Civil War, when slave ships could no longer take refuge under the American flag, that the slave trade across the Atlantic was effectively ended, with the last trickle not ceasing until perhaps 1880.

There is no way to accurately assess the number of slaves exported from Africa in the large-scale trade of modern times. A reasonable estimate is from ten to fifteen million. Millions more lost their lives in the raids, on the journey to the coast in slave coffles, while waiting for the ships to appear, in barracoons on the coast, and finally during the trip across the Atlantic to the Western Hemisphere or across the Indian Ocean to Arabia (Kamarck 1971, 6–10).

Slavery did not end in the nineteenth century. In 1926, a member of the ruling family in what is now Botswana described in court the social position of some of the people in his country:

> The Masarwa are slaves. They can be killed. It is no crime. They are like cattle. If they run away, their masters can bring them back and do what they like in the way of punishment. They are never paid. If the Masarwa live in the veldt, and I want any to work for me, I go out and take any I want. (Oliver 1991, 195)

Even though the slave trade was legally banned, slavery continued to be legal in Saudi Arabia and Oman until the 1970s. Today there are many complaints that female domestics recruited in the Philippines to work in oil-rich Middle Eastern countries find themselves in conditions of virtual slavery from which they cannot escape.

Mauritania officially abolished slavery three times between 1961 and 1980 but has not really eliminated it according to the International Labor Organization (ILO). The U.S. State Department's 1993 *Human Rights Report* stated that credible reports indicate that there are from thirty to ninety thousand black Africans living in slavery in the Islamic Republic of Mauritania. In the Sudan, Arabized northerners used to hunt slaves in the animist and Christian black African south up to the time of the British conquest at the end of the nineteenth century. During the current generation-long civil war between north and south, the Sudanese government's Arab tribal militias operating in the south take slaves as compensation according to United Nations investigators and the U.S. State Department. Members of the Dinka tribe are sold as slaves in the north for the equivalent of thirty to sixty dollars each. Girls are especially desirable as potential concubines. In the famine of 1988, some parents sold their girls to save them from starvation. The price of a healthy girl dropped from the equivalent of thirty dollars to five at that time (Horwitz 1989; *Economist* 1990, 42; Associated Press 1998, A16).

Trade in children is reported to be common in Benin and Nigeria. Traders visit poor farmers in Benin and offer parents the equivalent of twenty to forty dollars for a child, promising that he or she will be well taken care of and better off. The children are sold to households in Nigeria and Central Africa where they perform unpaid household work or they are forced into prostitution (*New York Times* 1997, 9).

Another contemporary trade in children is their sale for prostitution in Southeast Asia. Sex tourism is an important source of foreign exchange from the Philippines to Thailand. AIDS has increased the value of the youngest prostitutes because the risk of infection is less when the he or she has had fewer sexual contacts. The coordinator of the International Campaign to End Child Prostitution in Asiatic Tourism has reported that there are villages in northeastern Thailand where few children remain; the others have been sold into brothels in Bangkok (Kempton 1992). Burmese girls are sold into Thailand and Nepali girls into India; there are some twenty thousand of the latter in Bombay alone (*Economist* 1996b, 43).

Throughout the third world, millions of people, especially children, work in virtual or real slavery. Child slave workers are reported in Sri Lanka and Haiti. In India, millions of children work in conditions approaching slavery. The plight of children, age six and up, who work in the carpet industry around Varanasi (Benares) is well known. Their numbers in India have grown since the late 1970s, when the industry moved from Iran; there were around half a million in 1996 (*Economist* 1990, 42; 1996b, 43).

There are 15 million indentured servants in India, and, although it is against the law, 20 million laborers are held in bondage for their debts in Pakistan, according to the ILO. A similar system of debt bondage known as *enganche* (the hook) keeps workers in Peruvian gold mines. In Brazil, contractors called *gatos* (cats) hire rural workers and transport them long distances to jobs that pay less than promised while gunmen prevent the workers from leaving.

Piracy is a classic way of making a living through predation. It has been endemic throughout history wherever there has been maritime commerce. At times, as in the late Roman Republic, an effort comparable to a major war had to be undertaken to bring piracy under control.

In modern times, from the sixteenth to the early part of the nineteenth century, peaceful traders ran major risks from pirates (and from privateers, who often crossed the line into outright piracy). The risks were not restricted to the sea itself: in the Caribbean, for example, French privateers captured and burned Cartagena and Havana in 1559; Cartagena was sacked again in 1585 by Sir Francis Drake; the "Brethren of the Coast" controlled the island of Tortuga during most of the seventeenth century; and the Spanish colonial city of Panama was sacked in 1671. Blackbeard blockaded Charleston, South Carolina, in 1718 and held the town for ransom. For several centuries, Madagascar was used as a base for pirates preying on Indian Ocean trade and pilgrims on their way to Mecca.

The U.S. Navy owes its birth to piracy, for Congress had to vote funds for a permanent navy to protect American merchantmen against the Barbary pirates based in Algiers, Tunis, and Moroccan and Libyan ports. The young navy operated a Mediterranean squadron off the coast of North Africa from 1801 to 1806, fought several battles against the corsairs, and even had to pay ransom to free the crew of the frigate *Philadelphia,* which was captured off Tripoli. The campaigns are commemorated in the U.S. Marine Corps anthem's words, "to the shores of Tripoli." It took an attack on Algiers by a combined British and Dutch fleet in 1816 to eliminate most of the threat of Mediterranean piracy.

Even today, pirates exist. According to an informed observer, "In 1999, piracy constitutes a new and legitimate threat to shipping worldwide" (T. Hunter 1999, 72–74). In our postcolonial period, with the withdrawal of the colonial powers' fleets from the sub-Saharan African coasts, shipping in these waters has been scantily protected. Piracy is a threat to seagoing yachts in the Caribbean and Mediterranean and to commercial shipping off the coasts of Southeast Asia and Brazil. From around one hundred attacks on commercial shipping annually reported in 1994 and 1995, the numbers had increased to more than two hundred by 2000. In 1998, sixty-seven crew members were killed. Four ships have vanished off the Libyan coast, with no wreckage or survivors found. This is not unusual, as the pirates paint over the name of a seized ship and Belize, Honduras, and Panama offer temporary registration of ownership by fax, with little investigation, for a simple fee. More often, the pirates are more interested in the cargo: when a tanker is captured, another soon appears and the oil is pumped into it.

More than half of these attacks may go unreported. According to the director of the International Maritime Bureau, "The problem is the industry does not want incidents reported. They don't want their reputation scarred." Ship owners suspect that some of the pirates are off-duty members of national navies; one British captain reported that the pirate who put a sword to his throat was "obviously a military officer." Quite appropriately, the thirty pirates who seized the *Anna Sierra* in the Gulf of Thailand in September 1995 and sailed it into a Chinese port carried passports identifying themselves as "entrepreneurs" (Goh 1995, 91; Moulier 1997, 33–34; *Economist* 1997f, 40; *Economist* 1999, 87–89).

Crime

Every country has to live with crime. The best study to date (the International Crime Survey, which is coordinated by the Dutch Ministry of Justice) on the incidence of crime found that each year in the early 1990s 25 to 30 percent of the people in Australia, Canada, Holland, New Zealand, Poland, and the United States were victims of one or more crimes. In Britain, Italy, Spain, Sweden, and West Germany, the figure was 20 to 25 percent. In Belgium, Finland, France, Norway, and Switzerland, the percentage of people affected by crime was 15 to 20 percent. Only in Japan did the figure drop below 15 percent (*Economist* 1993e, 57).

In many cities across the world, a morass of social and economic pathology locks out millions of poor—in large part, ethnic or religious minorities in their societies—from normal, legal, economic occupations. Television shows and direct observation of the many luxuries available as well as the need for the necessities of life stimulate these poor to try to find ways to get money. With few jobs available to the untrained, poorly educated inhabitants of the inner cities the legal opportunities to earn money are limited. Demoralized, unaffected by the normal process of socialization, and without conventional family ties but with drug dealer and other criminal role models, many young people growing up in these cities find their most advantageous outlets in illegal predation on the rest of society.

Others find their best opportunities in businesses that supply illegal services or commodities. The more fortunate, enterprising, or ruthless may succeed through the use of force in organizing and managing others in these activities. With time, such successful managers may branch out and utilize their criminal skills and money to take over what otherwise are legal economic activities.

In one poor family from South Boston, one brother, William Bulger, went into politics, became the unchallenged leader of the Massachusetts State Senate, and by 2000 was president of the University of Massachusetts. Another brother, James (Whitey) Bulger, went into crime and became the leader of the Winter Hill gang, competing with the New England mafia. While acting as an informant for the Federal Bureau of Investigation, he levied racketeering tribute on bookies and escaped prosecution for three decades. He was finally indicted in 1995 for several murders (O'Neill, Lehr, and Cullen 1995, 1, 24). He went underground and was still free in 2001.

Criminal predation has widespread and pervasive costs. One can cite a few indications of this.

- In 1993, a fairly reliable official survey reported that nearly 11 million violent crimes and more than 32 million property crimes were experienced by U.S. residents over the age of twelve.
- In 1996 in the United States, 1.2 million convicted criminals were in prison. Two percent of the male labor force, and 9 percent of all black males were incarcerated at any one time. In addition to the prison population, another half a million persons were in jail awaiting trial or sentencing, 700,000 were on parole, and another 3 million were out on probation.
- Prison operating costs in Texas exploded from $91 million in 1980 to $1.84 billion in 1994. This is probably an extreme case, but it is representative of the trend.
- Private security guards in the United Kingdom and the United States are estimated to outnumber police officers—in America, by nearly three to one (see DiIulio 1996 and Freeman 1996).
- Shops have almost universally had to place electronic tags on much of the merchandise they sell to keep them from being shoplifted.

If you examine the course of your own life you can perceive the pervasive influence of predation, parasitism, and the costs they force you to undergo.[2] In Massachusetts, if you refinance your home you have to pay a lawyer a fee equal to 1 percent of the mortgage. The size of the fee has nothing to do with the amount of work involved: it is the *customary fee.* In fact, the lawyer may have very little to do when the only change in the mortgage is a drop in the interest rate. The whole legal cost is pure parasitism—the lawyer is there not to look after your interests but the interests of the bank. If the homeowner wants representation by a lawyer, he or she has to get another one. Of course, the bank has no concern about the size of the fee since it is not paying it; the homeowner is.

Most people receive a phone call or mail once or twice a week from someone trying to swindle them in some ingenious way, usually offering a "once in a lifetime opportunity." A substantial percentage of the charitable appeals we receive are from organizations that use very little of the money for their ostensible purpose. And so it goes.

Many people take costly precautions against crime. Some are prudent enough to purchase a security system that monitors all movement and is tied into a central office and the police. Many communities are "gatehouse developments" in which the area is accessible only through a single gate and security guards stop and check every person desiring entry. There are now more than 20,000 such gated communities, containing around 3 million homes, in the United States. A small number of rich people go further, building into their homes "God forbid rooms." If, "God forbid," it proves necessary, the owner can retreat to a safe room, which is an armored, bulletproof, impenetrable, electronically controlled, fortresslike space. It can be quickly shut off from the rest of the house and has its own power generator and separate buried phone line.

Both men and women pay a cost in time spent arranging behavior that will minimize the risk of becoming a victim of crime. A high proportion of men and women never go out after dark alone. People driving through a city keep their car doors locked and windows closed, especially while waiting for someone or for the traffic light to change. Many a woman will not take the elevator if the only other person in it is a male stranger. Other self-defense habits that steal time include passing up a convenient parking area for a safer one, ferrying children to and from school to shield them from dangerous strangers, and making social arrangements so that after a party no woman needs travel home alone.

Women in particular pay a special "predation cost" in modern American cities. These are everyday costs incurred just for being of the female sex. An apartment chosen because it is in a safer area will probably exact a higher rent. Safety features in an apartment—more secure locks, an alarm system, a doorman, grates on the windows—are additional costs. A woman may have to balance the higher wages of a job against the risks of working in a less safe neighborhood or at unusual hours. A taxi maybe taken instead of walking or taking mass transit. Some women take self-defense or karate lessons and carry mace or a police whistle. At night, women may avoid going to a movie, a play, or a restaurant or visiting friends or family because of the risks.

Sales of cellular phones have grown faster after their introduction than the sales of other consumer electronics products under comparable circumstances. Fear of predation is a principal reason. An industry survey in the United States found that two-thirds of all buyers of cellular phones purchase them for security reasons. One of the industry's most effective ads shows a young woman with a disabled car in an isolated area. The woman is fearfully talking into a car phone: "Please hurry, it's getting dark!"

While it helps to sell its services by arousing fear of predation in its customers, the industry itself has fallen victim to predators. It is only just awakening to the realization that cellular theft is also growing rapidly. Skillful thieves use scanners to pluck the electronic serial number codes of phones out of the air, clone the data into phones that can be programmed with up to ninety-nine stolen numbers, and sell these "lifetime" phones to drug dealers and others who want unidentifiable communications equipment. They also sell the opportunity for immigrants and others to call overseas for a fraction of the charges of the phone companies. The cellular trade group in the United States estimates that losses from theft are around half a billion dollars a year; industry consultants put the figure at around a billion dollars a year, that is, 7 percent of industry revenue (Naik 1995, 1996). To try to thwart the pirates, the companies have had to resort to measures such as requesting that their clients notify them in advance if they plan to use their phones outside of their usual calling areas!

There is no way of knowing how much wealth is siphoned off through successful fraud. During every recession, when the prices of some assets have fallen sharply and firms holding them are subject to financial strain, a number of previously respected individuals and firms are found to have been engaged in fraud or other criminal behavior.

Savings and loan institutions in the United States were one of the main avenues through which average Americans saved and financed the buying or building of their homes. They are still an important part of the American capital market. The savings and loan industry debacle in the United States in 1989–94, which cost the American government directly $153 billion (and, with the interest cost of the money over thirty years, a total of around $500 billion), was largely caused by fraud and corruption. Accountants and auditors who certified the books were often on the take. Professional appraisers were willing to provide any desired appraisal of the value of property for a suitable fee. Regulators proved amenable to influence. Alan Greenspan, for a fee of $40,000 testified that Charles Keating's savings and loan institution, which cost investors hundreds of millions of dollars, was a well-run thrift (Waldman 1990, 95). Charles Keating was only the most prominent among others who were eventually convicted of fraud and sentenced to jail (Mayer 1990).

George Staple, the head of the British Serious Fraud Office, estimated in 1993 that the amounts allegedly looted in Robert Maxwell's pension robbing (at least £400 million) and the Bank of Credit and Commerce International (BCCI, $9.5 billion missing) cases alone exceeded the annual total lost through burglary in England and Wales (*Economist* January 30, 1993). But the losses in the pension fund are only a small part of the total lost by creditors of Maxwell's empire. Two years after his disappearance at sea in 1991, administrators of his private holdings had recovered only £155 million of the total indebtedness of £1.4 billion and creditors of his defunct public company, Maxwell Communications Corp., may receive at a maximum

$1.35 billion of the $3.1 billion owed. Totaling everything, pensioners and creditors lost $4.5 to $5 billion.

The BCCI case was the greatest bank fraud in world financial history to date. It collected $20 billion in deposits from around 1 million people in seventy-two countries. When it was closed by banking regulators on July 5, 1991, $9.5 billion were missing. In total, $12 billion of depositors' claims were filed against the closed bank.

The BCCI was founded in 1972 with initial capital provided by Sheikh Zayed, the ruler of Abu Dhabi, and other Gulf states investors. It was active in the major financial centers. Incorporated in Luxembourg and the Cayman Islands, its head office was in London. BCCI was generous and hospitable to a whole array of influential people, including Lord Callaghan of Great Britain and former president Jimmy Carter, while bribing third world rulers to get their currency reserves as deposits and acting as the bank for Abu Nidal, the deadly Arab terrorist. It covertly bought and managed the former First American Bankshares in Washington, D.C., and three other banks in the United States. The true nature of its activities only began to be revealed when the American Customs Service in Miami discovered that BCCI was running a money-laundering service for the drug trade. It was the persistence of Senator John F. Kerry and two New York prosecutors that exposed the widespread fraud, corruption, and stealing that characterized the bank's activities. Its nickname in the financial community, the Bank for Crooks and Corruption International, was truly earned (Truell and Gurwin 1992).

In the United States, nine out of the ten top defense contractors admitted guilt or was found guilty of procurement fraud at least once during the 1980s (*Bulletin* 1993, 4). Usually the contractor paid a fine, was suspended from bidding on defense contracts for a period of time, and then was back in business.

Only a confirmed Dr. Pangloss would believe that every instance of fraud has been immediately detected and punished. For example, President Reagan's Commission on Organized Crime reported in 1985 that organized crime "controls entire industries in some areas of the country" (Shenon 1985, 4E). The FBI testified that mobsters ran the business of collecting and disposing of refuse in New York. Competition was eliminated through extortion, violence, and threats of violence. One new competitor promptly exited when the owner received a phone call. The voice at the other end described how the owner's ten-year-old daughter was dressed that day and warned him to shut his business down or his daughter would disappear.

Browning-Ferris Industries (BFI) bravely entered the commercial waste-hauling business in New York City in 1993. Its first customer, a large hospital, cut its monthly costs for waste removal from $100,000 to $40,000. BFI secured contracts with 500 companies, but most of these changed their minds after visits from large intimidating men. One BFI manager found the head of a German shepherd dog under his mailbox. Taped to the dog's mouth was the message "Welcome to New York." BFI's equipment was stolen and vandalized, and managers and drivers were harassed. With a potential customer market of 150,000 enterprises, in two and a half years BFI was able to persuade only 200 to take advantage of its lower prices and better service. It had to provide special compensation for its people and swallow losses in the hope of eventually being able to operate freely.

In 1995, Manhattan district attorney Robert Morgenthau secured indictments of a number of carting company men on charges of racketeering and antitrust violations. Fourteen pleaded guilty in 1997 and were sentenced to prison terms ranging from one to six years. The two top bosses were found guilty in October 1997 after a five-month trial. Three national companies are now competing for business in the city. The economic cost of the predation in this one service alone was enormous. As the result of the prosecution, the rate for collecting waste for an office building dropped from $200,000 to $150,000 a year, a supermarket from $25,000 to $20,000, and a restaurant from $15,000 to $12,000. The total savings of the 200,000 customers served should amount to around $400 million a year. All this does not include the indirect costs to the economy of the businesses that were driven out or discouraged from entering the city's market (Angell 1996, A16; Raab 1997a, A25; Raab 1997b, A18; Raab 1997c, A25).

For a century, criminal activities have permeated another of New York City's largest economic sectors, the construction industries. There are thousands of small and medium-sized construction firms and material suppliers, dozens of major developers, hundreds of general contractors, thousands of specialized subcontractors, and more than one hundred thousand workers belonging to about one hundred local unions in the building trades. Total yearly expenditures ran around $10 billion dollars a year in the late 1980s.

A state government crime task force found pervasive corruption and racketeering throughout the whole construction sector in New York City. Professional criminals have been involved in the industry for decades. There is long-established cooperation between organized crime and labor unions, contractors, and suppliers. Illegal payments flow from companies to union and public officials. Money is extorted to avoid sabotage, disruption in the delivery of materials, beatings, and so on. Former secretary of labor Raymond J. Donovan testified that to avoid labor shutdowns on a project being built by his company he had to put a teamster on the payroll to work as chauffeur for the local's business agent.

Bribes (in the form of "tips" or "grease") are paid to buy favors such as inspection approvals of unsatisfactory work, overlooking of legal requirements, and the granting of "sweetheart deals" (payment of substandard wages, allowing substandard or dangerous labor conditions, and so on). "Sometimes contractors claim not to know exactly why they pay; experience tells them that payoffs are necessary to assure that 'things will run smoothly'" (New York State 1990, 19). Extortion and bribery often extend into the day-to-day work on a project. It is common for a foreman on the job to demand a bribe for allowing access to the site or for a hoist, elevator, or crane operator to demand cash for taking supplies or workers up or down. Theft of materials and equipment by workers from a project is widespread, and a contractor often finds it is cheaper and more efficient to buy back the stolen property than to replace it from his usual suppliers.

Since extortion and bribes have to be factored in as a part of the cost of doing business, the work costs more and is of poorer quality. In fact, at times the work being paid for is nonexistent. These direct economic costs are bad enough, but even more devastating and incalculable is the warping of the whole sector by its acceptance of corruption and crime as normal: "The fact of the matter is that the construction industry in New York City has learned to live comfortably with pervasive corruption and racketeering. Perhaps those with strong moral qualms were long ago driven from the industry; it would have been difficult for them to have survived (New York State 1990, 5).

Some illegal predators are pillars of society. Descendants, left a sufficient fortune, after the lapse of a generation or two, can aspire to high rank on the social ladder. There is at least one respectable Canadian-American family whose fortune was made from illegal traffic in liquor during the American Prohibition era. While the Continental Group, a multibillion-dollar concern, was rebuked by the Federal Crime Commission for doing business with associates of racketeers, President Reagan, who appointed the commission, continued to maintain a close friendship with Frank Sinatra and even awarded him one of the highest American decorations, the Medal of Freedom. Sinatra's close connections with gangsters were public knowledge for a generation.

The criminal underworld is also important in economies of countries other than the United States and Russia. In India, for example, the film industry is financed by the underworld, as well as part of the construction industry in Mumbai (Bombay). Rich businessmen, as in Russia, need armor-plated cars and armed bodyguards (*Business Week* 1997a, 50, 52; *Economist* 1997g, 30).

Government Corruption

Government corruption occurs in many forms: tolls from gatekeeping, rent seeking, and outright predation or parasitism. In Pepys's time, the rewards of public office came from the opportunities to use the power of the office to enrich oneself. This was not only a British custom. Talleyrand, who served as foreign minister under the French Revolutionary government, Napoleon, and the restored monarch Louis XVIII, acquired immense wealth from his office (Ori and Perich 1978).

The Christian church has always condemned the sale of church offices. It is a grave sin, the sin of simony. With churchmen generally giving priority to their duties over their own personal interests, the Roman Catholic and Orthodox churches are the only institutions that survived the fall of the Roman Empire, feudalism, and communism in Eastern Europe and still flourish under the various modern varieties of capitalism.

When the pope, head of the church and governor of the Papal States, did resort to corruption, it encouraged the growth and success of the Protestant Reformation. Several popes looked to the sale of cardinal appointments, bishoprics, and benefices for a substantial part of their income. Between March and May 1503, one of the most venal popes, Alexander VI, created eighty new offices in the Curia to be sold for 780 ducats each and appointed nine new cardinals collecting a total of 120,000 to 130,000 ducats for these latter (Tuchman 1984, 89). Stendhal reported that the father of Pope Clemente XIII (1758–69) was a rich Venetian banker and bought a cardinal's appointment for his son for 300,000 thousand francs. The son was tormented the rest of his life by remorse for this great act of simony (1827, 89, 265).

It was not only Italian patriotism but also the deplorable way in which the Papal States were governed that made the papal subjects welcome enthusiastically their absorption into the Italian kingdom in the nineteenth century. While simony was a sin, nepotism was not. And it was by nepotism that the Papal States were mostly governed in the Renaissance and baroque periods. A new pope, an elective monarch, had no long-lasting dynastic loyalties to ensure having subordinates he could trust. He turned instead to family, his *nipoti,* that is, his nephews and other relatives. These were given the highest offices of state together with rich benefices, abbeys, and bishoprics whose revenues could be siphoned off to support them and enrich the family. A nephew, sometimes still in his teens or early twenties, by happy chance might be competent enough to be a capable secretary of state, general of the armies, or commander of the Castel Sant' Angelo. Generally, however, the theocratic, nepotistically chosen elite was more successful in adorning Rome with great baroque palaces and churches than in providing for the material welfare of their miserable subjects.

Many less developed countries today have standards of ethics even lower than those of Pepys's England. There are well-documented references to widespread corruption in a number of countries. Corruption is often the glue that holds the ruling party or clique together. Nicaragua under Somoza, the Dominican Republic under Trujillo, and Haiti under "Papa Doc" and his son were run like private plantations for the profit of the ruling families.

Countries are sometimes outright kleptocracies. The Philippines under Marcos was one such case. After his downfall, the equivalent of around $500 million was found in his bank accounts in Switzerland and repatriated to the Philippines. In the former Zaire, the loyalty of regional governors was ensured by allowing them to enrich themselves during their terms of office by placing levies on the public for their private purses. As one result, in much of the basin of the Congo River, roads have vanished back into the jungle and people have reverted from an exchange economy to subsistence. One Kamba cabinet minister in Kenya frankly explained to his fellow tribesmen that being in power meant that "We have been fed on bones for long, and it is our turn to feed on meat, while others feed on bones" (*Economist* 1993c, 47). Even in some of the better-governed African countries, like the Côte d'Ivoire, parasitism and predation are widespread. The World Bank representative in Abidjan reported:

> When I arrived in Côte d'Ivoire, I saw policemen stopping cars and asking for money. More recently, my day guard was attacked on the way to work. The thieves took his watch and broke his arm, but did not get his money. In the next few days, with the police and a doctor, he was less lucky. The police wanted a "tip" before filing a report on the incident. The doctor charged $12 for X-rays and a cast, but $80—half of the guard's monthly salary—to sign a medical certificate that he couldn't work. (Calderisi 1994, 20)

In Indonesia, "a willingness to enrich local and national officials is often considered the price of entry" (Sanger 1997, 38). President Suharto asked in December 1996 that foreigners working in the country donate 2 percent of their salaries to Indonesian charities controlled by him and his friends (Zachary 1997, A1).

The situation in India has been fairly public for decades. A complicated tangle of regulations and laws that ensnared the economy contributed to a disappointingly slow rate of growth—labeled by some Indian economists the "Hindu rate of growth"—and fostered ubiquitous corruption. Import quotas resulted in a discrepancy between foreign and domestic prices: whoever could secure an import permit had the opportunity for instant profit. Controlled prices for important commodities like cement in times of shortage were below open market or black market prices, and getting access to fixed-price cement quotas meant a quick profit.

Liberal government economic policies alone will not eliminate corruption in India, however. It has much in common with Pepys's England: the use of office for patronage and personal profit is sanctioned by tradition. Nepotism is more a virtue than a vice, for it is a duty to help one's family, caste, and religion. The way to get someone in authority to make a routine decision in one's favor—at a court, railroad station, or tax office—is to make a gift to the appropriate person. Even the gods can be influenced through the appropriate ritual sacrifice.

In China, widespread bribery is the way to oil the transactions of daily life. Officially, due to rules and restrictions, almost nothing is permitted. To survive and succeed, the most successful cheat and bribe. Official statistics indicate that 30 percent of state enterprises, 60 percent of joint ventures, 80 percent of private companies, and almost all shop owners cheat on their taxes (Xiao-huang Yin 1994, 46). As one policeman explained it, "we all take bribes. We know that our bosses and all the higher-ups do it. So why shouldn't we? Our salaries are too low to live on and every little bit helps" (Kiely 1991, 48).

There are countries where bribery does not even receive the tribute of official hypocrisy. In Thailand, Deputy Interior Minister Pairoj Lohsoonthorn told his Land Department officials that taking bribes was all right because it was part of traditional Thai culture: "It's like if we went to a restaurant and a young boy watched our car for us, we would give him a tip." Traditionally, officials in the king's service were not paid salaries and secured their incomes by taking a percentage of the taxes and fees paid by subjects. Today, Pairoj pointed out, bureaucrats' salaries are low, and this justifies their taking "tea money" (Associated Press 1996, A2).

In Bolivia and Colombia, a government official may be expected to refuse a fortune in bribes and risk his life if large areas of his country are to be kept out of the hands of drug growers and dealers. Not all officials are so dedicated and courageous.

Knowledge of the existence of corruption in much of the world is fairly common but the revelation of the pervasive corruption in Italy came as a shock. In 1990, an undertaker in Milan complained to a reporter that he had to kick back 100,000 lire (about $70) from each fee he collected for a corpse that he buried from a charity hospice run by the city. This public complaint initially resulted only in the undertaker being replaced by someone more compliant. However, it attracted the notice of a public prosecutor. When in 1991 a businessman who won the cleaning contract at the hospice revolted at the money demanded, the police had him wired for sound and the hospice head was caught with the marked money the businessman had handed over for the bribe.

As the prosecutor followed up this first arrest, he revealed a picture of widespread corruption in the Italian political class. In Milan itself, confessions from some of the people arrested, including two former mayors, revealed a system of kickbacks in virtually all public sector contracts. Investigators found that politicians routinely demanded kickbacks of as much as 10 percent on nearly every public works project in the country. Political parties were dependent on kickbacks to finance themselves. The corruption was systematic and efficient. The political parties split the money according to their percentage of the popular vote. Contracts and patronage jobs were divided in the same way.

The investigation implicated the head of the Socialist Party (former prime minister Bettino Craxi), several ministers from the Christian Democratic and Socialist Parties, the secretary of the Christian Democratic Party, and members of the Democratic Party of the Left and the Republican Party. A total of 150 members of Parliament were involved. Craxi was convicted in 1996 and sentenced to eight years and three months in prison for corruption. He fled to Tunisia, where he died in exile in 2000.

An Italian financial paper calculated that over a period of ten years total *tangenti* (kickbacks) received by 132 members of Parliament came to 580 billion lire (around $400 million). The mayors of Rome, Naples, Turin, Bologna, and Milan resigned, and local governments in many parts of Italy were paralyzed (Kramer 1992; *la Repubblica* 1993; *Economist* 1993a, 45–46).

The private counterparts engaged in this corruption were of course equally numerous but not as much in the public view. In the two years, February 1992 to February 1994, around a thousand businessmen were arrested on bribery charges. The finance director of Fiat and the chief executive officer of the Fiat insurance group were imprisoned in February 1993 and charged with corruption for alleged illegal payments made to win some construction contracts.

In the summer of 1993, the investigation reached Raul Gardini. Gardini was one of Italy's richest men, the chairman of Montedison and Ferruzzi Finanziaria. He had tried to corner the world soybean market in 1989.

He built the Italian challenger for the America's Cup. Along with Gardini, Gabriele Cagliari, chairman of ENI (Ente Nazionale Idrocarburi, the state-owned energy conglomerate), was involved in the 1990 purchase by ENI, at an unduly high price, of the equity owned by Montedison in Enimont, a chemicals joint venture. This transaction cost the equivalent of $50 million in bribes. Gardini killed himself on July 13, 1993, and Cagliari killed himself in prison five days later (Zampaglione 1993).

A businessman turned politician, Silvio Berlusconi, with his new party, Forza Italia, won election in March 1994 in a general voter revolt against the old parties. Eight months later he lost his office when it became apparent that his companies had also been involved in the widespread corruption. In 2001, he became prime minister again although questions about him of tax bribery, tax evasion, money laundering, and relations with the Mafia are still unresolved. The *Economist* commented "to all but the wilfully uncritical, he stands for sleaze, if not outright criminality" (2001, 14).

Carlo De Benedetti, a leading Italian industrialist, confessed that his company, Olivetti, beginning in 1983, had paid kickbacks to Italian political parties to get government contracts. He said he had to do it because it was the common practice. The payments were listed on Olivetti's balance sheet as "undocumented expenditures": "Tangentpoli [kickback city] caused a distortion of the market. Companies weren't even asked to make bids if they were on the black list of those who didn't pay kickbacks." He characterized the Italian system as "pseudo-capitalism," dominated by oligopolies and corrupt ties between business and politics. He went on to say that "Italian capitalism needs rules" (Bannon 1993a, A15, A13). Pietro Marzotto, who runs a large textile company, echoed Benedetti, saying, "What is needed is less statism and more state, in the sense of imposing clear rules on the game" (Gumbel and Bannon 1993).

Romano Prodi (1997 prime minister and an economics professor), estimated that the system of *tangenti* added 15 to 20 percent a year to business costs. The Einaudi Institute, the economics research institute in Turin, estimates that corruption cost the Italian economy 6.5 trillion lire (more than over $4 billion) annually. It also estimates that corruption has added around 15 percent to the Italian national debt, an amount equivalent to around 15 percent of GDP (Forman and Bannon 1993).

A wave of corruption scandals similar to those in Italy broke in France in 1994. Jacques Médecin, a former minister and mayor of Nice, was arrested and jailed in Uruguay while awaiting extradition to France on charges of tax fraud and misappropriation of municipal funds. Another former minister, Jean-Michel Boucheron, mayor of Angoulême, fled to Argentina to avoid charges of embezzlement of municipal funds. Bernard

Tapie, a businessman and politician whose new party enjoyed surprising success in the June 1994 European parliamentary elections, was arrested at the end of the month on fraud charges. Hundreds of other politicians, public officials, and businessmen were charged, arrested, and placed on trial on similar charges. By the middle of 1996, included in the hundreds of prominent people *mis en examen* were eight former government ministers and dozens of mayors and former and current members of Parliament. Business was not spared. One-fourth of the heads of the largest 140 companies were included. According to a poll published in September 1994, two-thirds of French business leaders believe that corrupt practices are normal (*Economist* 1996a, 49; 1994e, 55). With the courts proceeding at a slow pace, the most notable person convicted of corruption by June 2001 was Roland Dumas, a former foreign minister who had been head of the constitutional council when the investigation had forced him to resign. On May 30, 2001, Dumas was sentenced to six months in prison and a fine of 1 million francs ($130,000) for participating in a scandal involving slush funds from Elf Aquitaine, an oil company. Of the four others convicted and sentenced, the most important was Loik Le Floch-Frigent, Elf's chief executive, who was sentenced to three and a half years in prison and a fine of 2.5 million francs. He commented after his trial that the system of awarding contracts through "commission payments" via Switzerland was known and approved by every French president since Charles de Gaulle (*Financial Times* 2001, 15, 16).

On a smaller scale, there was also a rash of corruption scandals in Spain in 1994 that tainted some members of the Spanish central government as well as the regional government in Catalonia.

Even in Japan, where the standard of everyday ethics is high, corruption has proved to be widespread. The Liberal Democratic government lost a confidence vote in the lower house of the Diet in June 1993 because it had refused to take steps to reform an electoral system that puts a premium on raising and spreading around large sums of money. There have been a series of scandals over the years. In 1976, the revelation that Lockheed had bribed Japanese citizens to secure sales of its planes led to a jail sentence for Kauei Tanaka, a former prime minister. In 1989, the revelations of the Recruit Company's stock largess to politicians caused Prime Minister Takeshita to resign and ruined other leaders in business and government. In 1992, two companies, Sagawa and Kyowa, were found to have engaged in bribery. Sagawa, a package delivery firm, in addition to bribing legislators, gave nonrepayable "loans" to individuals in other companies. Some of these firms were fronts for one of Japan's largest crime syndicates. In return, Sagawa received strong-arm help in penetrating competitors' territories and bringing recalcitrant employees into line (*Economist* 1992, 28). In 1993, the National Tax Administration's investigators found the equivalent of $50 million in banknotes and boxes full of gold ingots in the home of Shin Kanemaru, the former paymaster of the Liberal Democratic Party. The administration charged him with having failed to declare the equivalent of $16.7 million that he allegedly received in kickbacks and donations from companies seeking favors from the government (Reuters 1993b).

Bribery of government officials is supposed to have been particularly widespread in the construction industry. The head of Shimizu Corporation, Japan's largest construction company, was arrested in September 1993 for allegedly paying the governor of Ibaraki Prefecture 10 million yen for directing business to his firm. This governor and two mayors were detained on accusations of taking bribes. The wave of arrests for business-government corruption led, as in Italy, to a crisis in the old governing party and the formation of a reformist government (Schlesinger and Kanabayashi 1993).

Tax evasion also appears to be widespread in Japan. Just as in the United States, it is the self-employed who comply least. Tax compliance rates are estimated at around 40 percent for farmers, 60 percent for non-farm self-employed persons, and 90 percent for employed workers (Hatta 1992, 233).

Predators, Parasites, and the Corporate Economy

While temptation to corruption is pervasive, the political process in modern democratic countries makes it difficult to keep corruption secret for long. Italy was more vulnerable than most because the Italian system of proportional representation kept the same collection of politicians ruling the country for decades, with individuals merely trading posts from time to time.

Corporations do not benefit from the harsh scrutiny of opposing parties out of power. The discussion on gatekeeping has illustrated one type of parasitism that may infect a corporation. Many of the perquisites, top corporate executives supply themselves with at the expense of their companies can also be classified as a parasitic toll. Many of these executive perks do not have to be disclosed in information available to stockholders.

The case is clearest that management perks are unrelated to performance when the executive is mismanaging his or her company. William Agee was fired as CEO of Morrison Knudsen in early 1995. While his company was losing money, it was providing him with a corporate jet for his private use, paying for a life-sized painting of him and his wife, and even planting petunia beds at his home. CEO Anthony J. F. O'Reilly of H. J. Heinz Company gave an annual three-day party at Dublin, Ireland, at company expense, of course. Some five hundred guests were flown in from around the world, housed at the best hotels, entertained at a gala ball at O'Reilly's Georgian mansion, and hosted in a white pavilion set up at the Leopardstown horse-racing track for the main race, the Heinz 57 Phoenix Stakes. O'Reilly's compensation totaled $182.9 million in the six years prior to 1997. While he was one of the best paid CEOs during these years, he was also cited by *Business Week* in five of these six years as being among the five CEOs who gave shareholders the least for their money (1997b, 107, 110).

The Wall Street Journal made a sample survey of some of the "imperial perks" of CEOs (1995. B1, B10). Here are some of their findings:

- Milan Panic, CEO of ICN Pharmaceuticals, received his salary of $584,000 in 1992 while he was on a leave of absence to serve as prime minister of Yugoslavia and promising the American government that he would not participate in the affairs of the company while prime minister. The company also paid for his personal support staff and some other expenses in the move to and from Yugoslavia.
- Don Tyson, chairman of Tyson Foods, received in addition to salary and bonus, $723,756 in 1994 for travel and entertainment costs; $759,000 to lease farm properties he owns, and $60,000 to lease his sixty-two-foot fishing boat. There were other company transactions with entities that Mr. Tyson owns or in which he has a major interest. In fiscal 1994, ending October 1, Tyson Foods reported a net loss of $2.1 million.
- Vernon Loucks, CEO of Baxter International, received $79,600 in 1993 in use of the company jet for personal travel, $33,450 for club membership fees, and car and financial counseling allowances. In fiscal 1993, Baxter reported a net loss of $198 million.

The so-called information superhighway is a magnificent example of human ingenuity and creativity. Unfortunately, some of it is being directed toward P&P. Predators take millions from banks through electronic financial transactions fraud. Computer programs are broken into and stolen. Information is extracted, deleted, or changed on personal computers by hackers. Electronic mail is easy to forge and can be read by unauthorized persons. A whole industry is being created to protect against and detect people who are trying to prey on Internet users.

Corporate law departments are sometimes used to intimidate. If a giant corporation has a dispute with a smaller company over a trademark, for example, a letter threatening legal action may be enough to force the small company to submit, whatever the merits of the case. The deep pockets of the large company cannot be taken lightly.

Corporate entertaining of customers is regarded as a cost and can be charged against income tax. Even casual observation shows flagrant abuse of this privilege: luxury yachts kept on the corporate tab that are used for weekend entertainment of the top corporate officers and their "business" friends, the corporate luxury boxes at football stadiums, theater parties, corporate apartments, and so on. But, abstracting from the abuse, consider what the substance of this type of transaction is. It is essentially a bribe, money being spent for the personal benefit of an individual to induce him or her to make a favorable decision on a corporate transaction. The individual should be deciding whether to award a contract, for example, based on the economic merits, not on which corporation provides the highest personal gain. A direct payment of money is frowned on and illegal, but receiving the equivalent in entertainment is not only legal but accepted by the tax laws. The real essence of what is involved is recognized only in the rigid restrictions on what government civil servants can accept.

Predators, Parasites, Capital, and the Financial Markets

The financial capital markets are crucial in the various forms of market capitalism in the world. The financial system mobilizes and allocates capital resources. The lifeblood of the economy flows through financial institutions. And confidence that the markets operate fairly and honestly is also the prime condition for maintaining the necessary trust of investors.

Predation may well be one of the principal means through which, historically, capital is accumulated. Schumpeter noted that robbery is one of the historic sources of commercial capital: "Phoenician as well as English wealth offers familiar examples" (1951b, 21). Keynes speculated that the booty brought back to England by Sir Francis Drake in the Golden Hind "may fairly be considered the fountain and origin of British Foreign Investment" (1930, 2: 156). Queen Elizabeth I invested part (£42,000) of her share of the loot in the Levant Company, and the profits from this financed the East India Company. Keynes, as a curiosity, calculated roughly that over the years since 1580 the continued reinvestment of this portion of Elizabeth's share of the booty would have accumulated to the aggregate total of British foreign investments (£4.2 billion) in 1930 (1930, 156–57).

There is a rich history of how war has often been little more than organized predation. The Fourth Crusade was devoted to the conquest and sacking of Byzantium. The Nazi occupations in World War II looted conquered territory both directly and indirectly through purchases of local goods and services with fiat occupation currency. At Potsdam in 1945, the Western Allies recognized the legal right of Soviet troops to take "war booty" from its occupation zone. The history of India is rich with stories of predation through war. The invasion and looting of Kuwait by Iraq's Saddam Hussein in 1990–91 is a contemporary example.

Extortion or inherited rights won by an ancestor's exercise of force were commonly accepted ways of securing services or income in feudal or slave societies. In the Middle Ages, predation was an honorable and esteemed occupation. Regular commerce and labor for gain were looked down on. Trade was regarded as motivated by avarice for money and as shot through with cheating and exploitation. To lust for land was noble, for money ignoble. When, with the coming of the Industrial Revolution, the land turned out to be in the center of a growing city or rich in minerals, the harvest in money was serendipity. That it is more socially prestigious to be descended from an ancient predatory ancestor than to have made a fortune by means of your own efforts is still a strong cultural prejudice in England, on large parts of the European continent, and in Japan.

In Britain, the royals and a ducal family are among the richest families in the kingdom, enjoying wealth that comes from the exercise of feudal right and might. Some Japanese fortunes likewise stem from positions of power seized in feudal times.[3] Social register family names whose wealth came from a robber baron ancestor are well known. Less well known is the fact that Franklin Delano Roosevelt's grandfather, Warren Delano, laid the foundations of his family fortune in the opium trade to China (Meyer 1997, 22). Elihu Yale came away from Madras rich enough to make a large donation to found Yale University. Stanford University had similar origins, except that the money in question (which Harvard refused to accept) came from Stanford's predatory success in the United States.

We can observe a similar process taking place in the former Soviet Union. The transition to capitalism brought both McDonald's and the *mafiya.* When the Soviet economy was liberalized, the persons who were best accultured to become successful entrepreneurs in a market economy were those who had lived as entrepreneurs in the socialist economy, that is, the black marketeers and corrupt bureaucrats. People in positions of power in the state or state-owned enterprises when enterprises were privatized could use their power to amass property. Other Russian *biznessmen* are founding their fortunes through crime and violence. When the transition to a market economy is completed, a very large portion of the wealth held by individuals will not measure the productive contribution they made to the economy but rather the magnitude of the ruthlessness and cunning the members of the *mafiya* and former *apparatchiks* possessed in cashing in on the opportunities available to them.

Experience in Russia suggests that the highest economic cost of P&P may come when it is disorganized, that is, when there are a number of individual freebooters, each operating independently for his or her own pocket, preying on enterprises. The International Institute of Strategic Studies in London estimated that four-fifths of Russian businesses have to pay, on average, a tenth to a fifth of their profits as protection money. A new business might have to pay tribute to a local and central government official, a neighborhood *mafiya*, and local police, fire, and water officials. Each tries to extort as much as possible. The result is a discouragement of new business. If the bribe taker were a monopolist, he or she would have had an incentive to hold down the total amount of the bribe to encourage a larger volume of business. In short, a monopoly in parasitism is more economically productive than competition! Just as in nature, it is to the long-run advantage of a parasite if it does not unduly weaken or kill its host (*Economist* 1997d, 6).

By 2000, crime in Russia had become better organized and less likely to be engaged in destructive feuds. The new rich are becoming strong advocates of law and order. With the interpenetration of crime, business, and government, the individuals who have been most successful in coming out on top are trying to legitimize their newly acquired wealth and power through government action and buying control of the press and television. Viktor Chernomyrdin, the managing director of Gazprom, Russia's gas monopoly, who became prime minister in December 1992, shared control of one of the three main television channels with the owner of a bank that helped pay for President Yeltsin's reelection. The president's national security adviser, a financier, controlled a second channel (Cottrell 1997, 30).

Drug dealers in the United States, drug cartels in Colombia, cocaine growers in Bolivia, and drug smugglers and money launderers across the globe are amassing wealth that will provide important pools of capital for the future. According to estimates of the "World Drug Report" prepared for the United Nations International Drug Control Program, the illicit drug trade generates as much as $450 billion annually in revenue, equal to about 8 percent of total international trade and comparable to the annual turnover in textiles. Of this total revenue, only 3 to 5 percent is received by the primary producers of the drugs; most of the rest fills the pockets of the traders and recipients of bribes (Wren 1997, A12).

The market in U.S. Treasury securities, with several trillion dollars outstanding, has an average trading volume of over $100 billion a day. It's a world market that is dominated by the forty investment and commercial banks that are authorized by the Federal Reserve Bank of New York to deal directly with it. Of these, almost half are non-American.

In 1990, Salomon Brothers was the largest securities dealer in the United States and one of the five largest in the world. In August 1991, it was discovered that the firm had been breaking the competitive rules and attempting to "squeeze" the market by cornering the supply of new Treasury securities and driving up prices. Two managing directors of the firm were fired, and the chairman and chief executive, the president, and the vice chairman resigned (Siconolfi August 19, 1991). Salomon Brothers and two hedge funds (Steinhardt Management, Inc., and Caxton Corporation), which also were involved, agreed in 1994 to settle a class action suit against them by paying $100 million to bond market participants who claimed to have suffered damages of up to $250 million from the squeeze. (*Wall Street Journal* 1994, C12).

The remaining four of the world's top five securities dealers were Japanese. Beginning in 1991, all four were implicated in major financial scandals. Nomura, the world's largest brokerage house, and the three others confessed publicly to having improperly compensated large favored clients for losses.

The Nomura and Nikko securities firms also admitted that affiliated companies had lent 40 billion yen ($290 million) to Susumu Ishii, the retired head of Japan's second-largest crime syndicate. Nomura manipulated the stock price of the Tokyu Corporation to allow this gangster to sell his shares at a large profit while small investors were losing money. Nomura's chairman and president were forced to resign but were reinstated to the board in 1995. In 1997, Nomura was again caught paying 49.7 million yen (around $400,000) to compensate for the trading losses of another client linked to a criminal gang; Nomura's president, chairman, and members of the board resigned.

The American subsidiaries of three of these four firms agreed to pay cash penalties to settle actions taken against them by the American Securities and Exchange Commission in February 1993. Among the charges settled were: assisting Salomon in illegal purchases of U.S. Treasury securities, improperly reimbursing losses incurred by a client, improperly maintaining licensing records, and improperly logging orders in client accounts. The fourth firm, Nikko, which refused to settle, was accused of concealing an $18 million loss in its accounts (Harlan 1993).

In June 1997, four former directors of Dai-Ichi Kangyo, Japan's fourth-largest bank, were indicted for making illegal payments of more than 11.7 billion yen (around $103 million) to a racketeer, Ryuichi Koike. Koike also received around $250 million in loans from Dai-Ichi Kangyo. After prosecutors questioned Kuniji Miyazaki, the former chairman of the bank, who had been involved in making these loans, he hanged himself.

In September 1997, the chairman, president, and four other executives of Daiwa, Japan's second-largest securities dealer, resigned after they were charged with having made illegal payments equivalent to $560,000 to racketeer Koike (Koike was sentenced to nine months in prison in April 1999).

Yamaichi, the smallest of the four major securities houses, was banned from underwriting government bonds, and five of its current and former employees were arrested on charges that the company had also made illegal payoffs to Koike. Yamaichi closed, bankrupt, on November 24, 1997, confessing that it had tremendous off-balance-sheet losses (*Economist* 1991a; *Economist* 1991b; Sterngold 1991; WuDunn 1997; Bloomberg News 1997a, D2; Bloomberg News 1997b, D15; Reuters 1997, D2).

The shares markets are a most important capital market. Prior to the founding of the Securities and Exchange Commission (SEC) in the United States, notorious Wall Street operators like Jay Gould would use their control of corporations to manipulate stock prices at the expense of legitimate investors and come away with the foundation of great fortunes. Today such manipulation is illegal in the United States, and there are no reports of it occurring on any appreciable scale.

There appears to be another kind of manipulation common today that is legal but costly to investors. In recent years, the total of initial public offerings (IPOs) of shares has run around $40 to $50 billion a year. Such shares, once launched, after the initial period often underperform the market. The record shows that the profits and cash flow of an IPO are generally attractive the year before the issue but fall in subsequent years. A study of this phenomenon found that it appeared that managers artificially boosted profits by "massaging" the accounts—legally. This can be done by changing the rates at which assets and liabilities are depreciated (Teoh et al., 1994).

For investors to maintain their confidence in the integrity of the market, the playing field has to be fair: all investors should have access to material information. Trading on insider information has been illegal in the United States since 1934. In many cases, when the SEC found reason to act, the individual concerned was penalized only by having to give up his or her ill-gotten gains.

In recent years, the SEC has become firmer. In 1985, Paul Thayer, the former deputy secretary of defense in the Reagan administration, was convicted for trading on insider information and given a four-year jail sentence. Then, in 1986, through a fortunate chance a series of insider traders were found and convicted. The unraveling began when some of the staff of an offshore bank noticed the extraordinary success of one of their clients in trading on the New York market. By piggybacking their transactions on his, they created enough suspicious activity in the stocks to alert the SEC. Once the first culprit was caught, following the trail led to others. The first, Dennis Levine, a Drexel Burnham Lambert managing director, exploited confidential information involving the shares of fifty-four companies over a period of four years. After being caught by the SEC, he paid $11.5 million in fines and drew a prison sentence to boot. The trail finally led to Michael Milken, who was the biggest catch of all.

In 1997, the Supreme Court strengthened the ban on insider trading by extending it to people who trade on confidential information even if they do not have any connection to the company whose shares are traded. The conviction of a lawyer, James H. O'Hagan, was sustained. O'Hagan had made a profit of $4.3 million by trading in the shares of the Pillsbury Company using information from his law firm, which was acting for a company planning a hostile takeover of Pillsbury.

The European Community (EC) issued a directive in 1989 to ban insider dealing, and most members of the EC that lacked such laws have since made it an offense. But enforcement is another matter. The British record is the best but still pitiful.

From 1980, when insider dealing became an offense, to July 1994, some three hundred cases were investigated by the British Department of Trade and Industry (DTI). Fifty were prosecuted and only twenty-three convicted. New, more stringent insider-trading laws came into effect on March 1, 1994. During the whole of 1994, the Stock Exchange referred seventeen suspected cases of insider trading for investigation; only two were successfully prosecuted.

In one notorious case, DTI announced in July 1994 that no action would be taken on referring Lord Jeffrey Archer, a prominent Tory politician and novelist, for prosecution. In January 1994, shortly after the board of Anglia TV, on which his wife was a director, had met to consider the takeover bid of another company, Lord Archer used a stockbroker with whom he had never before dealt to buy fifty thousand shares of the company. The shares were booked in the name of Broosk Saib, a Kurdish friend. Two hours after news of the merger became public on January 18, Archer sold the shares for a profit of £77,000 (*Economist* 1998, 98).

Share prices often rise suspiciously before a takeover bid. France banned insider trading in 1974. The enforcement agency, the Commission des Opérations de Bourse, secured the conviction of seven men (who were given suspended sentences) in September 1993 for insider dealing and fraud for trades made as Pechiney was about to take over American National Can Company.

German action was prompted by an insider-trading scandal in Germany's biggest bank, the Deutsche Bank. In Germany, the stock market is dominated by the banks, and their employees are allowed to speculate in the market. In the Deutsche Bank, employees were allowed to borrow an amount equal to one year's salary to speculate in the securities markets, it being understood that an unwritten code kept individuals from profiting from their insider information. As the result of an anonymous tip, in 1991 government authorities investigated possible tax evasion on profits derived from insider trading by Deutsche Bank employees (Protzman 1991).

On August 1,1994, a law finally took effect making insider trading a criminal offense and creating the Bundesaufsichtsamt für das Wertpapierwesen to administer it. The first conviction occurred in August 1995 when the son of the owner of a machinery company, Krones AG, was fined the equivalent of $1.3 million for trading on insider information. The case was flagrant: he sold his shares just days before the company announced big losses. The stock fell about 45 percent in a few days, and the volume was about ten times the normal level. Less obvious occurrences will be harder to detect, especially because the staff of the supervisory office is tiny and Germany has no automatic notification to the office by companies or stock exchanges that substantial changes in stock prices have occurred that require explanation (Marshall 1995, A5). The German law also bans "front running," that is, the situation that occurs when a broker gets such a large order to trade in a stock that the price will move and he or she deals on his or her own account first to take advantage of the anticipated price movement. No convictions have been reported. In most of Western Europe and Japan, investors who do not have access to insider information have to tread carefully and remain aware that they may have a substantial disadvantage in investing through the stock markets.

The world currency markets are secret and largely unregulated. Large amounts of "dirty" money, derived from the illegal trade in drugs and other forms of crime and terrorism, flow through the system each year. One estimate by British intelligence puts the volume of money that is "laundered" through the system at around $500 billion a year. This is fairly consistent with the United Nations' estimate that illicit drug sales total around $450 billion a year, making this industry the fourth-largest in the world (*Economist* 1994b, 81; 1998c, 45). Nonprofessional customers of traders in foreign exchange markets are usually ignorant or ill informed about prices. Since rules are few, money may be made from "front running" or exorbitant spreads.

With massive borrowing from banks, currency traders control multi-billion-dollar positions with a fraction of the amount in capital. In a small market, a trader with substantial resources can sometimes control currency prices all by himself. Andrew Krieger, the Bankers Trust New York currency trader, in 1987 made massive sales of the New Zealand currency, the kiwi, driving the price down with sales that eventually equaled 14 percent of New Zealand's foreign exchange reserves. This and other transactions netted Bankers Trust currency trading profits of $513 million in 1987 (Smith 1992, A7).

In September 1992, the currency speculators took on the EC central banks, which were defending the exchange rate mechanism (ERM) that linked the currencies of the European Community. In spite of massive efforts by the central banks defending their foreign exchange rates, Great Britain, Italy, and Spain were forced to devalue their currencies. Other countries were forced to follow suit. The economic case is not at all clear that the currency parities that the central banks were attempting to maintain were wrong. What is clear is that the speculators prevailed and walked away with billions of dollars in profit. One, George Soros's Quantum Fund, made a $1.7 billion profit speculating on the British pound's devaluation alone.

Bank Negara, Malaysia's central bank, in the 1980s used its resources to make "lightning raids" in currency markets. By coming in late in the afternoon with transactions as large as $250 million in the smaller markets of the 1980s, it was able at times to change the price of the targeted currency as much as 1 percent. Coming up against more able speculators in 1992, it lost more than $3 billion and in 1993 more than $2 billion. In early 1994, to prevent still more losses, Bank Negara changed Malaysia's banking rules abruptly to fight off attempts by hedge funds, banks, mutual funds, and other large speculators to drive up the value of the Malaysian dollar itself. This whole predatory adventure came to an end in April 1994 with the resignation of the central bank governor and his head of foreign exchange operations (Sesit and Jereski 1994; *Economist* 1994a, 82–83).

Minority shareholders in a firm are sometimes defrauded by tunneling, that is, transferring assets or profits out of a firm (as through an underground tunnel) for the benefit of controlling shareholders. There have been many cases of such looting of firms by their major shareholders in the emerging market economies. This also happens in developed civil law countries. A study by Johnson, LaPorta, Lopez-de-Silanes, and Shleifer has documented several cases in France, Italy, and Belgium, where courts, following their customary legal logic, allowed substantial expropriation of minority shareholders. These were cases in which a controlling shareholder simply transferred resources from the firm to himself through advantageous self-dealing transactions such as asset sales, contracts, transfer pricing, loan guarantees, and dilutive share issues (2000, 22–27).

Economies Dependent on Predators and Parasites

During most of human history, the relationship of governments with their hapless subjects—with few exceptions—is distilled in the pithy Italian saying "Governo, ladro" (When you say *government,* you say *thief*). For example, during the Spanish rule of Mexico from 1521 to 1821, the viceroys received no pay from the Crown but could keep whatever they could extort from the country, and the same was true of their subordinate officials. The resulting hopeless resignation of the subjects is likewise captured in the Neapolitan adage "Franza o Spagna, purchè se magna" (France or Spain, so long as we eat). The Vikings' home economy was largely supported by their raiding and plundering of Europe in the Dark Ages, and they then took over as overlords of Normandy and subsequently England and Sicily.

Small countries may derive substantial economic benefits by providing a base for parasitism or predation on larger countries. The Barbary pirate states in the seventeenth and eighteenth centuries profited from preying on and extorting blackmail from shipping in the Mediterranean. A modern spiritual descendent, Abu Nidal, although he controls only a small portion of the earth's surface directly, did equally well. Abu Nidal is a notorious Palestinian Arab terrorist who was responsible for the 1985 massacres in the Rome and Vienna airports. A 1988 French intelligence report suggested that Kuwait paid $80 million into Abu Nidal's account in the London branch of the also notorious Bank of Credit and Commerce International in 1987. Until this payment was made, Abu Nidal's men murdered Kuwaiti diplomats and detonated plastic explosives in crowded Kuwaiti cafes. After the payment was made, Kuwait enjoyed a period of freedom from terrorist attacks (Carley 1991).

In the seventeenth century, an important part of Bermuda's economy was its income from piracy. During the American Civil War, Bermuda was a base for blockade runners into southern ports. Prohibition in the United States during the 1920s gave a kick start to Bermuda's modern economy when thousands of American tourists visited Bermuda for the whisky and learned to enjoy its charm. After World War II, British, American, and Canadian firms set up headquarters in Bermuda to escape taxation at home. An important portion of modern Switzerland's high standard of living comes from its banking secrecy laws, which hide ethically earned assets but also assets derived from crime or corruption.

Paraguay's staple export industry, smuggling between its neighbors, has usually been responsible for around a quarter of its GDP. It has also been an important market for Brazil's and Argentina's car thieves; a third of Paraguay's automobiles are estimated to come from this source. Lack of a central registry for auto ownership facilitates the traffic. Autos stolen abroad usually are registered and receive license plates in small towns, which ask no embarrassing questions that might reduce the revenue from this source.

Some of the stolen autos imported into Paraguay are reexported to Bolivia. In May 1992, army colonel Luis Gonzalez Rojas, newly posted to the Chaco area, noticed a heavy traffic of trucks and four-wheel-drive vehicles on the dirty back roads leading into Bolivia. Investigating, he found that some border guards, with the approval of their superior officers, were taking bribes to let stolen vehicles pass. When he made his findings public, the army ordered him arrested on charges of divulging secret documents and slandering superiors. Only after the civil courts took over the case was Gonzalez released from jail (Associated Press 1992).

The Gambia, similarly exploiting the long protrusion of its territory into Senegal, profits from smuggling into and out of Senegal. And then there are all the offshore low-tax banking and insurance company refuges in the Bahamas, Belize, Mauritius, Western Samoa, and so on.

In recent years, the growth of paid telephone sex calls has allowed some countries to exploit this by deceiving customers who think they are making a cheap domestic long-distance call rather than an expensive international one. Moldava, the Netherlands Antilles, and Guyana have all profited. Forty percent (!) of Guyana's GDP was earned from international telecommunications traffic in 1993 (*Economist* 1998a, 67).

As of January 1, 2001, 20 percent of Africa's peoples were afflicted by civil wars, some of which spilled over national boundaries. Some of these wars have gone on for more than a generation. While ethnic differences have played a part in stimulating these conflicts, the ones that last longest are financed by predation. This appears to be true of the civil wars in Angola, Sierra Leone, Liberia, and Zaire/Congo, where exploitation of rich mineral deposits (diamonds or gold) led to competition among militarized predators (often the official government must be included in this category). The generations-long civil war in Colombia persists in part because traffic in narcotics is the source of finance that pays to arm and keep fighters in the field.

Conclusions

We know from economic theory that individuals usually have an interest in maximizing their incomes. The theory largely overlooks the primary choice that people have to make between trying to earn income through productive service or through predation and parasitism, exploiting coercive power. The P&P choice is often taken.

The discussion in this chapter has only scratched the surface of this subject. Ignoring P&P means ignoring an important force shaping the ways in which the regular economy works. An action as conventional as the founding of provincial banks in Britain was stimulated by the desire to avoid highwaymen preying on the transport of specie. Recent research has also shown that parasitism was widespread among artisans and craftsmen in Great Britain up to the eighteenth century. Workers supplemented their small money wages in ingenious ways of cheating their customers and employers (by substituting inferior materials in clothing and hats, stealing remnants, pilfering bits of cargo, etc.). One of the reasons for the introduction of the factory system was to shift production from the home to the factory so that the employer could supervise what was happening more closely (Linebaugh 1991). In a more recent example, most of the general merchandise moving in international trade these days is transported in containers—the use of which was stimulated by the need to avoid the widespread pilfering prevalent before.

Losses due to predation and parasitism and the costs people pay to protect themselves are huge. The obvious costs are losses from war, crime, and fraud and the costs of defending against these such as maintaining a military, the police, the courts, and penal systems. Americans spent $35 billion on local, state, and federal law enforcement in 1995 and almost double that sum, $65 billion, on private security services and products. The Internal Revenue Service (IRS) estimates that some 7 million citizens and 3 million corporations owe income taxes but avoid filing. Millions more cheat on the returns they file. Multinational corporations use creative transfer pricing or bogus transactions to shift income from the United States to lightly taxed jurisdictions. In total, the IRS estimates that about $150 billion in income taxes due on 1993 income, for example, were not paid. This was almost enough to have eliminated the federal government's deficit for that year.

While the parasitic behavior of corruption may be immediately profitable to the individuals concerned, it may also have large social and economic costs. When corruption is widespread in a government, inertia, inefficiency, and economic irrationality in the use of resources sap the economic life of the nation. If government officials sell import licenses and award construction contracts to whoever pays the biggest bribe, not only has an economically inferior choice been made but economic behavior across the whole economy is worsened as people observe that rewards flow to crooks rather than producers. Tax evaders reduce government revenues and force honest economic activity to be taxed more heavily. A company allowed to pollute a river may wreck the livelihood and health of thousands downstream. There are clearly social gains to be had if individuals in public life do not work to enrich themselves through corruption but instead are devoted to serving the community.

Some economies are stunted due to the ravages of predators or the costs of having to nourish parasites. Sicily is an attractive island, located at a crossroads of the Mediterranean, with many other natural advantages. In classical times, it was one of the centers of civilization. In modern times, Sicilians who emigrated to northern Italy and North and South America have shown the kind of energy and entrepreneurial skill that drives economic development. One of the reasons why Sicily has not lived up to its economic potential is clearly the heavy weight of the mafia succubus.

> Between 1978 and 1992, the Mafia killed the chief of detectives, the head of the fugitives squad, and the deputy chief of the Palermo police; the general heading the military police; Italy's leading anti-Mafia prosecutors; the leader of the leading opposition political party in Sicily and the head of the leading government party; two former mayors of Palermo; and the highest-ranking regional official, the President of the Sicilian Region. A good example of how the Mafia's stifled the economy is the story of Palermo's city opera house, the Teatro Massimo. It was closed for repairs for a quarter of a century. The equivalent of tens of millions of dollars were spent on repairs with the money going to Mafia-controlled construction firms that pocketed the money and made no progress in renovating the opera house. The job was done only after a series of indictments of Mafiosi. (Stille 1999, 49–52)

Southern Italy, also an economic laggard, has suffered from other criminal gangs, the Camorra and N'drangheta. The problems of New York City, described earlier, were exacerbated by the predators and parasites, legal and illegal, that preyed on vulnerable businesses trying to operate in the city.

If predation is sufficiently pervasive, economic regression may set in—as happened in Western Europe during the Viking raids, in African countries such as Angola and Zaire/Congo beginning around the time of their independence in the 1960s, in Equatorial Guinea and Uganda during the 1970s and 1980s, and in Sierra Leone and Liberia around the beginning of this millennium. A similar process destroyed parts of American cities in the 1970s. Residents fled, driven out by crime and fearing for their children, lives, and property. Areas decayed, burned, and were largely abandoned.

Economic analysis and economic policy that recognize only the existence of exchange transactions and overlook those dominated by power such as predation and parasitism can be woefully lacking. To understand the economy, vulnerability to P&P and its probability have to be taken fully into account. Obviously, in transition economies like those of Russia and other successor states, overlooking P&P means giving up any pretense of comprehension of the economy and its problems. But in all economies to neglect transactions influenced or driven by power is to fail to come to terms with the task.

CHAPTER 9

Summing Up

> [It is my] belief that in the present period economics as a practical art is ahead of economics as a science.
>
> —T. J. KOOPMANS.

Unless economics explains how the real economy works, it is not a science. Science is concerned with reality. To the extent that economics is a successful practical art it is, in fact, economic *science.* Empirical economists have often acquired a better understanding of the economy by dealing with the problems of the real world than can be gained from current economic theory. Economic theory can do better and secure a more effective grasp on the real economy by focusing on the real world. The National Bureau of Economic Research (NBER) organized a field project on sources of productivity change in industrial companies, and Martin Feldstein, president of NBER, reported rapturously on this unique venture into the real world:

> When I have described this project to non-economists, they were invariably surprised that the process of visiting companies, looking at production, and asking questions is an unusual part of economic research. It seems like such a natural thing to do. But as economists all know, it is unusual. We economists are generally accustomed to getting our insights by reading economic literature, going to seminars, and thinking hard about problems. We elaborate these insights in more or less formal models and then sometimes test these theories with aggregate statistics or micro data.
>
> But we rarely go and look and ask—I think that is a pity. Looking and asking provide insights and suggest hypotheses—and can shoot-down wrong ideas—in ways that go beyond introspection and reading. (2000, iii)

The lesson that to theorize about the real economy it is useful to actually look at it is one that I hope more theoretical economists will take to heart. As a first step and the first lesson after escaping from autism, it is necessary to accept that because of the difficulties inherent in all measurement and because economics is concerned with human adaptive and reactive activity it can never be precisely accurate. The best it can do, and it is sufficient, is to be roughly accurate.

Second, while economics can contribute to helping other social sciences in doing their job, economics also needs to call on the resources of other disciplines to help it understand the economy, for "the part of economics that is independent of history and social context is not only small but dull" (Solow 1997b, 54).

Finally, and this has been the main thrust of this book, in interfacing with the real economy theory needs to modify its fundamental assumptions to make them more realistic and it needs to discard the canonical and misleading hypothesis of "equilibrium," replacing it with the more accurate and less polarized concept of "outcome"—which carries no baggage of the implication that it is necessarily desirable in itself, that it will persist, and that if disturbed it will reassert itself.

The economy is an adaptive and complex but not a stable, balanced, or unchanging system. There is no fixed point, no stable equilibrium, toward which the economy is moving or to which it returns when it is disturbed. Everything is in the process of change away from the present and toward an unknown future. Change is the very essence of the capitalist market system; it is not only the result but the engine that drives the system and the growth of the economy.

The self-centered self-interest of neoclassical theory, as a positive description and normative prescription, should be replaced with Adam Smith's interpretation of self-interest as including regard for others. In addition to being affected by needs for food, shelter, sex, comfort, and enjoyment, human beings also crave recognition by others as being worthy of respect. People have various needs: to feel useful, to work toward an ideal, to avoid social shame, to live up to societal and community expectations, and to have prestige and power.

Human beings are more likely to be satisfied with acting "reasonably" (i.e., with bounded rationality, using rules of thumb, or satisficing) rather than driven by a maximizing hyper-rationality. Most transactions do not conform to the assumption of perfect rational maximization. The closeness of results in a transaction to perfect rational maximization, ceteris paribus, is likely to vary directly according to:

(1) The size (or importance) of the stake
(2) The degree of professionalism or specialization of the agent
(3) The degree of impersonal relationships among the parties
(4) The pressure of competition
(5) The availability of useful, pertinent knowledge
(6) The simplicity of the transaction

Beliefs as to how the economy works, herd psychology, and consumer and producer confidence all affect behavior and are crucial in influencing the way the economy works.

The market is a useful social and economic instrument, and its major, indispensable, and true contribution is as a means of collecting and disseminating information among its participants. This information is provided in the form of price signals or, if prices are not allowed to fluctuate freely, by the emergence of shortages or surpluses. The market is also a coordinating mechanism. As desires, technologies, and resources change, the market provides incentives to move resources to places where they are needed and from places where they are not.

Markets are social and historical constructs. The effective functioning of markets requires an orderly framework policed by the state or some other coercive power and a reasonable degree of implicit agreement among the participants on self-discipline and ethical behavior. Ethics are essential for a well-performing economy. Effective markets depend on the freedom of the individual to pursue self-interest as he or she wishes, but they also depend on a system of law and ethical and political systems that constrain people from pursuing self-interest too far or by antisocial methods. Ignoring this was one of the causes of Russia's disastrous transition from a centrally planned economy.

Pure atomistic competition exists in reality only in agriculture (and not even perfectly there). Monopolistic competition or differentiated oligopoly, the search for economic rents, nonprice competition in product and factor markets, and long-term relations with workers, customers, and suppliers are all more accurately characteristic of the real world than the conventional model that assumes atomistic pure competitive markets and competitive firms with production functions of diminishing or constant returns to scale that operate in a world of perfect information. Because of imperfect and asymmetric information and inequalities in power and capabilities, market outcomes are not necessarily optimal or socially just.

This also graphically demonstrates that the pursuit of personal ends, contrary to an unvoiced assumption of economics, is not always to the benefit of society. People can choose to try to accomplish their ends by producing or, if they are in a position to do so, may use power to try to live off the productive contributions of others. Even in the most law-abiding society, transactions motivated by power take place and predators and parasites are present. The standard of living and the growth or decline of an economy are results of the work of the productive factors, on the one hand, and the destructive behavior of the predators and parasites on the other.

Economics wandered off into a quicksand when, denying that one cannot compare the utility or welfare of one individual with that of another, it concluded that therefore one cannot rank one social state above another. This leaves the possibility of taking actions that may make one person better off only as long as this does not make anyone else worse off. There are very few such possibilities. In order not to be totally useless, attempts to avoid this Pareto-limitation have suggested various strategies for compensation to be paid (actually or hypothetically) to losers. This whole imbroglio can be avoided by going back to the original classical focus on material welfare. We do not need try to compare the mental state of one person to that of another but rather whether A is richer or poorer than B in command over goods and services. If we need to tax Bill Gates to provide housing for the homeless in Seattle, we do not need to worry that the few millions he will lose will make him more unhappy than the happiness the homeless will derive from having a roof over their heads and some warmth in the Seattle winter. Finally, only on the material welfare basis do national accounts (income distribution statistics) make sense and can policy be made rationally.

The market cannot set national and social ends. Conscious human thought has to be involved. The modern global and national economies are so complex and the responsibilities unavoidably placed on the governing authorities are so exacting that economists, if they are to be useful, need to use every bit of knowledge that affects the economy in making their diagnoses and providing policy help.

Notes

Chapter 1

1. Autistic behavior is not restricted to economists. Note, for example, the following statement by Venant Cauchy, honorary president of the International Federation of Philosophical Societies: "What strikes me as particularly worrisome in many areas of philosophical activity is the relative lack of relevance, even the refusal of relevance in the face of the fundamental social, economic, political, ethical, and technological problems which confront us today. The relative impotence or inability to cope significantly with the issues, the tendency to view philosophy as a game or a mere formal exercise, is very worrisome indeed" (quoted in Stoehr 1998, 31).

2. According to Barro's theory, an individual chooses a path of consumption and a bequest to the next generation by maximizing a utility function that has as its argument the individual's own annual consumption amounts and the utility of the next generation. A tax cut matched by a rise in the national debt to be serviced by taxes on future generations does not change the opportunity set of the individual. He or she maintains a consumption path and the utility level of the next generation by saving the whole of the tax cut, investing it, and leaving it to the next generation. This allows the next generation to maintain its consumption path and look out for its heirs. The process results in finite-lived individuals being equivalent to infinitely long-lived individuals (Barro 1974; Feldstein 1988).

John J. Seater finds exact Ricardian equivalence implausible (1993, 143) and believes that it requires too many stringent conditions to be believable (184), but he still accepts the articles supportive of it, rejects those opposed, and concludes that it is an attractive model of government debt's effects on economic activity (184). I can only echo James Tobin's question voiced on a similar occasion: "Why do so many talented economic theorists believe . . . elegant fantasies so obviously refutable by plainly obvious facts?" (1992, 400).

3. See Kamarck 2001.

Chapter 2

1. Der Mangel an mathematischer Bildung gibt sich durch nichts so aufallend zu erkennen, wie durch masslose Schaerfe im Zahlenrechnen.

2. In economic jargon, "*the* combined assumptions of maximizing behavior, market equilibrium and stable preferences, used relentlessly and unflinchingly . . . provides

a valuable unified framework for understanding *all* human behavior" (Becker 1976, 5, 14, emphasis in original; quoted in Elster 1989, 105). Economics megalomania is not unique. Compare this statement: "Unfortunately, psychology as a profession tends to assume that all questions about human action fall within its domain and that all can be eventually answered with the authority of science—this imperialism has gone largely unquestioned" (Staddon 1995, 88–89).

3. The following discussion draws heavily on Kamarck 2000.

4. See Kamarck 2001 for a development of this approach.

Chapter 3

1. That I might understand what / in final analysis holds the world together.

2. This translates into English as: "It is the social constraint, pure and simple. Society wills that men suffer and die at the front. Therefore they suffer and they die. That's it. . . . The fear that man has of society is much stronger than the fear he has of shells. Their fear of society isn't physical. It is intangible. Man is so made that for him a physical fear is almost always less strong than an intangible fear. The intangible fear of society knows how to take on forms that have an immediate effect in themselves. On one side, fear of shells. But on the other side, the fear of what your comrades or your commander will think, or if you are a commander what your men will think. It takes in one sense more courage for the average man to face up to a reputation of cowardice than to endure an explosion of shells."

Another reason for overriding self-interest by a soldier was illustrated by the letter, quoted by Ken Burns in his Civil War television series, that Major Sullivan Ballou, a Union officer, wrote to his wife.

> I have no misgivings about, or lack of confidence in, the cause in which I am engaged, and my courage does not halt or falter. I know how the triumph of American civilization now leans upon the triumph of the government, and how great a debt we owe to those who went before us through the blood and suffering of the Revolution; and I am willing, perfectly willing, to lay down all my joys in this life to help maintain this government, and pay that debt.
>
> Sarah, my love for you is deathless. It seems to bind me with mighty cable that nothing but omnipotence can break; and yet my love of country comes over me like a strong wind, and bears me irresistibly, with all those chains, to the battlefield.

Major Ballou was killed a week later in the First Battle of Bull Run (Rouner 1999, 1).

3. In modern economies, the effect of rising wages may be indeterminate: When wages rise, a worker may prefer to "buy" more leisure by working less. This is the so-called income effect. Or, with higher wages, a worker may decide to work more hours since each hour of leisure has a higher opportunity cost. This is the so-called substitution effect. In modern economies, it is usually assumed that at lower wage rates the substitution effect is stronger so that with a rise in wages more labor is supplied. In countries entering the market system, this turns out to be untrue. People here regard their working hours as time lost from their normal lives.

Chapter 4

1. Chapter 4 has benefited greatly from several thoughtful articles on rationality by Sheila C. Dow (1997), Robert L. Formaini (1994), Daniel R. Fusfeld (1996), Terence W. Hutchison (1996, 1997), Alan Kirman (1996), Tony Lawson (1995, 1997), Steven Rappaport (1996), Jochen Runde and Paul Anand (1997), Thomas Russell (1997), and Piet-Hein van Eeghen (1996).

2. A more detailed definition would be that rationality occurs when cognitive agents adopt beliefs or take actions with appropriate reasoning (i.e., using rigorous logical rules for deciding whether a proposition should be believed) on the basis of appropriate evidence (in empirical matters, this means having an adequate body of evidence) and yields results that are universal and necessary in the sense that they will be agreed upon by anyone who undertakes the same rigorous process.

3. But all is not lost. One economist has hastened to explain that economists who live up to the honor system must do so because they are reimbursed by their employers (*Journal of Economic Perspectives* 1997, 198).

4. I have had colleagues whose self-destructive behavior ruined any chance of a successful career. One highly competent economist in the Marshall Plan mission in Rome was declared persona non grata by the Italian government because he couldn't control his tongue. He lost one job after another for the same reason until he killed himself.

5. Formal theoretic economic models assume that they can capture the ranking of outcomes based on individual self-interest. It has been argued that one can likewise assume that these models can also capture outcomes that are based on a wider range of individual concerns than pure self-interest. That is, these models can take into account altruistic as well as self-interested motives. This, however, is not true—it is not possible for a model to capture the ranking of outcomes according to an individual's full range of concerns from self-interest to its polar opposite, negation of self-interest, in a single, all-purpose, preference ordering. Such a model would capture everything, that is, blot out the whole of our motivational spectrum. It would therefore be meaningless (McPherson 1993; Sen 1977).

6. Comments by Michael Ambrosi, David Colander, and Peter Doeringer helped clarify some of my thinking about reasonableness.

7. This approach owes much to Thomas Mayer (1999). But note how Alfred Marshall made a similar argument, stating that "stress is laid on the fact that there is a continuous gradation from the actions of 'city men,' which are based on deliberate and far-reaching calculations, and are executed with vigour and ability, to those of ordinary people who have neither the power nor the will to conduct their affairs in a business-like way" ([1920] 1952, vi).

Chapter 5

1. Ethical principles can be taught separately from religion. The Character Education Curriculum is being used successfully in many major school systems in the

United States. This program, based on a worldwide study of values shared by major cultures and religions, stresses honesty, kindness, courage, justice, tolerance, freedom, and sound use of talents (Goble 1988, 18).

2. Paul Streeten has commented, however, that British senior officials who retire at age sixty often get directorships on boards of companies. This expectation is bound to influence their behavior while in office (personal communication, April 25, 1998).

3. Forty years ago, before pleasure sailing was a mass participation sport, sailors looked out for each other and came quickly to one another's aid. See Bardhan 1993, 87–134.

Chapter 6

1. The range is from 74 percent in Korea, 73 percent in Switzerland, 49 percent in the European Union, and 24 percent in the United States to 6 percent in Australia and 2 percent in New Zealand.

2. This can be seen in any market and is strikingly evident in modern high-tech industries. The U.S. Justice Department maintained, for example, in its Microsoft suit that the company became dominant in operating systems through fair competition but then used its market power to try to maintain its dominance and extend it to related products.

3. Vernon reports that the "concentration index"—the ratio of sales of the four largest enterprises in each SIC five-digit industry as a percentage of the industry's total sales—came to 43.7 percent for the 187 multinationals in the Fortune 500 list, 40.8 percent for the rest of the Fortune 500, and 37.9 percent for U.S. industry as a whole in 1965 (1971, 285).

4. When I took singing lessons, it was obvious, even to me, that no matter how hard I tried I would never be able to sing like Pavarotti, as I had not been born with the requisite voice.

5. Ronald McKinnon was one of the principal proponents of the dominant orthodoxy of the 1970s and 1980s that the only strategy for successful economic development is to get the prices right and let the markets run freely. In 1991, older and wiser and confronting the problems of the former communist countries moving to a market system, he confessed that he was now more inclined to emphasize the pitfalls and underline the need for careful state management of the process. McKinnon, in fact, appears to be moving toward the belief that capitalism is a powerful means of economic growth but that to work effectively it has to be managed by the state or powerful responsible banks like those in the German or Japanese tradition (McKinnon 1991, 83; see also Taylor 1993, 279–80).

6. The *Harvard Crimson* commencement 1999 issue featured an open letter from a graduating student: "overcrowded lectures . . . make up the bulk of the undergraduate experience. . . . Most coursework is taught by inconsistently trained graduate students, while interaction with Faculty is limited to inconsistently offered office hours" (Chang 1999, A12). Another student said he knew what his professors looked like: "small dots" in the distance.

7. *Harvard Magazine* (1995, 112) presented a Charles Hefling satirical illustration of how, following such an event, professors would have to market their courses through

ads: for example, Social Analysis 20, from Plato to NATO; Deconstruct with the best of 'em in English 12a; Thrill to Rilke, German 55a; Music 9, not just a bunch of notes; and Math 14, it's integral.

8. The University of Central Arkansas as of 1999 offered new hires the option of tenure (or tenure track) or a 50 percent salary premium and a three-year rolling contract.

9. "From 1990 to 1995, countries of the former Soviet Union and of Eastern Europe experienced an extraordinary demographic crisis, most notably a startling fall in life expectancy. In Russia, life expectancy fell by 6 years, from 70 in 1989 to 64 in 1995, i.e. an estimated 1.3 to 1.7 million premature deaths. These deaths were disproportionately concentrated among prime age men" (Becker and Bloom 2000, 1). In 1999 alone, the Russian population dropped by 800,000.

10. I encountered Robert Kuttner's *Everything for Sale* after this essay was substantially complete and was delighted to find that his work and arguments parallel, support, and strongly supplement the shorter treatment of his points in a section of this chapter.

Chapter 7

1. In medicine, Dr. William Osler commented on the difficulty of getting acceptance of the need for aseptic treatment of wounds to prevent doctors from being agents of death by transporting germs from one patient to another: "It was . . . a long and grievous battle, . . . with the opposition of men who could not—not who would not—see the truth" (quoted in Horton 2000, 38).

2. Unfortunately, Walras was not aware that Newton, after buying into the South Sea bubble at the top and losing £20,000, had decided: "I can calculate the motions of the heavenly bodies, but not the madness of people" (Reed 1994, 40).

Walras was fearless in constructing his theory. Does economics as a physico-mathematical science require a measure of utility that escapes us? "Eh bien! This difficulty is not insurmountable. Let us suppose that this measure exists and we shall be able to give an exact and mathematical account" of the influence of utility on prices and the like (1896, 97, quoted and translated in Georgescu-Roegen 1971, 40). This may have been the inspiration for the joke about the engineer, the chemist, and the economist who, lost in the woods and possessing only a can of food with no way of opening it, solve the problem when the economist proposes a solution: "Assume a can opener."

3. David Colander alerted me to this.

4. It is not surprising, consequently, that economic history has been downgraded, has vanished as a subject in many universities, and is not even acceptable in some schools as a field for the general examination for the doctorate. In Bertrand Russell's words, "History makes one aware that there is no finality in human affairs; there is not a static perfection and an unimprovable wisdom to be achieved."

5. As it was in the beginning, is now, and ever shall be, world without end. Amen.

Chapter 8

1. The term *rent seeking* was coined by Anne Kreuger. Jagdish Bhagwati contributed *directly unproductive activities.* Gordon Tullock who invented the concept did

not provide a sufficiently catchy name by which to be memorialized. See Tullock 1993 for a history and overview of this valuable innovation in modern economics.

2. Although I live in a fairly safe area, Cape Cod, there are still large costs in guarding against crime. I have double locks on all my doors and locks on my windows. Whenever I leave my home, I take the time to lock up. Police routinely visit my street. I am always careful to close my garage doors by radio signal as I drive away. My automobile, of course, has locks on all the doors, which engage automatically when I lock the door on the driver's side. The car is further protected by a general alarm system that will sound if anyone should try to break in. On the window is a decal informing a prospective thief that identification numbers have been inscribed on all parts. The combination radio and cassette player has been specially engineered so that it cannot play if stolen from the car. The antenna of my radio emerges from the car body only when I turn the radio on. In my wife's car, the antenna has been etched into the rear window so that it cannot be broken off by vandals.

We have probably had less direct loss from predation than most, but during our lifetimes my wallet has been stolen twice, once in Washington, D.C., and once in Moscow; my wife's purse was stolen in Naples; a television set was stolen from our house on Capitol Hill in Washington; a pair of binoculars disappeared from my car on Cape Cod; my wife's car window was smashed and a cassette player was removed while she was parked in Boston; our dinghy and a jib were stolen from a mooring on Cape Cod Bay; and even a small blue spruce was removed from our yard. Some debentures we owned were called for redemption by the Bank of New York just before an interest payment was due. According to the small print, no compensation was owed to us, and none was paid.

3. There are examples of gains that came from predation all around us. In my town of Brewster ("The Town of Sea Captains"), a restaurant, the Gold Coast, carried on the name of the mansion built by a sea captain out of profits made from slaving off the Gold Coast in West Africa. There was obstinate resistance on Cape Cod in the 1850s to building the Nauset lighthouse to protect shipping passing the cape because it would injure the wreckage business then battening on ships driven ashore.

References

Adams, Henry. 1996. *The Education of Henry Adams: An Autobiography.* New York: Modern Library.

Adams, John. 1990. "Institutional Economic and Social Choice Economics: Commonalities and Conflicts." *Journal of Economic Issues* 24, no. 3 (September): 845–59.

Akerlof, George A. 1984. *An Economic Theorist's Book of Tales.* Cambridge: Cambridge University Press.

Alchian, Armen A. 1950. "Uncertainty, Evolution and Economic Theory." *Journal of Political Economy* 57:211–21.

——— and William R. Allen (1967). *University Economics.* Second Edition. Belmont, California: Wadsworth Publishing Company.

———, and H. Demetz. 1972. "Production, Information Costs, and Economic Organization." *American Economic Review* 62, no. 4 (December): 777–95.

Alexander, Robert J. 1986. "Is the United States Substituting a Speculative Economy for a Productive One?" *Journal of Economic Issues* 20, no. 2 (June): 365–74.

American Economic Association. 1999. "Minutes of the Executive Committee Meetings." *American Economic Review* 89, no. 2 (May):449–61.

Angell, Philip S. 1996. "Cleaning Up—in More Ways Than One." *Wall Street Journal* 228, no. 18 (December 16): A16.

Arendt, Hannah. 1978. "Hannah Arendt: From an Interview." *New York Review of Books* 25, no. 16 (October 26): 18.

Aristotle. 1926. *Aristotle's Politics.* Translated by Benjamin Jowett. First edition 1905. Oxford: Clarendon: 1926.

Arrow, Kenneth J. 1951. *Social Choice and Individual Values.* New York: Wiley.

———. 1996. *The Rational Foundations of Economic Behavior.* Edited by Enrico Colombatto, Mark Perlman, and Christian Schmidt. Hampshire, U.K.: Macmillan.

Arthur, W. Brian. 1989. "Competing Technologies, Increasing Returns, and Lock-in by Historical Events." *Economic Journal* 90, no. 394 (March): 116–31.

———. 1993. "Pandora's Marketplace." *New Scientist,* supplement, 6 (February): 6–8.

Associated Press. 1992. "Spectacular Scandal Astonishes Paraguay." *Cape Cod Times,* November 29, G4.

———. 1996. "Taking Bribes Is Proper in Thai Culture, Official Says." *Boston Globe* 250, no. 170 (December 17): A2.

———. 1997. "The Flamingo, at 50, Tries to Forget Its Sordid Past." *Cape Cod Times,* January 12, E6.

———. 1998. "Slavery Returns with War in Sudan: Arab Traders Prey on Southern Tribe." *Boston Globe* 253, no. 39 (February 8): A16, A17.

Auchincloss, Louis. 1986. *Diary of a Yuppie.* New York: Houghton Mifflin.

Averett, Susan, and Sanders Korenman. 1994. *The Economic Reality of the Beauty Myth.* NBER Working Papers, no. 4521. Cambridge, Mass.: National Bureau of Economic Research.

Bacon, Kenneth H. 1986. "U.S. Finds It Difficult to Catch Spies Who Sell Out for Cash, Not Ideology." *Wall Street Journal* 207, no. 126 (June 30): 26.

Balogh, T[homas], in collaboration with P. Balacs. 1973. "Fact and Fancy in International Economic Relations." *World Development* 2 (February): 76–92.

Banca d'Italia. 1986. *Ordinary General Meeting of Shareholders, Abridged.* Report for the year 1985. Rome: Banca d'Italia.

Bannon, Lisa. 1993. "De Benedetti Says Olivetti Kickbacks Date Back to 1983." *Wall Street Journal* 221, no. 96 (May 18): A15.

———. 1993. "De Benedetti Says Political Bribes Were Commonplace in the 1980s." *Wall Street Journal* 221, no. 98 (May 20): A13.

Barber, William J. 1997. "Reconfigurations in American Academic Economics: A General Practitioner's Perspective." *Daedalus* 126, no. 1 (winter 1997): 87–104. Issued as "American Academic Culture in Transformation: Fifty Years, Four Disciplines," vol. 126, no. 1, of the Proceedings of the American Academy of Arts and Sciences.

Bardhan, Pranab. 1993. "Symposium on Management of Local Commons." *Journal of Economic Perspectives* 7, no. 4 (fall 1993): 87–92.

Barro, Robert J. 1974. "Are Government Bonds Net Wealth?" *Journal of Political Economy* 82 (November–December): 1095–1117.

———. 1992. "A Gentleman's B for Bush on Economics." *Wall Street Journal* 220, no. 65 (September 30): A13.

Barzun, Jacques. 1983. *A Stroll with William James.* New York and Cambridge: Harper and Row.

Bator, Francis. 1998. "Excerpts from Workshop," 200–14, in Andrew M. Kamarck, *Economics for the Twenty-first Century.* 2001.

Bauer, P. T. 1981. *Equality, The Third World and Economic Delusion.* Cambridge: Harvard University Press.

Baumol, William J. 1967. "Macroeconomics of Unbalanced Growth." *American Economic Review* 57, no. 2 (May): 415–26.

———. 2000. "What Marshall *Didn't* Know: On the Twentieth Century's Contribution to Economics." *Quarterly Journal of Economics* 115, no. 1 (February): 1–44.

——— and Alan S. Blinder. 1988. *Economics: Principles and Policies.* 4th ed. San Diego: Harcourt Brace Jovanovich.

Becker, Charles M., and David E. Bloom. 2000. "The Mortality Crisis in the Former Soviet Union." *Research in the Developing World* 1, no. 1 (winter): 1–3.

Becker, Gary S. 1981. *A Treatise on the Family.* Cambridge: Harvard University Press.

———. 1976. *The Economic Approach to Human Behavior.* Chicago: University of Chicago Press.

———. 1995. "The Economics of Crime." Economics Lecture Series, *Cross Sections: Federal Reserve Bank of Richmond* (fall): 8–15.

Bell, Carolyn Shaw. 1994. "Data and the Economist." *Eastern Economic Journal* 20, no. 3 (summer): 349–55.

Benveniste, Guy. 1972. *The Politics of Expertise.* Berkeley and London: Glendessary and Croom Helm.

———. 1977. *Bureaucracy.* San Francisco: Boyd and Fraser.

———. 1987. *Professionalizing the Organization: Reducing Bureaucracy to Enhance Effectiveness.* San Francisco: Jossey-Bass.

Berle, Adolf A., and Gardiner C. Means. 1934. *The Modern Corporation and Private Property.* New York: Macmillan.

Berlin, Isaiah. 1969. *Four Essays on Liberty.* Oxford: Oxford University Press.

Bernstein, Aaron. 1999. "Why the Law Should Adopt More Family Leave." *Business Week,* February 1, 43.

Bertrand, Marianne, and Sendhil Mullainathan. 2000. "Agents with and without Principals." *American Economic Review* 90, no. 2 (May): 203–8.

Blaug, Mark. 1980. *The Methodology of Economics, or How Economists Explain.* Cambridge Surveys of Economic Literature. Cambridge: Cambridge University Press.

———. 1997. "Ugly Currents in Modern Economics." Paper presented at the conference Fact or Fiction? Perspectives on Realism and Economics, Erasmus University, Rotterdam, November.

———. 2001. "No History of Ideas, Please, We're Economists." *Journal of Economic Perspectives* 15, no. 1 (winter): 145–64.

Blanchard, Olivier J., and L. H. Summers. 1988. "Beyond the Natural Rate Hypothesis." *American Economic Review* 78, no. 2: 182–87.

———, and P. A. Muet. 1993. "Competitiveness through Disinflation: An Assessment of French Macroeconomic Policy since 1983."*Economic Policy* 16 (April): 12–56.

———. 2000. "Commentary." *Economic Policy Review* 6, no. 1 (April): 69–73.

———. 2000. "What Do We Know about Macroeconomics That Fisher and Wicksell Did Not." *Quarterly Journal of Economics* 115, no. 4 (November): 1375–1409.

Bleichrodt, Hans. 2000. Review of *Rational Risk Policy: Arne Ryde Memorial Lecture Series,* by W. Kip Viscusi. *Journal of Economic Literature* 38 (March 2000): 127–28.

Blinder, Alan S. 1988. "The Challenge of High Unemployment." *American Economic Review* 78, no. 2 (May): 1–15.

———. 1990. "Discussion." *American Economic Review* 80, no. 2 (May): 445.

Bloomberg News. 1997. "Ex-Head of Tainted Japan Bank, under Inquiry, Commits Suicide." *New York Times,* New England ed., 146, no. 50839 (June 30): D2.

———. 1997. "Tokyo Cracks Down on Yamaichi Securities." *New York Times,* New England ed., 147, no. 50919 (September 18): D15.

Bok, Sissela. 1978. *Lying: Moral Choice in Public and Private Life.* New York: Pantheon.

Boorstin, Daniel J. 1979. *Hidden History.* New York: Harper and Row.

———. 1988–89. "Remarks on Receiving Phi Beta Kappa's Distinguished Service to the Humanities Award." *Key Reporter* 54, no. 2 (winter): 6.

Boulding, Kenneth E. 1982. "Pathologies of the Public Grants Economy." In *The Grants Economy and Collective Consumption,* edited by R. C. O. Matthew and G. B. Stafford, 3–22. New York: St. Martin's.

———, and Thomas Frederick Wilson, eds. 1978. *Redistribution through the Financial System.* New York: Praeger.

Bourdieu, Pierre. 1990. *The Logic of Practice.* London: Polity.

Bowles, Samuel, and Herbert Gintis. 2000. "Walrasian Economics in Retrospect." *Quarterly Journal of Economics* 115, no. 4 (November): 1411–39.

Brandes, Stanley. 1987. *Forty: The Age and the Symbol.* Knoxville: University of Tennessee Press.

Break, George F. 1980. "Tax Principles in a Federal System." In *The Economics of Taxation,* edited by Henry J. Aaron and Michael J. Boskin, 317–26. Washington, D.C.: Brookings Institution.

Broder, David S. 1986. "Upgrading Education." *Boston Globe* 230, no. 65 (September 3): 17.

Brody, Hugh. 1982. *Maps and Dreams.* New York: Pantheon.

Browne, Lynn E. 1986. "Taking in Each Other's Laundry: The Service Economy." *New England Economic Review* (July–August): 20–31.

Browne, Lynn E., and Eric S. Rosengren. 1992. "Real Estate and the Credit Crunch: An Overview." *New England Economic Review* (November–December): 25–35.

Browning, Lynnley. 1999. "Heir Apparent Gifford to Gain Kingly Bundle after Fleet Merger." *Boston Globe* 256, no. 9 (July 9): C1, 10.

Buchanan, J. M. 1986. *Liberty, Market, and State: Political Economy in the 1980s.* New York: New York University Press.

———. 1987a. *Economics: Between Predictive Science and Moral Philosophy.* Compiled by Robert D. Tollison and Viktor D. Vanberg. College Station: Texas A&M University Press.

———. 1987b. "Tax Reform as Political Choice." *Journal of Economic Perspectives* 1, no. 1 (summer): 29–35.

Bulletin of the Atomic Scientists. 1993. "Make That Nine out of Ten." 49, no. 2 (March): 4.

Burghardt, Walter J. 1996. *Preaching the Just Word.* New Haven: Yale University Press.

Burrough, Bryan. 1993. "Barbarians in Retreat." *Vanity Fair* 56, no. 3 (March): 190–95.

———, and John Helyar. 1990. *Barbarians at the Gate: The Fall of RJR Nabisco.* New York: Harper and Row.

Business Week. 1997a. "Bloodshed and Terror in Bollywood—A True Story." September 8, 50, 52.

———. 1997b. "The CEO and the Board." September 15, 106–16.

———. 1997c. "The Year of the Punctured Myth." December 22, 110.

———. 1998a. "Needed: A New Financial Architecture." October 12, 162.

———. 1998b. "Bosses under Fire." November 30, 52–54.

Byrne, John A. 1999. "Management, Shareholder Activists: The Teddy Roosevelts of Corporate Governance." *Business Week,* May 31, 75–79.

———. 2000. "Pepsico's New Formula: How Roger Enrico is remaking the Company." *Business Week,* April 10, 172–84.

Cairnecross, Alec. 1969. "Economic Forecasting," Presidential Address to the Royal Economic Society, 3 July 1969. *Economic Journal,* 79 (316) 797–812.

Calderisi, Robert. 1994. "More Letters from Abidjan." *Bank's World* 113, no. 5 (May): 20–23.

Cannadine, David. 1992. "Cutting Classes." *New York Review of Books* 39, no. 21 (December 17): 52–58.

Carey, Richard Adams. 1987. "On the Corner of Hollywood and Quinhagak." *Harvard Magazine* 90, no. 1 (September–October): 10–15.

Carley, William M. 1985a. "Battle Tactics, Carl Icahn's Strategies in His Quest for TWA Are a Model for Raiders." *Wall Street Journal* 205, no. 120 (June 20): 1, 16.

———. 1985b. "TWA Pact Apparently Clears the Way for Investor Icahn to Acquire Carrier." *Wall Street Journal* 206, no. 54 (September 16): 17.

———. 1991. "Paying for Peace, To Finance Terrorism Abu Nidal Is Believed to Shake Down Arabs." *Wall Street Journal* 218, no. 29 (August 9): A1, A6.

Cassidy, John. 1996. "The Decline of Economics." *New Yorker* 72, no. 37 (December 2): 50–60.

Casson, Mark. 1991. *The Economics of Business Culture: Game Theory, Transaction Costs, and Economic Performance.* Oxford: Oxford University Press and Clarendon.

Chandler, Alfred D., Jr. 1977. *The Visible Hand: The Managerial Revolution in American Business.* Cambridge: Belknap Press of Harvard University Press.

———. 1992. "Organizational Capabilities and the Economic History of the Industrial Enterprise." *Journal of Economic Perspectives* 6, no. 3 (summer): 79–100.

Chang, Andrew S. 1999. "An Open Letter from a New Alum." *Harvard Crimson* 210, no. 75 (June 10): A12.

Chernow, Ron. 1998. "EndGame." Excerpt from *Titan: The Life of John D. Rockefeller Sr.* New York: Random House. Reprinted in *Business Week,* May 18, 67–84.

Chhibber, Ajay. 1997. "The State in a Changing World." *Finance and Development* 34, no. 3 (September): 17–20.

Clesse, Armand, and Christopher Coker, eds. 1997. *The Vitality of Britain.* Luxembourg: Luxembourg Institute for European and International Studies.

———, Takashi Inoguchi, E. B. Keehn, and J. A. A. Stockwin, eds. *The Vitality of Japan: Sources of National Strength and Weakness.* St. Anthony's Series; Houndmills, Basinstoke, etc, Great Britain: Macmillan Press Ltd; New York, USA: St. Martin's Press.

Clinton, William J. 2000. *Economic Report of the President.* Washington, D.C.: Government Printing Office.

Coase, Ronald. 1937. "The Nature of the Firm." *Economica,* n.s., 4 (November): 386–405.

———. 1991. "The Institutional Structure of Production." Alfred Nobel Memorial Prize Lecture in Economic Sciences.

Coffee, John C., Jr., Louis Lowenstein, and Susan Rose-Ackerman, eds. 1988. *Knights, Raiders, and Targets: The Impact of the Hostile Takeover.* New York and Oxford: Oxford University Press.

Cohen, David, and Glenn Follette. 2000. "The Automatic Fiscal Stabilizers: Quietly Doing Their Thing." *Economic Policy Review* 6, no. 1 (April): 35–67.

Cohen, Laurie. 1994. "Daddy Dearest: Victor Posner Lies Ill as Dysfunctional Clan Feuds over the Spoils." *Wall Street Journal* 224, no. 74 (October 14): A1, 4.

Cohen, Stephen S., and John Zysman. 1987. "The Myth of a Post-industrial Economy." *Technology Review* 90, no. 2 (February–March): 54–62.

Collander, David. 1992. "Retrospectives: The Lost Art of Economics." *Journal of Economic Perspectives* 6, no. 3 (summer): 191–98.

Collier, Paul, and Deepak Lal. 1986. *Labor and Poverty in Kenya, 1900–1980.* Oxford: Clarendon.

Collier, Paul, and Jan Willem Gunning. 1999. "Explaining African Economic Performance." *Journal of Economic Literature* 37, no. 1 (March): 64–111.

Commons, John R. [1934] 1963. *Institutional Economics.* Madison: University of Wisconsin Press.

Conlisk, John. 1996. "Why Bounded Rationality?" *Journal of Economic Literature* 34 (June): 669–700.
Connolly, Bob, and Robin Anderson. 1987. *First Contact: New Guinea's Highlanders Encounter the Outside World.* New York: Viking.
Conway, Jill Ker. 1994. *True North: A Memoir.* New York: Knopf.
Cooter, Robert, and Peter Rappoport. 1984. "Were the Ordinalists Wrong about Welfare Economics?" *Journal of Economic Literature* 22 (June): 507—30.
Cottrell, Robert. 1997. "Russia: The New Oligarchy." *New York Review of Books* 44, no. 5 (March 27): 28–30.
Coveney, Peter, and Roger Highfield. 1995. *Frontiers of Complexity: The Search for Order in a Chaotic World.* New York: Fawcett Columbine.
Cromie, William J. 1995. "Mind's Role in Healing the Body Is Probed." *Harvard University Gazette* 90, no. 16 (January 5): 3, 6.
———. 1998. "Study Finds Two Minds in Every Brain." *Harvard University Gazette* 94, no. 9 (November 12): 1, 4.
Crystal, Graff S. 1991. *In Search of Excess.* New York: Norton.
Darlin, Damon, and Roy J. Harris Jr. 1985. "GM, Hughes Face Culture Clash, Mixing Opposite Corporate Styles." *Wall Street Journal* 204, no. 110 (June 6): 14.
Darwin, Charles. 1952. *The Origin of Species by Means of Natural Selection. The Descent of Man and Selection in Relation to Sex.* Chicago, London, Toronto, Geneva, William Benton, Publisher. Encyclopedia Britannica, Inc.
David, Ronald. 1993. "The Demand Side of the Health Care Crisis." *Harvard Magazine* 95, no. 4 (March–April): 30–32.
Davidson, Cathy N. 1993. *36 Views of Mount Fuji.* New York: Dutton.
Davies, Adrian G. 1989. "The Economic War between the United States and Japan." Manuscript.
Davis, Tom E. 1963. "Eight Decades of Inflation in Chile, 1879–1959: A Political Interpretation." *Journal of Political Economy* 71 (August): 389–97.
Dawkins, Richard. 1998. "Science and Sensibility." *Free Inquiry* 19, no. 1 (winter): 37–40
Debreu, Gerard. 1984. "Economic Theory in the Mathematical Mode." *American Economic Review* 74, no. 3 (June): 267–78.
———. 1991. "The Mathematization of Economic Theory." *American Economic Review* 81, no. 1 (March): 1–7.
DeLong, J. B., A. Schleifer, L. H. Summers, and R. J. Waldman. 1990. "Noise Trader Risk in Financial Markets." *Journal of Political Economy* 98:703–38.
Delors, Jacques. 1992. *Our Europe.* New York: Verso.
Dewey, John. 1938. *Logic; The Theory of Inquiry.* New York: Holt.
Diamond, Peter A., and Jerry A. Hausman. 1994. "Contingent Valuation: Is Some Number Better Than No Number?" *Journal of Economic Perspectives* 8, no. 4 (fall): 45–64.
Dickens, Charles. [1854] 1981. *Hard Times.* Toronto: Bantam.
DiIulio, John J., Jr. 1996. "Help Wanted: Economists, Crime, and Public Policy." *Journal of Economic Perspectives* 10, no. 1 (winter): 3–24.
DiMaggio, Paul. 1990. "Cultural Aspects of Economic Action and Organization." In *Beyond the Marketplace: Rethinking Economy and Society,* edited by Roger Friedland and A. F. Robertson, 113–36. New York: Aldine de Gruyter.
Dow, Sheila C. 1997. "Critical Survey: Mainstream Economic Methodology." *Cambridge Journal of Economics* 21, no. 1 (January): 73–93.

Drucker, Peter F. 1994. "The Age of Social Transformation." *Atlantic Monthly* 274, no. 5 (November): 53–80.

Dunne, John Gregory. 1992. "Your Time Is My Time (to the End of Time: The Seduction and Conquest of a Media Empire by Richard M. Clurman)." *New York Review of Books* 39, no. 8 (April 23): 49–55.

Dyson, Freeman J. 1989. *Infinite in All Directions.* New York: Harper and Row.

Economist. 1986a. "The Gulf Learns the Meaning of Austerity." 300, no. 7459 (August 16): 45.

———. 1986b. "America's SEC: On the Insiders' Track." 300, no. 7460 (August 23): 74.

———. 1990. "Slavery by Any Other Name." 314, no. 7636 (January 6): 42.

———. 1991a. "Nomura Bows—halfway." 320, no. 7715 (July 13): 84

———. 1991b. "Japan's Financial Scandals: While Sleeping Watchdogs Lie." 320, no. 7721 (August 24): 70.

———. 1992. "Japan: Pass the Parcel." 322, no. 7747 (February 22): 28–29.

———. 1993. "Fraud-busters." 326, no. 7796 (January 30): 74.

———. 1993a. "The Fall of Montecitorio." 326, no. 7799 (February 20): 45–46.

———. 1993b. "Malaysia: Powerhouse Penang." 327, no. 7812, (May 22): 39.

———. 1993c. "If Kenya Goes." 327, no. 7815 (June 12): 47–48.

———. 1993d. "The Black Economy: Ghostbusters." 328, no. 7824 (August 14): 55.

———. 1993e. "The Britain Audit: Crime, Bewitched, Bothered and Bewildered." 328, no. 7826 (August 28): 56–57.

———. 1993f. "Taiwan: Buried Treasure." 329, no. 7836 (November 6): 37.

———. 1994a. "Asian Currencies: Malaise." 331, no. 7858 (April 9):82–83.

———. 1994b. "Dirty Money: Money-Launderers on the Line." 331, no. 7869 (June 25): 81–82.

———. 1994c. "The Texas Computer Massacre." 332, no. 7870 (July 2): 59–60.

———. 1994d. "Making a Meal of Mergers." 332, no. 7880 (September 10): 87–88.

———. 1994e. "Hands Up All Those Hit by Sleaze." 333, no. 7887 (October 29): 55–56.

———. 1995a. "Some Old Peculiar Practices in the City of London." 334, no. 7902 (February 18): 71–73.

———. 1995b. "Fat Cats and Their Cream." 336, no. 7924 (July 22): 19.

———. 1995c. "Managers and Shareholders, Acquisitive Egos." 336, no. 7927 (August 12): 52–53.

———. 1995d. "Financial Astrology." Advertisement. 336, no. 7928 (August 19): 56.

———. 1996a. "France, Who's Next?" 340, no. 7974 (July 13): 48–50.

———. 1996b. "The Flourishing Business of Slavery." 340, no. 7984 (September 21): 43–44.

———. 1996c. "Master and Slave in Mauritania" 340, no. 7984 (September 21): 44.

———. 1997a. "Why Too Many Mergers Miss The Mark." 342, no. 7998 (January 4): 57–58.

———. 1997b. "A Charter to Cheat." 342, no. 8004 (February 15): 61–62.

———. 1997c. "Economists as Gurus." 343, no. 8021 (June 14): 67.

———. 1997d. "A Survey of Russia." 344, no. 8025 (July 12): supplement, 1–18.

———. 1997e. "Reforming the Firm." 344, no. 8029 (August 9): 16–17.

———. 1997f. "Those in Peril on the Sea." 344, no. 8029 (August 9): 40.

———. 1997g. "The Real Gangster Films." 344, no. 8031 (August 23): 30.

———. 1998a. "Little Countries, Small but Perfectly Formed." 346, no. 8049 (January 3): 65–67.

———. 1998b. "America Bubbles Over." 347, no. 8064 (April 18): 67.
———. 1998c. "The UN and Drugs; Tremble, Medellin, Tremble." 347, no. 8072. June 13: 45–46.
———. 1998e. "Shareholder Voting, Voiceless Masses." 349, no. 8092 (October 31): 74, 79.
———. 1998f. "Lord Archer, Yours sincerely." 349, no. 8095 (November 21): 98.
———. 1998g. "Herd on the Street." 349, no. 8096 (November 28): 74.
———. 1999. "Dead Men Tell No Tales." 353, no. 8150 (December 18): 87–89.
———. 2000a. "The Taming of the Shrewd." 355, no. 8169 (May 6): 75–76.
———. 2001a. "So, Mr. Berlusconi . . ." 359, no. 8222 (May 19): 14.
———. 2001b. "R. K. Narayan." 259, no. 8223 (May 26): 88.
Ehrlich, Isaac. 1996. "Crime, Punishment, and the Market for Offenses." *Journal of Economic Perspectives* 10, no. 1 (winter): 43–68.
Eichenwald, Kurt. 1997. "A Health Care Giant's Secret Payments Taint a Texas Deal." *New York Times,* New England Edition, 146, no. 50746 (March 29): 25, 27.
Eichner, Alfred S. 1983. *Why Economics Is Not Yet a Science.* Armonk, N.Y.: M. E. Sharpe.
Einstein, Albert. 1954. *Ideas and Opinions.* New York: Bonanza.
Elster, Jon. 1989. "Social Norms and Economic Theory." *Journal of Economic Perspectives* 3, no. 4 (fall): 99–117.
Exeter, Julian, and Steven Fries. 1998. "The Post-communist Transition: Patterns and Prospects." *Finance and Development* 35, no. 3 (September): 26–29.
Fairbank, John King. 1983. *The United States and China.* 4th ed, enl. Cambridge: Harvard University Press.
Feldstein, Martin. 1988. "The Effects of Fiscal Policies When Incomes Are Uncertain: A Contradiction to Ricardian Equivalence." *American Economic Review* 78, no. 1 (March):14– 23.
———. 2000. "Preface: The NBER-Sloan Project on Productivity Change." In *NBER/Sloan Project Report: Industrial Technology and Productivity: Incorporating Learning from Plant Visits and Interviews into Economic Research,* ii–iv. Cambridge: NBER. Papers presented at the annual meetings of the American Economic Association, January 2000. Pamphlet.
Fenton, James. 1996. "Degas in the Evening." *New York Review of Books* 43, no. 15 (October 3): 48–53.
Ferguson, Tim W. 1994. "Tissues Turnaround Comes in Shades of Goldsmith." *Wall Street Journal* 224, no. 51 (September 13): A19.
Feynman, Richard P. 1995. *Six Easy Pieces: Essentials of Physics Explained by Its Most Brilliant Teacher.* Reading, Mass.: Addison-Wesley. Originally prepared for publication by Robert B. Leighton and Matthew Sands.
Fialka, John J. 1993. "Auditors' Lapses at BNL-Atlanta Helped to Hide Iraq Loans, Ex-Manager Says." *Wall Street Journal* 222, no. 93 (November 10): B12.
Fidelity Investments. 1993. *Fidelity Focus* (fall).
Ford, Daniel. 1988. "A Reporter at Large: Crown of Thorns." *New Yorker,* July 25, 34–63.
Formaini, Robert L. 1994. Review of Roy Cordato, *Welfare Economics and Externalities in an Open Ended Universe. Journal of Economic Methodology* 1, no. 1 (June):180–85.
Forman, Craig, and Lisa Bannon. 1993. "Mounting Outcry: A Corruption Scandal

Leaves Italy's Leaders Weakened and Scorned." *Wall Street Journal* 221, no. 40 (March 1): A1, 8.

Forman, Judy. 1996. "Loneliness Can Be the Death of Us." *Boston Globe* 249, no. 113 (April 22): 25–27.

Frank, Richard G., and David S. Salkever. 1994. "Nonprofits in the Health Sector." *Journal of Economic Perspectives* 8, no. 4 (fall): 129–44.

Frank, Robert H. 1990. "Rethinking Rational Choice." In *Beyond the Marketplace: Rethinking Economy and Society,* edited by Roger Friedland and A. F. Robertson, 53–87. New York: Aldine de Gruyter.

———. 1994. "Talent and the Winner-Take-All Society." *American Prospect* 17 (spring): 97–107.

———, Thomas Gilovich, and Dennis T. Regan. 1993. "Does Studying Economics Inhibit Cooperation?" *Journal of Economic Perspectives* 7, no. 2 (spring): 159–71.

Freedman, Craig. 1995. "The Economist as Mythmaker: Stigler's Kinky Transformation." *Journal of Economic Issues* 29, no. 1 (March): 175–209.

Freeman, Richard B. 1996. "Why Do So Many Young American Men Commit Crimes and What Might We Do About It?" *Journal of Economic Perspectives* 10, no. 1 (winter): 25–42.

———, and James L. Medoff. 1984. *What Do Unions Do?* New York: Basic Books.

Frey, Bruno S., and Reiner Eichenberger. 1992. "Economics and Economists: A European Perspective." *American Economic Review (AEA Papers and Proceedings)* 82, no. 2 (May): 216–20.

———. 1993. "American and European Economics and Economists." *Journal of Economic Perspectives* 7, no. 4 (fall): 185–93.

Friedland, Roger, and A. F. Robertson. 1990. *Beyond the Marketplace: Rethinking Economy and Society.* New York: Aldine de Gruyter.

Friedman, Milton. 1953. "The Methodology of Positive Economics." In *Essays in Positive Economics.* Chicago: University of Chicago Press.

Fromm, Erich. 1947. *Man for Himself: An Inquiry into the Psychology of Ethics.* New York: Holt, Rinehart and Winston.

Fuerbringer, Jonathan. 1997. "Why Both Bulls and Bears Can Act So Bird-Brained." *New York Times,* New England edition, 146, no. 50746, (March 30): C1, 6.

Fusfeld, Daniel R. 1996. "Rationality and Economic Behavior." *Journal of Economic Methodology* 3, no. 2 (December): 307–15.

Galbraith, James K. 1999. "The Levy Report Interview: James K. Galbraith Discusses the State of the American Economy and the Field of Economics." *Jerome Levy Economics Institute of Bard College Report* 9, no. 2 (May): 8–14.

Galbraith, John Kenneth. 1951. "Conditions for Economic Change in Underdeveloped Countries." *Journal of Farm Economics* 33 (November), 689–96.

———. 1974. *The New Industrial State.* Harmondsworth: Penguin.

Gallup, John Luke, Jeffrey D. Sachs, and Andrew D. Mellinger. 1998. *Geography and Economic Development.* NBER Working Papers, no. 6849. Cambridge: National Bureau of Economic Research.

Gardner, Bruce L. 1992. "Changing Economic Perspectives on the Farm Problem." *Journal of Economic Literature* 30 (March): 62–101.

Gazzaniga, M. 1985. *The Social Brain.* New York: Basic Books.

Geertz, Clifford. 1998. "The Pinch of Destiny (Religion as Experience, Meaning, Identity, Power, The William James Lecture)." *Harvard Divinity Bulletin* 27 (4): 7–12.

Gell-Mann, Murray. 1994. *The Quark and the Jaguar.* New York: Freeman.

Georgescu-Roegen, Nicholas. 1971. *Analytical Economics, Issues, and Problems.* Cambridge: Harvard University Press.

Gerlin, Andrea. 1995. "Former J. C. Penney Housewares Buyer Is Sentenced to Prison for Taking Bribes." *Wall Street Journal* 226, no. 40 (August 28): B6A.

Gibbons, Robert. 1998. "Incentives in Organizations." *Journal of Economic Perspectives* 12, no. 4 (fall): 115–32.

Gillett, J. D. 1974. "Direct and Indirect Influences of Temperature on the Transmission of Parasites from Insects to Man." In *The Effects of Meteorological Factors upon Parasites,* edited by Angela E. R. Taylor and R. Muller, Symposia of the British Society for Parasitology, no. 12, 79–95. Oxford: Blackwell Scientific Publications.

Goble, Frank G. 1988. "Building Ethics from the Classroom Up." *Wall Street Journal* 211, no. 5 (January 8):18.

Goh, Leong Huat. 1995. "From Singapore's Humble Beginning." *Proceedings of the U.S. Naval Institute* 121, no. 1,105 (March): 90–91.

Gompers, Paul, and Andrew Metrick. 1999. *Institutional Investors and Equity Prices.* NBER Working Papers, no. 6723. Cambridge, Mass.: National Bureau of Economic Research.

Gordon, Robert J. 1996. *Problems in the Measurement and Performance of Service-Sector Productivity in the United States.* NBER Working Papers, no. 5519. Cambridge, Mass.: National Bureau of Economic Research.

Gramlich, Edward M. 1985. "Government Services." In *Managing the Service Economy: Prospects and Problems,* edited by Robert P. Inman, 273–89. Cambridge: Cambridge University Press.

Granovetter, Mark. 1990. "The Old and the New Economic Sociology: A History and an Agenda." In *Beyond the Marketplace: Rethinking Economy and Society,* edited by Roger Friedland and A. F. Robertson, 89–112. New York: Aldine de Gruyter.

———, and Richard Swedberg, eds. 1992. *The Sociology of Economic Life.* Boulder: Westview.

Gray, Cheryl W. 1997. "Reforming Legal Systems in Developing and Transition Countries." *Finance and Development* 34, no. 3 (September): 14–16.

Greenwald, B., and Joseph E. Stiglitz. 1986. "Externalities in Economics with Imperfect Information and Incomplete Markets." *Quarterly Journal of Economics* (May): 229–64.

Gregory, J. W. 1896. *The Great Rift Valley,* London: John Murray.

Grossman, Sanford J., and Joseph E. Stiglitz. 1980. "On the Impossibility of Informationally Efficient Markets." *American Economic Review* 70, no. 3 (June): 393–408.

Gumbel, Peter, and Lisa Bannon. 1993. "Italians Engage in Fierce Self-Scrutiny in Midst of Wide Corruption Scandals." *Wall Street Journal* 222, no. 51 (September 13): A13.

Hahn, Frank H. 1981. "General Equilibrium Theory." In *The Crisis in Economic Theory,* edited by Daniel Bell and Irving Kristol, 123–38. New York: Basic Books.

———. 1985. "In Praise of Economic Theory: The 1984 Jevons Memorial Fund Lecture," University College, London.

———. 1987. Review of *The Rhetoric of Economics,* by Donald N. McCloskey. *Journal of Economic Literature* 25 (March): 110–11.

———. 1992. "The Next Hundred Years." In *The Future of Economics,* edited by John D. Hey. 47–50. Oxford: Blackwell.

———, and Robert Solow. 1997. *A Critical Essay on Modern Macroeconomic Theory.* Cambridge: MIT Press.

Hahn, Robert W. 1998. "Policy Watch: Government Analysis of the Benefits and Costs of Regulation." *Journal of Economic Perspectives* 12, no. 4 (fall): 201–10.

Halberstam, David. 1984. "Yes We Can." *Parade,* July 8, 4–7.

Hall, Robert E., and Charles I. Jones. 1997. "Levels of Economic Activity across Countries." *American Economic Review* 87, no. 2 (May): 173–77.

Haltiwanger, John C. 1999. "Understanding Aggregate Fluctuations: The Importance of Building from Microeconomic Evidence." *NBER Reporter* (spring): 4–7.

Hamermesh, Daniel S., and Jeff E. Biddle. 1994. *Beauty and the Labor Market.* NBER Working Papers, no. 4518. Cambridge, Mass.: National Bureau of Economic Research.

Hamilton, Gary G., and Nicole Woolsey Biggart. 1992. "Market, Culture, and Authority: A Comparative Analysis of Management and Organization." In *The Sociology of Economic Life,* edited by Mark Granovetter and Richard Swedberg, 181–224. Boulder: Westview.

Hampshire, Stuart. 1993. "Liberalism: The New Twist." *New York Review of Books* 40, no. 14 (August 12): 43–47.

Hanemann, W. Michael. 1994. "Valuing the Environment through Contingent Valuation." *Journal of Economic Perspectives* 8, no. 4 (fall): 19–43.

Hannah, Leslie. 1998. "Survival and Size Mobility among the World's Largest 100 Industrial Corporations, 1912–1995." *American Economic Review (AEA Papers and Proceedings)* 88, no. 2 (May): 62–65.

Hansen, Robert G., and John R. Lott Jr. 1991. "The Winner's Curse and Public Information in Common Value Auctions: Comment." *American Economic Review* 81, no. 1 (March): 347–61.

Harlan, Christi. 1993. "U.S. Accuses Nikko of Concealing Loss in Actions against Japanese Concerns." *Wall Street Journal* 221, no. 39 (February 26): A4.

Harvard Gazette. 1993. "Report Cites Disparities in Day Care Services Nationwide." 99, no. 2 (September 17): 1, 7.

Harvard Magazine. 1995. "Verities." 98, no. 1 (September–October): 112.

Hatta, Tatsuo. 1992. "The Nakasone-Takeshita Tax Reform: A Critical Evaluation." *American Economic Review (AEA Papers and Proceedings)* 82, no. 2 (May): 231–36.

Hausman, Daniel M., and Michael S. McPherson. 1993. "Taking Ethics Seriously: Economics and Contemporary Moral Philosophy." *Journal of Economic Literature* 31 (June): 671–731.

Hawking, Stephen W. 1988. *A Brief History of Time.* Toronto: Bantam.

Heilbroner, Robert. 1990. "Seize the Day." *New York Review of Books* 37, no. 2 (February 15): 30–31.

———. 1990. "Analysis and Vision in the History of Modern Economic Thought." *Journal of Economic Literature* 28 (September): 1097–1114.

Herman, Edward S. 1981. *Corporate Control, Corporate Power.* A Twentieth Century Fund Study. Cambridge: Cambridge University Press.

Hessen, Robert. 1980. *Corporate Legitimacy and Social Responsibility.* Los Angeles: International Institute for Economic Research.

Hicks, John R. 1946. *Value and Capital.* 2d ed. Oxford: Clarendon.

———. 1977. *Economic Perspectives: Further Essays on Money and Growth.* Oxford: Clarendon.

———. 1983. *Classics and Moderns.* Oxford: Blackwell.

Hill, Dennis S. 1975. *Agricultural Insect Pests of the Tropics and Their Control.* Cambridge: Cambridge University Press.

Hirshleifer, Jack. 1985. "The Expanding Domain of Economics." *American Economic Review* 75, no. 6 (December): 53–68.

Hobbes, Thomas. [1651] 1934. *Leviathan.* Everyman's Library, no. 691. London and New York: J. M. Dent and E. P. Dutton.

Hoover, Herbert. 1958. *The Ordeal of Woodrow Wilson.* New York: McGraw-Hill.

Horton, Richard. 2000. "An Autopsy of Dr. Osler." *New York Review of Books* 47, no. 9 (May 25): 36–39.

Horwitz, Steven. 1995. "Feminist Economics: An Austrian Perspective." *Journal of Economic Methodology* 2, no. 2 (December): 259–79.

Horwitz, Tony. 1989. "Dinka Tribes Made Slaves in Sudan's Civil War." *Wall Street Journal* 213, no. 70 (April 11): A19.

Howells, William Dean. [1890] 1965. *A Hazard of New Fortunes.* New York, New American Library.

Hughes, Robert. 1987. *The Fatal Shore.* New York: Knopf.

Hulten, Charles R. 1985. "Measurement of Output and Productivity in the Service Sector." In *Managing the Service Economy: Prospects and Problems,* edited by Robert P. Inman, 127–30. Cambridge: Cambridge University Press.

Hunt, Albert R. 1999. "Clinton Strikes Out on Health Research." *Cape Cod Times* 63, no. 32 (February 6): A13.

Hunter, Robert W. 1999. *Spy Hunter: Inside the FBI Investigation of the Walker Espionage Case.* Annapolis: Naval Institute Press.

Hunter, Thomas B. 1999. "The Growing Threat of Modern Piracy."*U.S. Naval Institute Proceedings* 125, no. 7 (July): 72.

Hutchison, Terence W. 1996. "On the Relations between Philosophy and Economics, Part 1: Frontier Problems in an Era of Departmentalized and Internationalized 'Professionalism.'" *Journal of Economic Methodology* 3, no. 2 (December):187–214.

———. 1997. "On the Relations between Philosophy and Economics, Part 2: To What Kind of Philosophical Problems Should Economists Address Themselves?" *Journal of Economic Methodology* 4, no. 1 (June):127–51.

Hutton, Will. 1994. "Back by Popular Demand." *American Prospect* 16 (winter 1994): 50–57.

Ikenberry, David, Josef Lakonishok, and Theo Vermaelen. 1995. *Market Under-reaction to Open Market Share Repurchases.* NBER Working Papers, no. 4965. Cambridge, Mass.: National Bureau of Economic Research.

Ingrao, Bruno, and Giorgio Israel. 1990. *The Invisible Hand: Economic Equilibrium in the History of Science.* Translated by Ian McGilvray. Cambridge: MIT Press.

Inter-American Development Bank. 1997. "Indicators of Structural Reform." *Latin American Economic Policies* 1 (3d qtr.): 8.

Ito, Takatoshi. 1997. "Japan's Economy Needs Structural Change." *Finance and Development* 34, no. 2 (June):16–19.

Jacobs, Michael. 1991. *The Green Economy.* London: Pluto.

Jaffé, W., ed. 1965. *Correspondence of Léon Walras and Related Papers.* 3 vols., Amsterdam: North-Holland.

James, William. [1902] 1987. "The Varieties of Religious Experience." In *William James, Writings, 1902–1910.* 1–477. New York: Library of America.

———. [1907] 1987. "The Present Dilemma in Philosophy." In *William James, Writings, 1902–1910*, 487–504. New York: Library of America.

John Paul II. 1991. *On the Hundredth Anniversary of Rerum Novarum, Centesimus Annus.* Publication no. 436–38. Washington, D.C.: Office for Publishing and Promotion Services, United States Catholic Conference.

Johnson, Harry G. 1977. "Methodologies of Economics." In *The Organization and Retrieval of Economic Knowledge,* edited by Mark Perlman, 496–509. Boulder: Westview.

Johnson, S., L. J. Kotlikoff, and W. Samuelson. 1987. *Can People Compute? An Experimental Test of the Life-Cycle Consumption Model.* NBER Working Papers, no. 2183. Cambridge, Mass.: National Bureau of Economic Research.

Johnson, Simon, Rafael LaPorta, Florencio Lopez-de-Silanes, and Andrei Shleifer. 2000. "Tunneling." *American Economic Review* 90, no. 2 (May): 22–27.

Journal of Economic Perspectives. 1997. "Correspondence: AEA Dues and Ethics." 11, no. 3 (summer): 198.

Kagel, John H., and Dan Levin. 1991. "The Winner's Curse and Public Information in Common Value Auctions: Reply." *American Economic Review* 81, no. 1 (March): 362–69.

Kaldor, Nicholas. 1985. *Economics without Equilibrium.* Armonk, NY: M. E. Sharpe.

———. 1996. *Causes of Growth and Stagnation in the World Economy.* Cambridge: Cambridge University Press.

Kamarck, Andrew M. 1965. "Notes on Underemployment." In *Economic Development in Africa:* edited by E. F. Jackson. 78–85. Oxford: Basil Blackwell and Augustus M. Kelley.

———. 1970. "The Appraisal of Country Economic Performance." *Economic Development and Cultural Change* 18, no. 2 (January 1970): 153–65.

———. 1971. *The Economics of African Development.* Rev. ed. London and New York: Praeger.

———. 1976. *The Tropics and Economic Development.* Baltimore and London: Johns Hopkins University Press for the World Bank.

———. 1977. *Politica finanziaria degli alleati in Italia (luglio 1943, febbraio 1947).* Rome: Carecas.

———. 1982a. "McNamara's Bank." *Foreign Affairs* 60, no. 2 (spring): 951–53.

———. 1982b. "The Resources of Tropical Africa." *Daedalus* 111, no. 2 (spring): 149–64.

———. 1983. *Economics and the Real World.* Oxford: Blackwell.

———. 1986. "Donato Menichella: La Commissione di controllo alleata e l'IRI, l'ECA e la Banca d'Italia." In *Donato Menichella, Testimonianze e Studi Raccolti dalla Banca d'Italia.* 37–44. Roma-Bari: Editori Laterza.

———. 2000. "Slow Growth in Africa." *Journal of Economic Perspectives* 14, no. 2 (spring): 235–36.

———. 2001. *Economics for the Twenty-first Century.* Aldershot, U.K.: Ashgate.

Kaplan, Steven N. 1992. *Top Executive Rewards and Firm Performance: A Comparison of Japan and the United States.* NBER Working Papers, on. 4065. Cambridge, Mass.: National Bureau of Economic Research.

———. 1993. *The Evolution of Buyout Price and Financial Structure.* NBER Reprints, no. 1835. Cambridge, Mass.: National Bureau of Economic Research.

Katz, Lawrence F. 1986. *Efficiency Wage Theories: A Partial Evaluation.* NBER Working Papers, no. 1906. Cambridge, Mass.: National Bureau of Economic Research.

Kay, Neil M. 1995. "Alchian and 'the Alchian Thesis.'" *Journal of Economic Methodology* 2, no. 2: 281–86.

Keehn, E. B. 1997. "Organized Dependence: Politicians and Bureaucrats in Japan." In *The Vitality of Japan: Sources of National Strength and Weakness,* edited by Armand Clesse, Takashi Inoguchi, E. B. Keehn, and J. A. A. Stockwin, 131–48. Houndmills, U.K., and New York: Macmillan and St. Martin's.

Kempton, Murray. 1992. "A New Colonialism." *New York Review of Books* 39, no. 19 (November 19): 39.

Kendrick, John W. 1985. "Measurement of Output and Productivity in the Service Sector." In *Managing the Service Economy: Prospects and Problems,* edited by Robert P. Inman, 111–23. Cambridge: Cambridge University Press.

Kessler, Ronald C., Katherine A. McGonagle, Shanyang Zhao, Christopher B. Nelson, Michael Hughes, Suzann Eshleman, Hans-Ulrich Wittchen, Kenneth S. Kendler, 1994. "Lifetime and 12-month Prevalence of DSM-III-R Psychiatric Disorders in the United States: Results from the National Comorbidity Survey." *Archives of General Psychiatry.* 51, no. 1 (January): 8–19.

Keynes, John Maynard. 1925. "Alfred Marshall, 1842–1924." In *Memorials of Alfred Marshall,* edited by A. C. Pigou, 1–65. London: Macmillan.

———. 1930. *A Treatise on Money.* New York: Harcourt, Brace.

———. 1936. *The General Theory of Employment, Interest, and Money.* New York: Harcourt, Brace.

———. 1949. *Two Memoirs: Dr. Melchior: A Defeated Enemy and My Early Beliefs.* New York and London: Augustus M. Kelley and Rupert Hart-Davis.

———. 1951. *Essays in Biography.* New ed. New York: Horizon Press.

Kiely, Robert. 1991. 'White Swan, Gray Turtle." *Harvard Magazine* 93, no. 6 (July–August): 45–50.

Kindleberger, Charles P. 1965. *Economic Development.* 2d ed., New York: McGraw-Hill.

———. 1984. *A Financial History of Western Europe.* London: Allen and Unwin.

———. 1996. *World Economic Primacy, 1500 to 1990.* New York: Oxford University Press.

Kinsley, Michael. 1986. "How to Succeed in Academia by Really Trying." *Wall Street Journal* 208, no. 86 (October 30): 33.

Kirman, Alan. 1996. "Micro-foundations Built on Sand? A Review of Maarten Janssen's *Microfoundations: A Critical Inquiry. Journal of Economic Methodology* 3, no. 2 (December): 322–33.

Kirzner, Israel M. 1997. "Entrepreneurial Discovery and the Competitive Market Process: An Austrian Approach." *Journal of Economic Literature* 35 (March): 60–85.

Kitch, Edmund W., ed. 1983. "The Fire of Truth: A Remembrance of Law and Economics at Chicago, 1932–1970." *Journal of Law and Economics* 26 (April): 163–233.

Klamer, Arjo, and David Colander. 1990. *The Making of an Economist.* Boulder: Westview.

Korda, Michael. 1996. "Annals of Tycoonery: The Last Business Eccentric." *New Yorker* 72, no. 39 (December 16): 82–91.

Kornblut, Anne E. 1998. "McGovern Vows Revamp of Child Care." *Boston Globe* 253, no. 82 (March 23): B8.

Kramer, Jane. 1992. "Letter from Europe." *New Yorker* 68, no. 27 (September 21): 108–24.
Kreps, David M. 1997. "Economics: The Current Position." *Daedalus* 126, no. 1 (winter): 59–86.
Kuntz, Mary. 1985. "A Price on Your Head." *Forbes* 136, no. 7 (September 16): 92–93.
Kurkjian, Stephen. 1993. "Papers Show New Links between Ferber, Firm." *Boston Globe* 244, no. 170 (December 17): 1, 44.
Kuttner, Robert. 1998. *Everything for Sale: The Virtues and Limits of Markets.* New York: Knopf.
Kuznets, Simon. 1966. *Modern Economic Growth.* New Haven and London: Yale University Press.
———. 1971. *Economic Growth of Nations.* Cambridge: Belknap Press of Harvard University Press.
Lambert, Craig. 2000. "Deep Cravings." *Harvard Magazine* 102, no. 4 (April): 60–68.
Landes, David S. 1970. *The Unbound Prometheus: Technological Change And Industrial Development In Western Europe from 1750 to the Present.* Cambridge: At the University Press.
Langan, Fred. 1993. "Ban on Profits in Sperm, Embryos Urged in Canada." *Boston Globe* 244, no. 154 (December 1): 2.
La Porta, Rafael, Florencio Lopez-de-Silanes, Andrei Shleifer, and Robert Vishny. 1997. "Trust in Large Organizations." NBER Working Papers. no. 5864. Cambridge, Mass.: National Bureau of Economic Research.
la Repubblica. 1993. "La top ten delle tangenti." 18, no. 192 (August 22–23): 9.
Larsen, Ralph S. 2000. "Letter to Shareowners." In *Johnson and Johnson 1999 Annual Report: "Leading from Our Strengths".* New Brunswick, New Jersey: Johnson & Johnson.
Latham, Robert, ed. 1983. *The Diary of Samuel Pepys.* Vol. 19, *Companion.* Berkeley and Los Angeles: University of California Press.
Lavoie, Don. 1985. *National Economic Planning: What Is Left?* Washington, D.C.: Cato Institute.
Lawrence, Robert Z. 1993. "Japan's Different Trade Regime: An Analysis with Particular Reference to *Keiretsu.*" *Journal of Economic Perspectives* 7, no. 3 (summer): 3–19.
Lawson, Tony. 1995. "A Realist Perspective on Contemporary 'Economic Theory.'" *Journal of Economic Issues* 29, no. 1 (March): 1–32.
———. 1997. "Situated Rationality." *Journal of Economic Methodology* 4, no. 1 (June): 101–26.
Lazear, Edward P. 2000. "Economic Imperialism." *Quarterly Journal of Economics* 115, no. 1 (March): 99–146.
Lazonick, William. 1998. *The Japanese Financial Crisis, Corporate Governance, and Sustainable Prosperity.* Working Papers, no. 227. Annandale-on-Hudson, N.Y.: Jerome Levy Economics Institute.
Le Monde. 1997. "Les pays de l'OCDE adoptent une convention anti-corruption." [*The World.* "OECD countries adopt an anti-corruption convention"] (cinquante-troisième année) (16430) (24 novembre): 28.
Leontief, Wassily. 1982. Letter to the editor. *Science* 217 (July 9): 104–5.
Leroy, Stephen. 1989. "Efficient Capital Markets and Martingales." *Journal of Economic Literature* 28:1583–1621.

Le Roy Ladurie, Emmanuel. 1978. *Montaillau: the promised land of error.* Translation of Montaillou, village occitan de 1294 à 1324. New York: George Braziller.

Letiche, John M. 1987. Foreword to Amartya Sen, *On Ethics and Economics.* Oxford and New York: Blackwell.

Levy, Brian. 1997. "How Can States Foster Markets?" *Finance and Development* 34, no. 3 (September): 21–23.

Lewis, W. Arthur. 1955. *The Theory of Economic Growth.* London: Allen and Unwin.

Lichtenberg, Frank, and George Pushner. 1992. *Ownership Structure and Corporate Performance in Japan.* NBER Working Papers, no. 4092. Cambridge, Mass.: National Bureau of Economic Research.

Lind, Barry, and Charles R. Plott. 1991. "The Winner's Curse: Experiments with Buyers and with Sellers." *American Economic Review* 81, no. 1 (March): 335–46.

Lindbeck, A., and D. Snower. 1988. *The Insider-Outsider Theory of Employment and Unemployment.* Cambridge: MIT Press.

Linder, Stefan B. 1970. *The Harried Leisure Class.* New York: Columbia University Press.

Linebaugh, Peter. 1991. *The London Hanged: Crime and Civil Society in the Eighteenth Century.* New York and Cambridge: Cambridge University Press.

Lipman, Marvin M. 1996. "Office Visit: The Power of Placebos." *Consumer Reports on Health* 8, no. 2 (February): 23.

Livingstone, David. 1871. "Journey in Manyema Country." *East African Explorers,* selected and introduced by Charles Richards and James Place. London: Oxford University Press, 1960, pp. 86–88.

Loeb, Gerald M. [1935] 1996. *The Battle for Investment Survival.* New York: Wiley.

Loewenstein, George, and Richard H. Thaler. 1989. "Anomalies: Intertemporal Choice." *Journal of Economic Perspectives* 3, no. 4 (fall): 181–93.

Lowenstein, Roger. 1995a. *Buffett.* New York: Random House.

———. 1995b. "Intrinsic Value: Turner's Pay Deal Is a Lesson in Socialism." *Wall Street Journal* 226, no. 67 (October 5): C1.

Lublin, Joann S. 1996. "The Great Divide." *Wall Street Journal* 227, no. 72 (April 11): R1, 4.

Macaulay, Stewart. 1992. "Non-contractual Relations in Business." In *The Sociology of Economic Life,* edited by Mark Granovetter and Richard Swedberg, 265–83. Boulder: Westview.

Macaulay, Thomas Babington. 1833. "Samuel Johnson" and "Walpole's Letters to Sir Horace Mann." In *Essays, Historical and Literary, from the 'Edinburgh Review,'* 194–216. London: Ward, Lock.

Maddison, Angus. 1987. "Growth and Slowdown in Advanced Capitalist Economies: Techniques of Quantitative Assessment." *Journal of Economic Literature* 25 (June): 649–98.

Malabre, Alfred L., Jr., and Lindley H. Clark Jr. 1992. "Dubious Figures." *Wall Street Journal* 210, no. 31 (August 12): A1, 5.

Mankiw, N. Gregory. 1998. *Principles of Economics.* Fort Worth: Dryden Press and Harcourt Brace College Publishers.

———. 2000a. Review of *Monopolistic Competition and Macroeconomic Theory,* by Robert M. Solow. *American Economic Review* 38 (June): 426–27.

———. 2000b. "The Savers-Spenders Theory of Fiscal Policy." *American Economic Review* 90 no. 2 (May): 120–25.

Mansfield, Edwin. 1970. *Macroeconomics: Theory and Applications.* New York: Norton.
———. 1982. *Microeconomics: Theory and Applications.* 4th ed., abridged. New York: Norton.
Marais, Eugene N. 1947. *My Friends the Baboons.* 2d ed. London: Methuen.
Marcial, Gene G. 1998. "That Was Just the Warm-Up." *Business Week,* December 28, 151.
Marshall, Alfred. [1920] 1952. *Principles of Economics.* 8th ed. London: Macmillan.
Marshall, Matt. 1995. "Germany's Law on Inside Trading Brings a Conviction." *Wall Street Journal* 226, no. 35 (August 21): A5.
Maruna, David F., II. 1994. "Duty, Honor, and the Commission." *US Naval Institute Proceedings* 120, no. 6 (June): 36–38.
Matthews, R. C. O., and G. B. Stafford. 1982. *The Grants Economy and Collective Consumption.* New York: St. Martin's.
Maugham, Somerset. [1951] 1955. *The Complete Short Stories.* Vol. 2. London: Heinemann.
Maxwell, Kenneth. 1997. "Pirate Democracy." Review of *Under the Black Flag: The Romance and the Reality of Life among the Pirates,* by David Cordingly. *New York Review of Books* 44, no. 4 (March 6): 34–37.
Mayer, Martin. 1990. *The Greatest-Ever Bank Robbery: The Collapse of the Savings and Loan Industry.* New York: Scribner's.
Mayer, Thomas. 1993. *Truth versus Precision in Economics.* Aldershot, U.K., and Brookfield, Vt.: Edward Elgar.
———. 1999. "The Domain of Hypotheses and the Realism of Assumptions." *Journal of Economic Methodology* 6, no. 3 (November): 319–30.
McClelland, David C. 1961. *The Achieving Society.* Princeton: D. van Nostrand Company, Inc.
———, and David Burnham. 1976. "Power Is the Great Motivator." *Harvard Business Review* 54, no. 2 (March–April): 100–10.
McDonough, William J. 1997. "Asia and the World Economy." In *Federal Reserve Bank of New York, Eighty-Second Annual Report, for the Year Ended December 31, 1996,* 1–12. New York: Federal Reserve Bank.
McGinley, Laurie. 1993. "Lorenzo's Bid to Start Airline Is Set Back." *Wall Street Journal* 222, no. 50 (September 10): A5.
McKinnon, Ronald I. 1991. *The Order of Economic Liberalization: Financial Control in the Transition to a Market Economy.* Baltimore and London: Johns Hopkins University Press.
McPherson, Michael S. 1993. Review of *Thoughtful Economic Man: Essays on Rationality, Moral Rules, and Benevolence,* edited by J. Gay Tulip Meeks. *Journal of Economic Literature* 31 (December 1993): 1964–66.
McUsic, Molly. 1987. "U.S. Manufacturing: Any Cause for Alarm?." *New England Economic Review* (January–February): 3–15.
Medoff, James L., and Katharine G. Abraham. 1984. *Years of Service and Probability of Promotion.* NBER Working Papers, no. 1191. Cambridge, Mass.: National Bureau of Economic Research.
Meyer, Karl E. 1997. "Editorial Notebook: The Opium War's Secret History." *New York Times,* New England Edition, 146, no. 50837 (June 28): 22.
Michels, Robert. 1962. *Political Parties.* Glencoe, Ill.: Free Press.
Mill, John Stuart. 1892. *Principles of Political Economy.* 6th ed. London: Longman.

Miller, Edythe S. 1993. "The Economic Imagination and Public Policy: Orthodoxy Discovers the Corporation." *Journal of Economic Issues* 27, no. 4 (December): 1041–58.

Moore, Francis D. 1985. "Who Should Profit from the Care of Your Illness." *Harvard Magazine* 88, no. 2 (November–December): 45–54.

Morgenstern, Oskar. 1963. *On the Accuracy of Economic Observations.* Second Edition. Princeton, New Jersey: Princeton University Press.

Morita, Akio. 1993. "Toward A New World Economic Order." *Atlantic Monthly* 271, no. 6 (June): 88–98.

Morris, Betsy. 1987. "Big Spenders." *Wall Street Journal* 210, no. 22 (July 30): 1, 13.

Moulier, Philippe B. 1997. "Pirates? What Pirates? A Growing Problem the Shipping Industry Would Like to Ignore." *U.S.. News and World Report* 122, no. 24 (June 23): 33–34.

Mumford, Lewis. 1973. *The Condition of Man.* New York: Harcourt Brace Jovanovich.

Murphy, Jerome. 1993. "A Conversation with Jerome Murphy." *Harvard Gazette* 98, no. 31 (April 16): 5–6.

Myers, Milton L. 1983. *The Soul of Modern Economic Man: Ideas of Self-Interest, Thomas Hobbes to Adam Smith.* Chicago and London: University of Chicago Press.

Myrdal, Gunnar. 1968. *Asian Drama.* 3 vols. New York: Pantheon.

Nagel, Thomas [T.N.]. 1995. "Egoism, Psychological." In *The Oxford Companion to Philosophy,* edited by Ted Honderich, 220–21. Oxford: Oxford University Press.

Naik, Gautam. 1995. "Cellular Carriers Try New Tricks to Beat Bandits." B1, B6; "How Cellular Pirates Have Thwarted Efforts to Outsmart Them." B2 *Wall Street Journal* 225, no. 52 (March 16).

———. 1996. "U.S., Using E-Mail Tap, Charges Three with Operating Cellular-Fraud Ring." *Wall Street Journal* 227, no. 2 (January 2): 16.

New York State Organized Crime Task Force. 1990. *Corruption and Racketeering in the New York City Construction Industry.* New York and London: New York University Press.

New York Times. 1997. "Slave Trade in Africa Highlighted by Arrests" *New York Times,* New England edition, 146, no. 50,580 (August 10): 9.

Niebuhr, Reinhold. 1986. *The Essential Reinhold Niebuhr: Selected Essays and Addresses.* Edited by Robert McAfee Brown. New Haven and London: Yale University Press.

Norgaard, Richard. 1992. *Sustainability and the Economics of Assuring Assets for Future Generations.* Washington, D.C.: World Bank.

Norris, Floyd. 1998. "Q. Who Lost in Continental Airlines Deal?" *New York Times* 147, no. 51,051 (January 28): D1, D6.

Okun, Arthur M. 1981. *Prices and Quantities: A Macroeconomic Analysis.* Washington, D.C.: Brookings Institution.

Oliver, Roland. 1991. *The African Experience.* New York: HarperCollins.

Olson, Mancur, Jr. 1996. "Big Bills Left on the Sidewalk: Why Some Nations Are Rich and Others Poor."*Journal of Economic Perspectives* 10, no. 2 (spring): 3–24.

O'Neill, Gerard, Dick Lehr, and Kevin Cullen. 1995. "New Team, Tactics Hastened Whitey Bulger's Fall." *Boston Sunday Globe* 247, no. 64 (March 5): 1, 24.

Ori, Pier D'Amiano, and Giovanni Perich. 1978. *Talleyrand.* Milano: Rusconi.

Osterman, Paul, ed. 1984. *Internal Labor Markets.* Cambridge and London: MIT Press.

Ostrom, Elinor. 1990. *Governing the Commons: The Evolution of Institutions for Collective Action.* Cambridge: Cambridge University Press.
Ostrom, Elinor, and Roy Gardner. 1993. "Coping with Asymmetries in the Commons: Self-Governing Irrigation Systems Can Work." *Journal of Economic Perspectives* 7, no. 4 (fall 1993): 93–112.
Paddock, William, and Elizabeth Paddock. 1973. *We Don't Know How: An Independent Audit of What They Call Success in Foreign Assistance.* Ames: Iowa State University Press.
Page, John, et al. 1993. *The East Asian Miracle: Economic Growth and Public Policy.* New York: Oxford University Press.
Pareto, Vilfredo. 1971. *Manual of Political Economy.* Translated by Ann S. Schwier. New York: A. M. Kelly.
Parkinson, C. Northcote. 1958. *Parkinson's Law.* London: John Murray.
———. 1962. *In-Laws and Outlaws.* London: John Murray.
Patucchi, Marco. 1993. "Capitalismo tra resole e Far West." *la Repubblica* 18, no. 187 (August 17): 39.
Pearl, Daniel. 1994. "Lorenzo Bid to Reenter Airline Business Is Rejected by Transportation Officials." *Wall Street Journal* 223, no. 67 (April 6): A3.
Pearce, David W. 1981. *The Dictionary of Modern Economics.* Cambridge: MIT Press.
Persky, Joseph. 1997. "Retrospectives: Classical Family Values, Ending the Poor Laws as They Knew Them." *Journal of Economic Perspectives* 11, no. 1 (winter): 179–89.
Phelps, Edmund S. 1981. "Okun's Micro-Macro System: A Review Article." *Journal of Economic Literature* 19 (September): 1065–73.
Pines, Shlomo. 1963. Introduction to *Moses Maimonides, The Guide to the Perplexed.* Chicago: University of Chicago Press.
Pistor, Katharina and Jeffrey D. Sachs. 1998. "The Rule of Law and Economic Reform in Russia." *HIID research Review* 11, no. 2 (Winter/Spring): 2, 6.
Polinsky, A. Mitchell, and Steven Shavell. 2000. "The Economic Theory of Public Enforcement of Law." *Journal of Economic Literature* 38 (March): 45–76.
Pool, Daniel. 1993. *What Jane Austen Ate and Charles Dickens Knew: From Fox Hunting to Whist, the Facts of Daily Life in Nineteenth-Century England.* New York: Simon and Schuster.
Portney, Paul R. 1994. "The Contingent Valuation Debate: Why Economists Should Care." *Journal of Economic Perspectives* 8, no. 4 (fall): 3–17.
Posner, Richard A. 1993. "Nobel Laureate Ronald Coase and Methodology." *Journal of Economic Perspectives* 7, no. 4 (fall): 195–210.
Powell, Alvin. 1998. "Taking the Pulse: Cutler Monitors the Vital Signs of U.S. Health Care System." *Harvard University Gazette* 93, no. 18 (February 12): 3–4.
———. 1999. "Study: Parents' Presence Helps Heal Children." *Harvard University Gazette* 95, no. 8 (November 4): 1, 6.
Pradhan, Sanjay. 1997. "Improving the State's Institutional Capability." *Finance and Development* 34, no. 3 (September): 24–27.
Protzman, Ferdinand. 1991. "Germany: Insider Trading Scandal Grows." *New York Times* 140, no. 48670 (July 23): D6.
Quine, W. V. 1987. *Quiddities: An Intermittently Philosophical Dictionary.* Cambridge: Belknap Press of Harvard University Press.
Raab, Selwyn. 1997a. "Battling Mob, New York Cuts Hauling Rates for Garbage." *New York Times,* New England Edition, 146, no. 50743 (March 26): A25.

———. 1997b. "Testimony to Start in Trash Carting Trial." *New York Times,* New England Edition 146, no. 50805 (May 27): A18.

———. 1997c. "Two Convicted as Masterminds of Mob's Hold on Private Garbage Collection." *New York Times,* New England Edition, 147, no. 50953 (October 22): A25.

Rabin, Matthew. 1998. "Psychology and Economics." *Journal of Economic Literature* 36 (March): 11–46.

Ram, Rati. 1997. "Tropics and Economic Development: An Empirical Investigation." *World Development* 25:1443–52.

———. 1999a. "Tropics, Income, and School Life Expectancy: An Intercountry Study." *Economics of Education Review* 18 (1999): 253–58.

———. 1999b. "Tropics and Income: A Longitudinal Study of the U. S. States." *Review of Income and Wealth* 45, no. 3 (September): 1–6.

Rappaport, Steven. 1996. "Abstraction and Unrealistic Assumptions in Economics." *Journal of Economic Methodology* 3, no. 2 (December): 215–36.

Reed, Christopher. 1999. "The Damn'd South Sea." *Harvard Magazine.* 101, no. 5 (May–June): 36–42.

Regan, Donald T. 1988 *For the Record: From Wall Street to Washington.* San Diego: Harcourt Brace Jovanovich.

Reich, Robert B. 1991. *The Work of Nations: Preparing Ourselves for 21st Century Capitalism.* New York: Knopf.

Reingold, Jennifer, with Brad Wolverton. 1998. "When Bosses Get Rich from Selling the Company." *Business Week,* March 30, 32–33.

Reuters. 1993a. "Bonn Tries to Fire Up Engine."*International Herald Tribune,* no. 34,367 (August 27): 5.

———. 1993b. "Report Names Kanemaru Biggest Tax Evader in '92." *Wall Street Journal* 221, no. 120 (June 22): A11.

———. 1997. "Brokerage Scandal Widens in Japan." *New York Times,* New England Edition, 147, no. 50926 (September 25): D2.

Ridley, Matt. 1997. *The Origins of Virtue: Human Instincts and the Evolution of Cooperation.* New York: Viking.

Robbins, Lionel. 1954. *The Economist in the Twentieth Century and Other Lectures in Political Economy.* London: Macmillan; New York: St. Martin's Press.

———. 1981. "Economics and Political Economy," *AEA Papers and Proceedings.* 71, no. 2 (May): 1–10.

Robinson, Joan. 1964. *Economic Philosophy.* Harmondsworth, U.K.: Penguin Books.

Romains, Jules. 1938. *Les Hommes de Bonne Volonté.* Vol. 16: *Verdun.* Paris: Flammarion.

Rosen, Sherwin. 1997. "Austrian and Neoclassical Economics: Any Gains from Trade?" *Journal of Economic Perspectives.* 11, no. 4 (fall): 139–52.

Rouner, Leroy S. 1999. "Civil Religion, Cultural Diversity, and American Civilization." *Key Reporter* 64, no. 3 (spring): 1, 3–6.

Routh, Guy. 1984. *Economics: An Alternative Text.* London: Macmillan.

Rowley, Charles K. 1993. *Liberty and the State.* Shaftesbury Papers, no. 4. Aldershot, U.K., and Brookfield, Vt.: Edward Elgar.

Ruhm, Christopher. 1998. "The Well-Being of Children." *NBER Reporter* (summer): 27–28.

Runde, Jochen, and Paul Anand. 1997. Introduction to special issue on rationality and methodology. *Journal of Economic Methodology* 4, no. 1 (June): 1–21.

Russell, Thomas. 1997. "The Rationality Hypothesis in Economics: From Wall Street to Main Street." *Journal of Economic Methodology* 4, no. 1 (June): 83–100.

Ryback, Timothy W. 1998. "The Man Who Swallowed Chrysler." *New Yorker*, November 16, 80–89.

Sachs, Jeffrey D., and Andrew M. Warner. 1997. "Fundamental Sources of Long-Run Growth." *American Economic Review* 87, no. 2 (May): 184–88.

Sachs, Jeffrey D., and Wing Thye Woo. 1999. "The Asian Financial Crisis: What Happened and What Is to Be Done." Manuscript.

Saffran, Bernard. 1996. "Recommendations for Further Reading." *Journal of Economic Perspectives* 10, no. 3 (summer): 181–88.

Sagan, Carl, and Ann Druyan. 1992. *Shadows of Forgotten Ancestors.* New York: Random House.

Sala-I-Martin, Xavier X. 1997. "I Just Ran Two Million Regressions." *American Economic Review* 87, no. 2 (May): 178–83.

Samuels, David. 1996. "Presidential Shrimp: Bob Dole Caters the Political Hors d'Oeuvres." *Harper's Magazine* 292, no. 1750 (March): 45–52.

Samuelson, Paul Anthony. [1947] 1975. *Foundations of Economic Analysis.* Cambridge and London: Harvard University Press.

———. 1964. "A Brief Post-Keynesian Survey." In *Keynes's General Theory: Reports of Three Decades*, edited by R. Lekachman, 331–47. New York: St. Martin's Press, London: Macmillan.

———. 1989. "Robert Solow: An Affectionate Portrait." *Journal of Economic Perspectives* 3, no. 3 (summer): 91–97.

Sanger, David E. 1997. "29 Nations Agree to a Bribery Ban." *New York Times*, New England Edition, 146, no. 50802 (May 24): 1, 38.

Saxenian, Anna Lee. 1994. *Regional Advantage: Culture and Competition in Silicon Valley and Route 128.* Cambridge: Harvard University Press.

Schelling, Thomas. 1960. *The Strategy of Conflict.* Cambridge: Harvard University Press.

Schlesinger, Jacob M., and Masayoshi Kanabayashi. 1993. "Shimizu Chairman's Arrest Weakens Often Corrupt Basis of Japan Economy." *Wall Street Journal* 222, no. 58 (September 22): A14.

Schmid, A. Allan. 1994. Review of *A Framework for Cognitive Economics*, by Roger A. McCain." *Journal of Economic Issues* 28, no. 1 (March): 261–64.

Schumpeter, Joseph A. [1912] 1934. The *Theory of Economic Development: An Inquiry into Profits, Capital, Credit, Interest, and the Business Cycle.* Harvard Economic Studies, no. 46. Cambridge,: Harvard University Press.

———. [1942] 1947. *Capitalism, Socialism, and Democracy.* 2d ed. New York and London: Harpers and Allen and Unwin.

———. 1951a. *Essays.* Edited by Richard V. Clemence. Cambridge, Mass.: Addison-Wesley.

———. 1951b. *Ten Great Economists. From Marx to Keynes.* New York: Oxford University Press.

———. 1954. *History of Economic Analysis.* Edited by Elizabeth Boody Schumpeter. New York: Oxford University Press.

Schwartz, Hugh. 1998. *Rationality Gone Awry? Decision Making Inconsistent with Economic and Financial Theory.* Westport, Conn., and London: Praeger.

Seabright, Paul. 1993. "Managing Local Commons: Theoretical Issues in Incentive Design." *Journal of Economic Perspectives* 7, no. 4 (fall 1993): 113–34.
Seabrook, John. 1994. "A Reporter at Large: E-Mail from Bill." *New Yorker,* January 10, 48–61.
Seater, John J. 1993. "Ricardian Equivalence (Sic!)." *Journal of Economic Literature* 31 (March): 142–90.
Seers, Dudley. 1967. "The Limitations of the Special Case." In *The Teaching of Development Economics,* edited by Kurt Martin and John Knapp, 1–27. Chicago: Aldine.
Sen, Amartya K. 1977. "Rational Fools: A Critique of the Behavioral Foundations of Economic Theory." *Philosophy and Public Affairs* 6, no. 4: 317–44.
———. 1987. *On Ethics and Economics.* Oxford and New York: Blackwell.
———. 1991. "Economic Methodology, Heterogeneity and Relevance." *Methodus.* 3, no. 1: 67–80.
———. 1995. "Rationality and Social Choice." *American Economic Review* 85, no. 1 (March): 1–24.
Sesit, Michael R., and Laura Jereski. 1994. "Malaysia's Bank Negara Plays Hard Ball with Traders." *Wall Street Journal* 223, no. 19 (January 27): C1, C21.
Seth, Vikram. 1994. *A Suitable Boy.* New York: HarperCollins.
Shapiro, Carl, and Joseph Stiglitz. 1984. "Equilibrium Unemployment as a Discipline Device." *American Economic Review* 74:433–44.
Shapiro, Robert. 1992. *The Human Blueprint: The Race to Unlock the Secrets of Our Genetic Code.* New York: Bantam.
Sharpe, Rochelle. 1994. "To Boost IQs, Aid Is Needed in First Three Years." *Wall Street Journal* 223, no. 71 (April 12): B1, B10.
Shattuck, Roger. 1996. "Emily Dickinson's Banquet of Abstemiousness." *New York Review of Books* 43, no. 8 (June 20): 55–59.
Shenon, Philip. 1985. "The Mobsters Who Lurk behind the Corporate Veil." *New York Times* 134 (December 8): 4E.
Siconolfi, Michael, and Laurie P. Cohen. 1991. "Sullied Solly: How Salomon's Hubris and a Quiet U.S. Trap Led to the Downfall." *Wall Street Journal* 218, no. 35 (August 19): A1, A4.
Silvestre, Joaquim. 1993. "The Market-Power Foundations of Macroeconomic Policy." *Journal of Economic Literature* 31 (March 1993): 105–41.
Simon, Herbert A. 1991. "Organizations and Markets." *Journal of Economic Perspectives* 5, no. 2 (spring): 25–44.
Simons, Katerina, and Joanna Stavins. 1998. "Has Antitrust Policy in Banking Become Obsolete?" *New England Economic Review* (March–April): 13–16.
Sissman, L. E. 1997. "The April Almanac. 25 Years Ago." *Atlantic Monthly* 279, no. 4 (April): 16.
Smart, Molly. 1994. "Gaijin." *The World: Journal of the Unitarian Universalist Association* 8, no. 3 (May–June): 30–31.
Smith, Adam. [1776] 1937. *The Wealth of Nations.* New York: Modern Library.
———. 1976. *The Theory of Moral Sentiments.* Edited by David D. Raphael and Alec L. Macfie. London: Oxford University Press.
Smith, Randall. 1992. "The Big Casino: How Currency Traders Play for High Stakes Against Central Banks." *Wall Street Journal* 22, no. 57 (September 18): A1, A7.
Smith, Vernon L. 1982. "Microeconomic Systems as an Experimental Science." *American Economic Review* 72, no. 5 (December): 923–55.

———. 1994. "Economics in the Laboratory." *Journal of Economic Perspectives* 8, no. 1 (winter): 113–31.
Solow, Robert M. 1997a. "It Ain't the Things You Don't Know That Hurt You, It's the Things You Know That Ain't So." *American Economic Review* 87, no. 2 (May): 107–8.
———. 1997b. "How Did Economics Get That Way and What Way Did It Get?" *Daedalus* (winter): 39–58.
———. 1998. *Monopolistic Competition and Macroeconomic Theory.* Cambridge: Cambridge University Press.
Specter, Michael. 1997. "In Modern Russia, a Medieval Witch Hunt." *New York Times,* New England Edition, 146, no. 50753 (April 5): 1, 4.
Spring, William J. 1987. "Youth Unemployment and the Transition from School to Work: Programs in Boston, Frankfurt, and London." *New England Economic Review* (March–April): 3–16.
Staddon, John. 1995. "On Responsibility and Punishment." *Atlantic Monthly* 275, no. 2 (February): 88–94.
Stanfield, J. Ron. 1983. "Institutional Analysis: Toward Progress in Economic Science." In *Why Economics Is Not Yet a Science,* edited by Alfred S. Eichner, 187–204. Armonk, N.Y.: M. E. Sharpe.
Stanley, Henry M. 1872. *How I Found Livingstone.* London: Sampson Low.
Stavro, Barry. 1985. "A House Undivided." *Forbes* 136, no. 6 (September 9): 36, 40.
Stein, Jeremy C. 1991. "What Went Wrong with the LBO Boom:, *Wall Street Journal* 217, no. 119 (June 19): A12.
Stendhal. [1827]. 1991. *Passeggiate Romane. Bari: Storia e Memoriae, Editori Laterza.* Translated from the French by Marco Cesarini Sforza. Bari: Editori Laterza.
Stéphane, Roger. 1984. *André Malraux: Entretiens et précisions.* Paris: Gallimard.
Sterngold, James. 1991. "2 Top Nomura Officials Quit In Effort to Curb Scandal." *New York Times* 140, no. 48670 (July 23): D1, 18.
Stevenson, Glenn C. 1991. *Common Property Economics: A General Theory and Land Use Applications.* Cambridge: Cambridge University Press.
Stewart, James B. 1992. *Den of Thieves.* New York: Simon and Schuster.
———. 1993. "Annals of Law: Michael Milken's Biggest Deal." *New Yorker,* March 8, 58–71.
Stigler, George J. 1982. "Do Economists Matter?" In *The Economist as Preacher,* edited by George J. Stigler, 54–67. Oxford: Blackwell.
———. 1988. *Memoirs of an Unregulated Economist.* New York: Basic Books.
Stiglitz, Joseph E. 1983. "Samuelson and Neoclassical Economics." *Journal of Economic Literature* 21, no. 3 (September): 997–99.
———. 1991. "Symposium on Organizations and Economics." *Journal of Economic Perspectives* 5, no. 2 (spring): 15–24.
———. 1992. "Another Century of Economic Science." In *The Future of Economics,* edited by John D. Hey, 134–41. Oxford and Cambridge, Mass.: Blackwell.
———. 1998. "Distinguished Lecture on Economics in Government: The Private Uses of Public Interests—Incentives and Institutions." *Journal of Economic Perspectives* 12, no. 2 (spring): 3–22.
———. 2000. "The Contributions of the Economics of Information to Twentieth Century Economics." *Quarterly Journal of Economics* 115, no. 4 (November): 1441–78.

Stille, Alexander. 1999. "Palermo: The Photography of Death." *New York Review of Books* 46, no. 12 (July 15): 49–52.

Stoehr, Kevin L. 1998. "Twentieth World Congress of Philosophy: A Historical Meeting of the Minds." *Humanist* 58, no. 2 (March–April): 31–33.

Stolper, Wolfgang F. 1968. "Schumpeter, Joseph A.." In *International Encyclopedia of the Social Sciences*, 67–72. New York: Macmillan and Free Press.

Streeten, Paul. 1972. *The Frontiers of Development Studies.* New York: Wiley.

———. 1986. "Aerial Roots." *Banca Nazionale del Lavoro Quarterly Review* 157 (June): 135–59.

———. 1997. "Contemporary Economics: A Critique." In *Zukuntsfähige Entwicklung, Herausforderungen an Wissenschaft und Politik, Festrschrift für Udo E. Simonis zum 60. Geburtstag*, edited by Frank Biermann, Sebastian Büttner, and Carsten Helm, 33–52. Berlin: Edition Sigma.

Sugden, Robert. 1989. "Spontaneous Order." *Journal of Economic Perspectives* 3, no. 4 (fall): 85–97.

———. 2000. "Credible Worlds: The Status of Theoretical Models in Economics." *Journal of Economic Methodology* 7, no. 1 (March): 1–31.

Summers, Lawrence H. 2000. "International Financial Crises: Causes, Prevention, and Cures." *American Economic Review* 90, no. 2 (May): 1–16.

Sundrum, R. M. 1983. *Development Economics: A Framework for Analysis and Policy.* New York: Wiley.

Tanzi, Vito, and L. Schuknecht. 1995. *The Growth of Government and the Reform of the State in Industrial Countries.* Washington, D.C.: International Monetary Fund.

Taylor, John B. 2000. "Teaching Modern Macroeconomics at the Principles Level." *American Economic Review* 90, no. 2 (May): 90–94.

Taylor, Lance. 1993. Review of *The Order of Economic Liberalization: Financial Control in the Transition to a Market Economy*, by Ronald I. McKinnon. *Journal of Economic Literature* 31 (March): 279–80.

Tevlin, Stacey. 1996. "CEO Incentive Contracts, Monitoring Costs, and Corporate Performance." *New England Economic Review* (January–February): 39–50.

Teoh, Siew Hong, T. J. Wong and Gita Rao. 1994. *Incentives and Opportunities for Earnings Management in IPOs and Earnings Management and the Long-term Market Performance of IPOs.* Los Angeles: University of California at Los Angeles.

Thaler, Richard H. 1988. "Anomalies: the Winner's Curse." *Journal of Economic Perspectives* 2, no. 1 (winter): 191–202.

———. 1991. *Quasi Rational Economics.* New York: Sage Foundation.

———. 1992. *The Winner's Curse: Paradoxes and Anomalies of Economic Life.* New York and Toronto: Free Press and Macmillan.

Theil, Henri, and Dongling Chen. 1995. "The Equatorial Grand Canyon." *De Economist* 143, no. 3: 317–27.

———, in association with Dongling Chen, Kenneth Clements, and Charles Moss. 1996. *Studies in Global Econometrics.* Dodrecht: Kluwer.

Thomas, Lewis. 1980. "On the Uncertainty of Science." *Harvard Magazine* 83, no. 1 (September–October): 19–22.

Thomas, Michael M. 1990. "Greed." *New York Review of Books* 37, no. 5 (March 29): 3–5.

Thurow, Lester C. 1983. *Dangerous Currents: The State of Economics.* New York: Random House.

Titmuss, Richard. 1997. *The Gift Relationship: From Human Blood to Social Policy.* Rev. ed. New York: New Press.
Tobin, James. 1987. *Policies for Prosperity: Essays in a Keynesian Mode.* Cambridge: MIT Press.
———. 1992. "An Old Keynesian Counterattack." *Eastern Economic Journal,* 18, no. 4 (fall): 387–400.
Train, John. 1994. "Going into Wall Street." *Harvard Magazine* 96, no. 5 (May–June): 22–23.
Tribe, Keith. 1999. "Adam Smith: Critical Theorist?" *Journal of Economic Literature* 37 (June): 609–32.
Truell, Peter, and Larry Gurwin. 1992. *BCCI.* New York: Houghton Mifflin.
Tuchman, Barbara W. 1984. *The March of Folly from Troy to Vietnam.* New York: Knopf.
Tullock, Gordon. 1993. *Rent Seeking.* The Shaftesbury Papers, 2. Aldershot, England: Edward Elgar.
Turnbull, Colin. 1972. *The Mountain People.* New York: Simon and Schuster.
Tversky, Amos, and Daniel Kahneman. 1981. "The Framing of Decisions and the Psychology of Choice." *Science* 211:453–58.
Tversky, Amos, and Richard H. Thaler. 1990. "Anomalies: Preference Reversals." *Journal of Economic Perspectives* 4, no. 2 (spring): 201–11.
United Nations. 1971. *Basic Principles of the System of Balances of the National Economy.* Studies in Methods, series F, no. 17. New York: Department of Economic and Social Affairs, Statistical Office, United Nations.
U.S. Department of Commerce, Economics and Statistics Administration, Bureau of Economic Analysis. 1992. *Business Statistics, 1963–91.* 27th ed. Washington, D.C.: Government Printing Office.
Urquhart, Brian. 1987. *A Life in Peace and War.* New York: Harper and Row.
van Eeghen, Piet-Hein. 1996. "Towards a Methodology of Tendencies." *Journal of Economic Methodology* 3, no. 2 (December): 261–84.
Vernon, Raymond. 1971. *Sovereignty at Bay: The Multinational Spread of U.S. Enterprises.* New York, London: Basic Books.
Vickers, Douglas. 1995. *The Tyranny of the Market; A Critique of Theoretical Foundations.* Ann Arbor: University of Michigan Press.
———. 1991. *Essays on the Intellectual History of Economics.* Edited by Douglas A. Irwin. Princeton: Princeton University Press.
von Neumann, John. 1963. "The General and Logical Theory of Automata." In *Design of Computers, Theory of Automata, and Numerical Analysis,* 288–323. Vol. 5 of *Collected Works.* Oxford: Pergamon Press.
von Neumann, John, and H. H. Goldstine. 1963. "Numerical Inverting of Matrices of High Order." In *Design of Computers, Theory of Automata, and Numerical Analysis,* 479–572. Vol. 5 of *Collected Works.* Oxford: Pergamon Press.
Wagner, Richard E. 1997. "Choice, Exchange, and Public Finance." *American Economic Review* 87, no. 2 (May): 160–63.
Walcott, John. 1987. "War of the Spies." *Wall Street Journal* 210, no. 106 (November 27): 1, 7.
Waldman, Michael. 1990. *Who Robbed America? A Citizen's Guide to the S and L Scandal.* New York: Random House.
Waldman, Peter, and Brenton R. Schlender. 1987. "Falling Chips." *Wall Street Journal* 209, no. 32 (February 17): 1, 24.

Waldrop, M. Mitchell. 1992. *Complexity.* New York: Simon and Schuster.

Wall Street Journal. 1994. "Damages Estimated at up to $250 Million in Treasury Squeeze." 223, no. 72 (April 13): C12.

———. 1995. "In a Cost-Cutting Era, Many CEOs Enjoy Imperial Perks." 225, no. 45 (March 7): B1, B10.

———. 1996. "The Boss's Pay: The Wall Street Journal/William M. Mercer 1995 CEO Compensation Survey." 227, no. 72 (April 11): R15–17.

Walras, Léon. 1896. *Eléments d'économie politique pure.* 3d ed. Lausanne: Corbaz.

———. 1965. *Correspondence of Léon Walras and Related Papers.* Edited by W. Jaffé. 3 vols. Amsterdam: North-Holland.

Warsh, David. 1984. *The Idea of Economic Complexity.* New York: Viking.

———. 1989. "Economic Principals: Where the Pink Slip Is Only an Undergarment." *Boston Globe* 235 (January 8): 75, 79.

Webb, Susan. 1995. "Bowling Leagues: Answer to Good Government." *John F. Kennedy School of Government Bulletin* (summer 1995): 10–11.

Weber, Max. 1958. *The Protestant Ethic and the Spirit of Capitalism.* Translated from the German by Talcott Parsons. New York: Charles Scribner's Sons.

Weiermair, Klaus. 1986. "On the Economics of Institutional Change: An Institutional Change in Economics?" *Journal of Economic Issues* 20, no. 2 (June): 571–82.

Weinstein, Michael M. 2000. "Students Seek Some Reality amid the Math of Economics." *Items and issues* 1, no. 1 (winter): 1–3.

Weintraub, E. Roy. 1983. "On the Existence of a Competitive Equilibrium: 1930–1954." *Journal of Economic Literature* 41, no. 1 (March): 1–39.

Weithman, Paul J. 1989. "Sex and Sin." *New York Review of Books* 35, no. 10 (June 15): 61.

Welch, John F., Jr. 1994. "To Our Share Owners." *1993 Annual Report,* 1–5. General Electric Company.

Westphal, Larry. 1990. "Industrial Policy in an Export-Propelled Economy: Lessons from South Korea's Experience." *Journal of Economic Perspectives* 4, no. 3 (summer): 41–59.

Whitehead, Alfred North. [1933] 1954. *Adventures of Ideas.* New York: Macmillan.

Wiener, Martin. 1981. *English Culture and the Decline of the Industrial Spirit.* Harmonsworth, U.K.: Penguin.

Wiener, Norbert. 1964. *God and Golem, Inc.: A Comment on Certain Points where Cybernetics Impinges on Religion.* Cambridge: MIT Press; London: Chapman and Hall.

Wiles, Peter. 1983. "Ideology, Methodology, and Neoclassical Economics." In *Why Economics Is Not Yet a Science,* edited by Alfred S. Eichner, 61–89. Armonk, N.Y.: M. E. Sharpe.

Williams, Bernard. 1985. *Ethics and the Limits of Philosophy.* Cambridge: Harvard University Press.

Williamson, Jeffrey G. 1991. "Productivity and American Leadership: A Review Article." *Journal of Economic Literature* 29 (March): 51–68.

Williamson, Oliver E. 1996. *The Mechanism of Governance.* New York and Oxford: Oxford University Press.

Willoughby, Jack. 1985. "The Human Factor." *Forbes* 136, no. 1 (July 1): 36.

Wilson, Edward O. 1992. *The Biodiversity of Life.* New York and London: Norton.

Wilson, James Q. 1993. *The Moral Sense.* New York and Toronto: Free Press and Macmillan.

———, and Richard J Herrnstein. 1985. *Crime and Human Nature.* New York: Simon and Schuster.

Wired. 1995. "Fast, Cheap, and Very Polite." 3, no. 12 (December): 49.

Woo, Henry K. H. 1986. *What's Wrong with Formalization in Economics: An Epistemological Critique.* Hong Kong and Newark, Calif.: Victoria Press.

World Bank. 1993. *Getting Results: The World Bank's Agenda for Improving Development Effectiveness.* Washington, D.C.: World Bank.

World Health Organization. 1999. *World Health Report 1999.* Geneva: World Health Organization.

Wren, Christopher S. 1997. "UN Report Says Tens of Millions Use Illicit Drugs." *New York Times,* New England Edition, 146, no. 50835 (June 26): A12.

WuDunn, Sheryl. 1997. "Scandal Stains Nomura, but Will It Stick?"*New York Times,* New England Edition, 146, no. 50807 (May 29): D1–2.

Xiao-huang Yin. 1994. "China's Gilded Age." *Atlantic Monthly* 273, no. 4 (April): 42–53.

Young, Allyn A. 1928. "Increasing Returns and Economic Progress." *Economic Journal* 38 (December): 527–42.

Zachary, G. Pascal. 1997. "The Outlook: Anticorruption Drive Starts to Show Results." *Wall Street Journal* 229, no. 18 (January 27): A1.

Zagorin, Adam. 1994. "The Sins of a Sainted Bank." *Time* 144, no. 8 (August 22): 54–55.

Zakaria, Fareed. 1994. "Culture Is Destiny, A Conversation with Lee Kuan Yew." *Foreign Affairs* 73, no. 2 (March–April): 109–26.

Zampaglione, Arturo. 1993. "Chicago: La Waterloo di Raul." *la Repubblica* 18, no. 184 (August 13): 7.

Zhilin, Aleksandr. 1995. "Criminal Financial Dealings Dramatically Increased in Russia." *Transition: The Newsletter about Reforming Economies* 6, nos. 11–12 (November–December): 9–10.

Zinman, John. 1978. *Reliable Knowledge: An Exploration of the Grounds for Belief in Science.* Cambridge: Cambridge University Press.

Zuckerman, Mortimer B. 1998. "A Second American Century." *Foreign Affairs* 77, no. 3 (May–June): 18–31.

About the Author

Andrew Martin Kamarck is the retired director of the World Bank Institute and the founding director of the bank's economics complex.

Born in upstate New York, he was educated at Harvard University, receiving an S.B. in economics (summa cum laude), M.A. in public administration, and Ph.D. in political economy and government. He also worked for a year for the CIO Textile Workers Organizing Committee.

In 1939, Kamarck joined the International Section of the Federal Reserve Board. At the outbreak of World War II, because of his peculiar qualifications (economics, a reserve commission, and reading knowledge of German), he was borrowed by the Secretary of the Treasury to follow war developments for him. After America's entrance into the war, Kamarck was called to active duty and became an instructor at the Field Artillery School.

In 1943, Kamarck was posted to the Allied Control Commission for Italy. He supervised the Banca d'Italia in southern Italy and then, in Rome, the Instituto per Ia ricostruzione industriale, which controls much of Italian finance and industry. In December 1944, he was released from the army, given the assimilated rank of lieutenant colonel, and assigned as chief of U.S. financial intelligence in Germany. In Berlin, he became deputy director of the Control Council's U.S. Finance Division and U.S. deputy on the Allied Finance Directorate for Germany.

Back at the Treasury in 1946, Kamarck chaired the Staff Committee for the cabinet-level National Advisory Council for International Monetary and Financial Problems. This committee set the financial, fiscal, foreign exchange, and monetary policy guidelines for the Marshall Plan. The final estimates of U.S. aid were coordinated by a State and Treasury committee, which he chaired.

Following two years in Italy as U.S. Treasury representative, chief of the Marshall Mission's Finance Division, and financial attaché to the embassy, Kamarck returned to the United States in 1950 and joined the World Bank as an economic adviser for Europe, Australasia, and Africa. In 1964–65, he was Regents Professor at UCLA and then returned to the bank as director of a new Economics Department. In 1971, he was research associate at the Harvard Center of International Affairs, returning to the bank as director of the Economic Development Institute (now called the World Bank Institute). He was responsible at one time or another for writing, supervising, or reviewing economic studies that in total covered most of the members of the bank.

On retiring from the bank, Kamarck served for eight years as a visiting and associate fellow of the Harvard Institute of International Development. He has published five books: *The Economics of African Development,* with French, Swedish, Portuguese, and Spanish editions; *The Tropics and Economic Development,* with French and Spanish editions; *La Politica Finanziaria degli Alleati; Economics and the Real World;* and *Economics for the Twenty-first Century.*.

He is the coauthor of seventeen books on a range of economic subjects, most recently: *The Role of the Economist in Government;* and *The Bretton Woods-GATT System: Retrospect and Prospect after Fifty Years.* He is listed in *Who's Who in the World* and *International Who's Who.*

Kamarck lives with his wife, Margaret, an artist, on Cape Cod in Brewster, Massachusetts.

Index